WE REMEMBER
D-DAY

Frank and Joan Shaw

Dedicated to the memory of all those who died.

"Their sun went down whilst it was yet dawn"

HINCKLEY · LEICESTERSHIRE · ENGLAND · 1994

Typeset and Printed in England by
ECHO PRESS (1983) LTD
Loughborough and London

ISBN 1 872779 01 8

John Martin
Mayor of Southampton

Alan Martindale J.P.
Mayor of Weymouth

Alex Bentley
Lord Mayor of Portsmouth

FOREWORD

On 6th June, 1944, 50 years ago, a great Allied Armada landed on the coast of Normandy between Quinneville in the west and Ouistreham in the east. 150,000 soldiers were landed, and more than 6,000 ships and 11,000 combat aircraft were involved in a vast operation the like of which had never been seen before and will certainly never be seen again. The success of that assault led 11 months later to the final liberation of Europe from a Fascist tyranny that had threatened to permanently enslave it.

Such an undertaking on such a scale could not have been achieved without tremendous co-operation between the Land, Sea and Air Forces but we must remember also the "unofficial" Forces of the French Resistance who worked fearlessly against the Nazi Occupation for so many years. They harassed the enemy and supplied vital information to the Allies right up to the moment of the invasion and beyond.

This book tells the stories of the men and women who were involved. It tells of those who gave their lives and risked their lives so that we today can enjoy our freedoms and a better world that perhaps we take for granted. It tells the stories of human bravery and endeavour. It tells how men felt as they came ashore and what happened to them. It tells of the pain and heartache of those left behind in Britain, and the joy of those in Occupied Europe. But most importantly it tells of a hope that was born again in Europe on 6th June, 1944 which has flourished as we now accept how dependant we are on each other and how closely we are in fact linked together.

Do not forget what happened. Do not forget why it happened. But the greatest memorial we can give to those who sacrificed so much in the Battle of Normandy is to make certain it never happens again. For that reason we give full approval to this book "We Remember D-Day", and call on everyone to give it their total support and assistance in whatever way they are able.

Mnsr. D. Lecomte,
Mayor of Arromanches,
with Her Majesty
Queen Elizabeth II.

Mnsr. Jean le Carpentier
Mayor of Bayeux
Vice-President du Conseil Général

Mnsr. Marc LeFèvre
Mayor of St. Mere Eglise

Sur le 6 de Juin, 1944, 50 annees passé, un enorme armada allie sont arrivee sur les plages de Normandie entre Quinneville dans l'ouest et Ouistreham dans l'est. 150,000 soldats, ont debarqué, et plus de 6,000 bateaus et 11,000 avions combattants on participer dans une grande entreprise le quelle qui était jamais vu et pour sur un spectacle pas repeter. Le success de cette attaque a commencer 11 mois plus tard la liberation finale de Europe de une regime Fascist avec menaces permanent.

Une entreprise si enorme n'ete pas possible sans le corporation le meilleur entre les forces de l'Aire, Terre et de Mer, mais il faut aussi rappeler les "pas-Officialle" de la Resistance Francais avec leur travails sans peur contre l'occupation Nazi pour beaucoup d'anneés. Ils ont tourmentci l'ennemi et a fourni les aillies avec l'information trés importante jus'qua le moment de l'invasion et au dela.

Ce livre rencontre les histoires de les hommes et femmes de cette entreprise. Les personnes qui ont donne leur vie, qui ont risque leur vie pour nous donner aujourd'hui l'opportunite de prendre le plaisir de notre liberté et une manier de vie le plus meilleurs.

Ca rencontre des histoires de bravoure, courage et effort.

Ca rencontre les pensees de les hommes en arrivons sur les plages et les resultats.

Ca rencontre la douleur et le mal de coeur de celle lui qui éte laissez en Grand Bretagne et la joie de celle lui arrivee dans Europe occupé au moment de liberation. Mais plus importante ca rencontre de un espoire qui etait née encore en Europe sure le 6 de Juin, 1944 qui a fleurir commes nous acceptons a ce moment la dependance de une sur l'autre et le savoire que nous somme accrocher ensemble trés proche.

Ne oubliez pas les evenements. Ne oubliez pas les raisons pour les evenements.

Mais le plus grand mémorial on peut donner a ceux qui ont fait les sacrifice enorme dans la Bataille de Normandie c'est de donner les assurances que jamais, jamais ca va commence un autre fois.

Pour cette raison nous dons notre approbation en plein a cette livre "Nous Souvenons D-Day," et demande a tout le monde de donner le livre leur supporte total et assistance dans le quel maniere possible.

iii

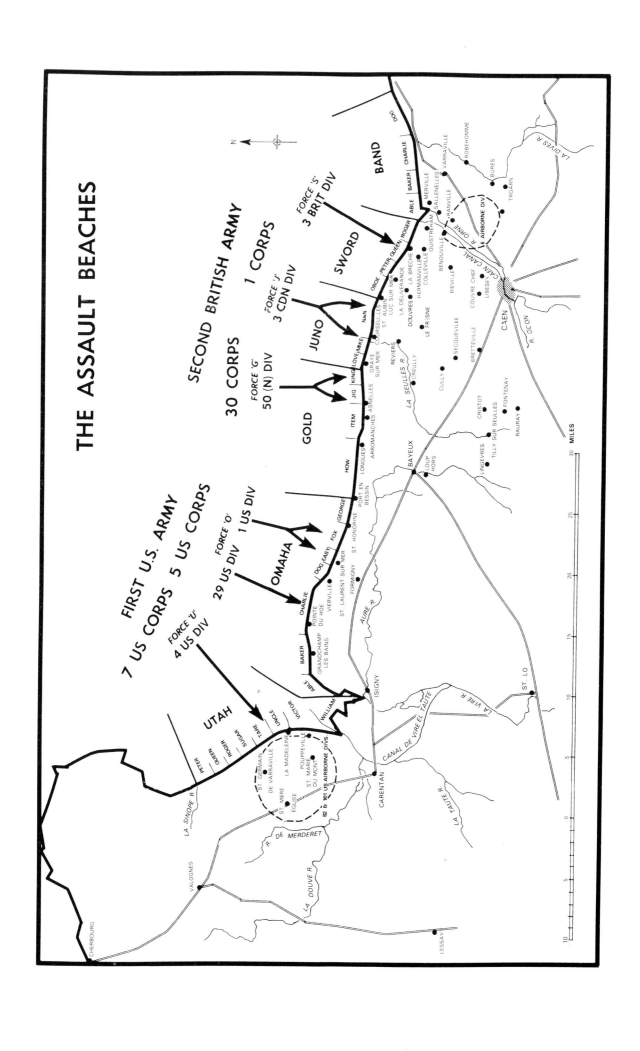

THE ASSAULT BEACHES

INTRODUCTION

The invasion force launched on D-Day was of a size never seen before and never likely to be seen again. There were more than 6,000 warships, transports and landing craft including 6 Battleships and 23 Cruisers. In the air were more than 11,000 combat aircraft, 2,300 transport planes, and 2,600 gliders. In the Armada would be 3½ million men, of whom over 150,000 were to be landed on D-Day alone. Never again would an operation of this size be contemplated let alone undertaken.

To defend Holland, Belgium and France the German Commander in Chief in the West, Field Marshall Rundstedt, had 38 Infantry and 10 Panzer Divisions, plus 7 reserve Divisions in the Pas-de-Calais and 3 in Normandy. It was a formidable force, but he had only a handful of destroyers and torpedo boats, and only 497 aircraft. And 18 of the 38 Divisions were stationed in the Pas-d-e-Calais because Rundstedt was convinced that was where the invasion would come. There were only 9 Divisions in Normandy.

However, to supplement these forces there was a defensive system of minefields, fortifications, machine-gun nests, mortar batteries and mined obstacles. It was a daunting defence system – for example on the beaches alone there were 1,400 obstacles and mines to the mile! To deal with all this was the job of "Hobart's Funnies", the name given to various armoured vehicles adapted by Major-General Sir Percy Hobart of the 79th Armoured Division. These included bulldozer tanks which could clear the beaches with impunity, the "Crocodile" flame-thrower tank which could incinerate anything within a range of 120 yards, and the "Bobbin" tank which was adapted to lay a roadway over sand or soft ground. There was also the "Crab" tank with whirling flails at the front which literally exploded a 10ft. wide path through the minefields, and the "Flying Dustbin" tank which could fire a 40lb shell three times a minute to smash concrete strongpoints. But most important of all for a landing from the sea were the Duplex Drive ("DD") amphibious tanks, fitted with twin propellors which could "swim" ashore independently.

However, there was a problem. Many of the obstacles of the Atlantic Wall were just below water level at high tide. They would rip open the bottom of any landing craft like a tin-opener. To avoid these the landings would have to be at least three or four hours before high tide so that the "hedgehogs" as they were called could be seen. But because of the need to start the assault at dawn, this meant there were only a few days each month when the tides were just right at first light.

The original date had finally been set for 5th June, 1944 but wind and heavy seas had forced a postponement. But then Group Captain James Stagg cautiously forecast that for the evening of the 5th June and the morning of 6th June conditions might improve sufficiently for a short period to allow the operation to proceed. But if the forecast proved to be wrong...? Well, it didn't bear thinking about. On the other hand the troops had already embarked and the Navy had sailed, only to be recalled. Not to proceed now would mean a delay of at least two weeks, with all the enormous problems of refuelling and resupplying. But most of all the security risks would be horrendous. Too many people now knew not only that the invasion was imminent, but where the attack was to take place.

A meeting of the Commanders was held at 21.30 on 4th June and another at 03.30 on 5th June. The decision rested with General Dwight Eisenhower, Supreme Allied Commander. He had asked for the views of his Commanders. Air Chief Marshalls Tedder and Leigh-Mallory were apprehensive. "Chancy" said Leigh-Mallory. Two votes against. Admiral Ramsey said they should proceed. General Montgomery was asked. His answer was crisp and precise. "I would say – go". Two votes for! Eisenhower sat for some minutes, silent and alone with his thoughts. Then he spoke the words that were to go down in history. "O.K. – let's go." It was a momentous decision. The invasion fleet headed to "Piccadilly Circus" the Assembly Area just south of the Isle of Wight, and then along the 10 channels swept clear of mines by 12 flotillas of minesweepers of the Royal Navy. During this period the weather remained foul, and the troops suffered badly with the smaller craft in particular in difficulty in the rough seas. But the bad weather had its advantages – the invasion fleet remained undetected because an attack seemed inconceivable and so all German air and sea patrols were cancelled! Total surprise was achieved.

Rundstedt's belief that the invasion would be in the Pas-de-Calais area had in fact been confirmed by Operation FORTITUDE, a calculated and complex deception started by the

Allies weeks before D-Day. Thousands of dummy tanks, guns, planes and landing craft had been constructed and then sited in Kent and Sussex. The RAF bombed Normandy, but concentrated its efforts on the Pas-de-Calais to add to the illusion. The deception of the German Intelligence Service succeeded beyond all expectations. For seven whole weeks AFTER D-Day the German High Command remained convinced that Normandy was a diversion and that the real attack was still awaited.

But it had already started at 00.16 on Tuesday, 6th June, 1944. To safeguard the beaches on which the troops and supplies would be landing in a few hours time, the bridges over the River Orne and the Caen Canal at Benouville had to be captured and held to prevent any German counter-attack on the invasion flank or the bringing up of reinforcements. A detachment of the Oxs. and Bucks. Light Infantry led by Major John Howard landed in three gliders bang on target and within 15 minutes had secured their objective. At 00.30 Corporal Ted Tappenden sent out the historic signal "Ham and Jam" confirming that these vital bridges were now held by the Airborne troops. They were the very first to set foot on French soil.

At Merville, eight miles away, the 9th Battalion of British Parachutists followed shortly afterwards. Their job was to silence the Merville Gun Battery. Immediately things went wrong, At 00.30 the plane which was to mark the target for 120 Lancaster bombers "marked" the nearby village of Gonneville by mistake due to thick cloud. The result was that Merville was untouched but Gonneville was turned into a furnace by 400 tons of bombs. Then the Battalion lost the gliders carrying its heavy assault equipment and out of 750 men who jumped, 192 were never to be seen again – drowned in the sea or marshes under the weight of their equipment. By 02.30 only 150 paratroops had reached the Assembly Point. But the job had to be done and so the attack went ahead and in a desperate hand to hand struggle the Battery was taken. It was a fight without mercy as the figures show. 100 of the 130 Germans in the Battery were killed. 66 of the 150 paratroops were killed and 30 more were wounded. Amazingly a carrier pigeon they had brought from England survived and so was sent off with the news that the Battery had been captured!

Across to the west of Normandy on the neck of the Cotentin peninsula the United States 82nd and 101st Airborne Battalions were landing. The 82nd was to capture both banks of the Merderet to the south and south west of St. Mere Eglise. The 101st was to seize the beach exits and the bridges over the River Douve north of Carentan.

The 101st landed nearest to Utah beach but in an area of meadows flooded by the Germans. They had their own recognition system of mechanical "clicking crickets". Some paratroops were captured and the Germans quickly recognised the significance of the "toy". Other paratroops were lured into gunfire by the "friendly" clicks of the now German held devices, and the whole operation degenerated into a nightmare of confusion, saved eventually only by the heroism and sheer "guts" of those paratroops who survived.

For the 82nd Airborne Division it was even worse. They lost more than 60 per cent of their equipment in the drop and were scattered for miles around St. Mere Eglise. Those who landed in the town came down through a hail of "flak", but nevertheless, through grim determination they achieved most of their objective, and even added substantially to the success of D-Day by cutting every telephone wire in the Cotentin they could lay their hands on!

Whilst these events were taking place the Allied Air Force was softening up the defences for the invading troops. Between midnight and 08.00 on 6th June the Air Force dropped 10,000 tons of bombs on the invasion coast defences. At the height of the bombing, in one concentrated period, 2,000 tons of bombs were dropped in just one 10 minute period. In that same bombing period of eight hours over 7,500 sorties were flown by Allied planes. On D-Day itself a total of over 14,000 sorties were flown, bombing, strafing, dropping leaflets and confusing radar. It is very often forgotten in our preoccupation with the Army and Navy that the Allied Air Force lost 127 planes on D-Day.

Before the bombings came to an end with the actual landings, the Navy had arrived offshore with the invasion fleet, and to the terror of the aerial devastation was now added the naval bombardment. The 16" shells from 6 Battleships and 23 Cruisers pounded the German defences. Then 101 destroyers joined in, as did the Rocket Launchers mounted on landing craft. The devastation was terrible and continuous, and yet many of the fortifications remained operational because of the immense concrete protection that can still be seen to this day.

The seaborne landings were timed to begin one hour after low water. But because the tide rises earlier in the west of the English Channel the invasion started with the arrival of the 4th US Infantry Division at 06.30 on Utah Beach. As early as 05.30 276 Marauder bombers of the US Army Air Corps. had begun to pound the coastal defences at Utah, and the 4th Division soon had the beaches cleared with few losses. By 10.00 the first Support Regiment was ashore, and by noon the troops had made breaches in the anti-tank wall and were pushing inland to join up with the 82nd Airborne Division. All the defences in the area were quickly crushed, and the beaches under control by the evening by which time 23,550 men were ashore together with 1,700 vehicles plus supplies.

The contrast could not have been greater at Omaha Beach. There the 1st US Infantry Division landed shortly after 06.30 but with heavy losses. The landing craft had been launched 12 miles offshore and in the still rough seas many sank or lost their bearings and foundered on Rommel's mined obstacles. Out of 29 amphibious tanks launched at Omaha only 2 made it to the beaches. When the second wave of troops went in at 07.30 they were pinned down on the beaches by German artillery and small arms fire. The beaches had still not been cleared of anti-invasion devices and the tide was now rising. To make the problem worse General Omar Bradley had refused to use "Hobarts Funnies" and so there was no equipment to sort things out. Two destroyers moved in to shell the German positions but the slaughter continued to the stage where abandoning the landing was seriously considered. It was not until noon that the Americans were able to make some progress and get inland off the now bloodied beaches. This was the most difficult of all the landings and by nightfall only a small bridgehead six miles wide and two miles deep had been established. But even that had cost 3,000 casualties.

The British and Canadian beaches were Gold, Juno and Sword, and here the sea was even rougher than at Omaha. The assault troops on all three beaches all came under heavy fire from German strongpoints, but the use of the specialised tanks so disastrously rejected by General Bradley at Omaha proved decisive in allowing the infantry to make rapid progress. On Gold Beach the 50th Infantry Division and the 8th Armoured Brigade landed at 07.25 in front of Ver, Meuvaines and Asnelles. The nearby village of Le Hamel was garrisoned by a detachment of the crack German 352nd Division and it was here that the heaviest fighting took place. But despite this they fought their way rapidly inland establishing a bridgehead eight miles deep. No. 47 Royal Marine Commando reached its objective in the west, Port-en-Bessin, on D-Day+2, linking up with the Americans at Omaha Beach.

On Juno Beach the 3rd Canadian Infantry Division landed at 07.00 and encountered strong opposition as they came ashore, but the 7th Brigade was established in Creully by 17.00. The 8th Brigade landed at Bernieres and St. Aubin but there two heavily defended and fortified radar stations held out until 17th June, a truly remarkable achievement. However, a considerable bridgehead was established, even though one objective, Carpiquet, was not reached, and a link up with the 3rd British Division on the left was not made.

On Sword Beach the 3rd British Infantry Division began landing at 07.30 between Lion-sur-Mer and Ouistreham/Riva Bella. Its mission was to take Caen. But although the towns of Hermanville, Periers, Beuville, Bieville and Blainville were overrun, a vigorous counter attack was launched by the 21st Panzer Division which recaptured Bieville and then Periers. No. 4 Commando which had landed at 08.45 quickly put the fortified position at Riva Bella out of action and by 13.30 had linked up with the Airborne Troops still holding the bridges at Benouville. By nightfall the British and Canadians had established a combined bridgehead 12 miles wide and 6 miles deep, but Caen had still not been reached.

But within five days the Allies had established a bridgehead 50 miles wide and 12 miles deep. Over 325,000 troops had landed with nearly 55,000 vehicles and over 100,000 tons of supplies. The Mulberry Harbours, consisting of vast steel and concrete sections towed across the Channel and sunk off the beaches, then allowed the level of supply and unloading to be increased enormously even though the Allies had still not captured a seaport. The contrast with Rommel's situation was stark – when finally released his Panzers found themselves short of petrol and lacking essential air cover. Already it was effectively all over.

The rest, as they say, is history. The small but significant perimeter established on D-Day was pushed ever outwards. Some 3,000 British and Canadian troops had been killed or wounded, plus 600 men of the 6th Airborne Division. Over 6,000 American troops were killed or wounded. Large though these figures were, they were substantially less than expected. On 22nd August, 1944 the "Falaise Pocket" was sealed and the Normandy Campaign effectively ended. Over 50,000 German troops surrendered, the remnants of the German 7th Army and the 5th Panzer Army. They had suffered slaughter and destruction on a vast scale. On 19th August the escape route was only two miles wide and crossed by the River Dives. Although 30,000 German troops did escape, over 10,000 died and the carnage was so terrible that the Germans called it "Das Korridor des Todes" — The Corridor of Death.

But let no-one underestimate what a close run thing it all was. What if D-Day had been delayed by Eisenhower? What if the invasion had failed? These are now hypothetical questions, but if either of these events had happened remember that only ONE WEEK later, on 13th June, 1944, Hitler launched the first of his Vergeltungswaffen (Reprisal Weapons) the V1 "Flying Bomb". Over 2,000 were launched, followed later by the bigger, faster and even more deadly V2.

If Eisenhower had put back D-Day and security had been breached then surely these weapons would then have been targetted not on London but on Portsmouth, Weymouth and Southampton. The effect on the troops, supplies, equipment and communications would have been catastrophic. If the invasion had failed, how many years would it have been before nerves would have been braced for a second attempt? And in either case what even more horrendous weapons could by then have been developed by the Nazi regime?

For those of us living today it is all now hypothetical – but that very fact is a measure of the debt we owe, and will always owe, to all those men and women who played their part (however small) in the success of the D-Day landings. Remember that.

Frank and Joan Shaw.

ACKNOWLEDGEMENTS

Our grateful thanks go again to the Imperial War Museum for many of the photographs in this book. Also to John Frost of John Frost Newspapers, who has a fabulous collection of old newspapers, for the newspapers at the front and back of the book. John's own story appears on page 197.

But a special "thank you" has to be reserved for Philip Buss of Blean near Canterbury, Kent, who has provided so much detailed information to us about the Regiments and equipment involved in D-Day. His help and advice has proved invaluable.

We also wish to gratefully acknowledge the support so willingly given to us by the following Cross-Channel Ferry Companies. Brittany Ferries on the Portsmouth/Caen route. P and O on the Portsmouth/Cherbourg and Portsmouth/Le Havre routes. Stena Sealink on the Southampton/Cherbourg route.

This ready assistance has helped ensure we raise the maximum funds for all the veterans of the Normandy Campaign.

D-DAY – LIST OF REGIMENTS

AMERICAN ASSAULT
DIVISIONS
OMAHA BEACH
1st US Division
16 Infantry
18 Infantry
26 Infantry
115 Infantry
116 Infantry
2nd Rangers
5th Rangers
741 Tank Bn.
111 Field Artillery Bn.
7 Field Artillery Bn.
81 Chemical Bn.

UTAH BEACH
4th US Division
8 Infantry
12 Infantry
22 Infantry
359 Infantry
   (attached from 90th Div.)
70 Tank Bn.

BRITISH ASSAULT DIVISIONS – SWORD BEACH
3rd British Division
8th Brigade
1st Bn. The Suffolk Regt.
2nd Bn. The East Yorkshire Regt.
1st Bn. The South Lancashire Regt.
9th Brigade
2nd Bn. The Lincolnshire Regt.
1st Bn. The King's Own Scottish Borderers
2nd Bn. The Royal Ulster Rifles
185th Brigade
2nd Bn. The Royal Warwickshire Regt.
1st Bn. The Royal Norfolk Regt.
2nd Bn. The King's Shropshire Light Infantry
Divisional Troops
3rd Reconnaissance Regt. RAC
3rd Divisional Engineers
3rd Divisional Signals
7th, 33rd and 76th Field, 20th Anti-Tank and 92nd Light
   Anti-Aircraft Regts. RA
2nd Bn. The Middlesex Regt. (Machine Gun)
51st (Highland) Division
152nd Brigade
2nd and 5th Battalions The Seaforth Highlanders
5th Battalion The Queen's Own Cameron Highlanders
153rd Brigade
5th Battalion The Black Watch
1st and 5th/7th Battalions The Gordon Highlanders
154th Brigade
1st and 7th Battalions The Black Watch
7th Battalion The Argyll and Sutherland Highlanders
Divisional Troops
2nd Derbyshire Yeomanry RAC
51st Divisional Engineers
51st Divisional Signals
126th, 127th and 128th Field
61st Anti-Tank and 40th Light Anti-Aircraft Regiments RA
1/7th Battalion The Middlesex Regiment (Machine Gun)

GOLD BEACH
49th (West Riding) Division
70th Brigade (to 20.8.44)
10th and 11th Battalions The Durham Light Infantry
1st Battalion The Tyneside Scottish
146th Brigade
4th Battalion The Lincolnshire Regiment
1/4th Battalion The King's Own Yorkshire Light Infantry
Hallamshire Battalion The York and Lancashire Regiment
147th Brigade
11th Battalion The Royal Scots Fusiliers
6th Battalion The Duke of Wellingtons Regiment (to 6.7.44)
7th Battalion The Duke of Wellingtons Regiment
50th British (Northumbrian) Division
69th Brigade
5th Bn. The East Yorkshire Regt.
6th and 7th Bn. The Green Howards
151st Brigade
6th, 8th and 9th Bns. The Durham Light Infantry
231st Brigade
2nd Bn. The Devonshire Regt.
1st Bn. The Hampshire Regt.
1st Bn. The Dorsetshire Regt.
Divisional Troops
61st Reconnaissance Regt. RAC
50th Divisional Engineers

50th Divisional Signals
74th, 90th and 124th Field, 102nd Anti-Tank and 25th Light
   Anti-Aircraft Regts. RA
2nd Bn. The Cheshire Regt. (Machine Gun)
Divisional Troops
49th Reconnaissance Regiment RAC
49th Divisional Engineers
49th Divisional Signals.
69th, 143rd and 185th Field, 55th Anti-Tank and 89th Light
   Anti-Aircraft Regiments RA
2nd Princess Louise's Kensington Regiment (Machine-Gun)

CANADIAN ASSAULT DIVISIONS – JUNO BEACH
3rd Canadian Division
7th Brigade
The Royal Winnipeg Rifles
The Regina Rifle Regt.
1st Bn. The Canadian Scottish Regt.
8th Brigade
The Queen's Own Rifles of Canada
Le Régiment de la Chaudière
The North Shore (New Brunswick) Regt.
9th Brigade
The Highland Light Infantry of Canada
The Stormont, Dundas and Glengarry Highlanders
The North Nova Scotia Highlanders
Divisional Troops
7th Reconnaissance Regt. (17th Duke of York's Royal
   Canadian Hussars)
3rd Canadian Divisional Engineers
3rd Canadian Divisional Signals
12th, 13th and 14th Field, 3rd Anti-Tank and 4th Light
   Anti-Aircraft Regts. RCA
The Cameron Highlanders of Ottawa (Machine-Gun)

OTHER FORMATIONS
79th Armoured Division
30th Armoured Brigade
22nd Dragoons
1st Lothian and Border Horse
2nd County of London Yeomanry (Wesminster Dragoons)
141st Regt. RAC
1st Tank Brigade
11th, 42nd and 49th Bns. RTR
1st Assault Brigade R.E.
5th, 6th and 42nd Assault Regts. RE
79th Armoured Div. Signals
1st Canadian Armoured Personnel Carrier Regt.
1st Special Service Brigade
Nos. 3, 4 and 6 Commandos
No. 45 (Royal Marine) Commandos
4th Special Service Brigade
Nos. 41, 46, 47 and 48 (Royal Marine) Commandos
Royal Marine Support Group
1st and 2nd Royal Marine Armoured Support Regts.
Units of the Royal Artillery and Royal Engineers

AIRBORNE FORCES
6th Airborne Division
3rd Parachute Brigade
8th and 9th Bns. The Parachute Regt.
1st Canadian Parchute Bn.
5th Parachute Brigade
7th, 12th and 13th Bns. The Parachute Regt.
6th Airlanding Brigade
12th Bn. The Devonshire Regt.
2nd Bn. The Oxfordshire and Buckinghamshire
   Light Infantry
1st Bn. The Royal Ulster Rifles
Divisional Troops
6th Airborne Armoured Reconnaissance Regt. RAC
6th Airborne Div. Engineers
53rd Airlanding Light Regt. RA
6th Airborne Div. Signals

US 82nd and 101st Airborne Divisions
501st, 502nd, 505th, 506th, 507th, 508th Parachute Infantry.
325th and 327th Glider Infantry.

D-DAY – LIST OF SHIPS

BRITISH
Battleships
Ramillies
Rodney
Warspite

Cruisers
Ajax
Arethusa
Argonaut
Belfast
Bellona
Black Prince
Danae
Diadem
Emerald
Enterprise
Frobisher
Glasgow
Hawkins
Mauritius
Orion
Scylla
Sirius

Monitors
Erebus
Roberts

HQ Ships
Bulolo
Hilary
Largs

Destroyers
Algonquin
Ashanti
Beagle
Blankney
Bleasdale
Brissenden
Campbell
Cattistock
Cotswold
Cottesmore
Duff
Eglinton
Faulkner
Fury
Grenville
Haida
Hambledon
Hotham
Huron
Impulsive
Isis
Jervis
Kelvin
Kempenfelt
Melbreak
Middleton
Obedient
Offa
Onslaught
Onslow
Opportune
Oribi

Orwell
Pytchley
Saumarez
Savage
Scorpion
Scourge
Serapis
Sioux
Stevenstone
Swift
Talybont
Tanatside
Tartar
Ulster
Ulysees
Undaunted
Undine
Urania
Urchin
Ursa
Venus
Versatile
Verulam
Vesper
Vidette
Vigilant
Vimy
Virago
Vivacious
Volunteer
Wensleydale
Westcott
Wrestler

Frigates
Chelmer
Halsted
Holmes
Retalick
Riou
Rowley
Stayner
Thornborough
Torrington
Trollope
Nith

Corvettes
Alberni
Armeria
Azalea
Campanula
Clarkia
Clematis
Clover
Godetia
Kitchener
Lavender
Mignonette
Mimico
Narcissus
Oxlip
Pennywort
Petunia
Pink

Sloops
Hind

Magpie
Redpole
Stork

Asdic Trawlers
Bombardier
Bressay
Coll
Damsay
Fiaray
Flint
Foulness
Fusillier
Gairsay
Gateshead
Grenadier
Hugh Walpole
Lancer
Lindisfarne
Lord Austin
Northern Foam
Northern Gem
Northern Gift
Northern Pride
Northern Reward
Northern Sky
Northern Spray
Northern Sun
Northern Wave
Olvina
Sapper
Skye
Texada
Veleta
Victrix

Fleet
  Minesweepers
Ardrossan
Bangor
Beaumaris
Blackpool
Blairmore
Bootle
Boston
Bridlington
Bridport
Britomart
Caraquet
Catherine
Cato
Cockatrice
Cowichan
Dornock
Dunbar
Eastbourne
Elgin
Fancy
Fort William
Fort York
Fraserburgh
Friendship
Gazelle
Georgian
Gleaner
Gorgon
Gozo
Grecian

Guysborough
Halcyon
Harrier
Hound
Hussar
Hydra
Ilfracombe
Jason
Kellet
Kenora
Larne
Lennox
Lightfoot
Llandudno
Loyalty
Lydd
Lyme Regis
Malpeque
Melita
Milltown
Minas
Onyx
Orestes
Pangbourne
Parrsboro
Pelorus
Persian
Pickle
Pincher
Pique
Plucky
Poole
Postillion
Qualicum
Rattlesnake
Ready
Recruit
Rifleman
Romney
Ross
Rye
Salamander
Saltash
Seagull
Seaham
Selkirk
Shippigan
Sidmouth
Speedwell
Steadfast
Sutton
Tadoussac
Tenby
Vestal
Wasaga
Wedgeport
Whitehaven
Worthing

USA
Battleships
Arkansas
Nevada
Texas

Cruisers
Augusta
Quincy
Tuscaloosa

Destroyers
Baldwin
Barton
Butler
Carnick
Cherardi
Corry
Doyle
Ellyson
Endicott
Fitch
Forrest
Frankford
Glennon
Hambleton
Harding
Herndon
Hobson
Jeffers
Laffey
McCook
Meredith
Murphy
Nelson
O'Brien
Plunkett
Rodman
Satterlee
Shubrick
Thompson
Walker

HQ Ships
Ancon
Bayfield

Frigates
Borum
Maloy

Patrol Craft
484 617 1233
552 618 1252
564 619 1261
565 1176 1262
567 1225 1263
568 1232

Minesweepers
Auk
Broadbill
Chickadee

Nuthatch
Pheasant
Staff
Swift
Threat
Tide

FRENCH
Cruisers
Georges Leygues
Montcalm

Destroyer
La Combattante

Corvettes
Aconit
Renoncule

Frigates
La Decouverte
L'Aventure
La Surprise
L'Escaramouche

POLISH
Cruiser
Dragon

Destroyers
Krakowiak
Slazak

NORWEGIAN
Destroyers
Glaisdale
Stord
Svenner

GREEK
Corvettes
Kriezis
Tompazis

NETHERLANDS
Sloops
Flores
Soemba

TOTAL VESSELS

Principal vessels listed	325
Landing Ships	
and Craft	4,126
Ancillary Ships	
and Craft	736
Merchant Ships	864
	6051

U.S. Engineers moving in on "Bloody Omaha" Beach at H.Hour + 25 minutes.

THE FIRST TO DIE

The very first Allied soldier to be killed on D-Day was Lieutenant Herbert Denham "Den" Brotheridge from Smethwick. He was a Platoon Leader in D Company, 2nd Battalion Oxfordshire and Buckinghamshire Light Infantry (The Oxs. and Bucks.) who were a formation within the Air Landing Brigade of the 6th Airborne Division of the British Army. He was in one of three gliders, each carrying 30 men, assigned the task of capturing the bridge over the Caen Canal to safeguard the flanks of the beachhead. Three other gliders carried the men who had to capture the nearby River Orne bridge for the same reason.

Den Brotheridge was in the first glider to land, along with Major John Howard the Commander. That glider came down very hard at 00.16 and embedded itself in a barbed wire fence, smashing the nose. It can be seen in the photograph opposite. The pilot and co-pilot were thrown out unconscious, and inside everyone else was momentarily stunned. Major Howard had his helmet smashed over his eyes and when he revived at first thought he had been blinded. One minute later the second glider landed close by without damage and both groups now charged together to attack the east end of the bridge. Even as they were running to do so the third glider landed just behind them.

Private Bill Gray a Bren Gunner later recalled Lieutenant Brotheridge saying: "Here we go," as their glider came in and then there was the most mind-numbing crash. The undercarriage was ripped off, and pieces of the cockpit flew back inside the glider. Nevertheless, within a few moments they were out, with Brotheridge leading his Platoon in the dash for the bridge. The whole scene was one of chaos as 90 superbly trained and fit men stormed the bridge and the nearby German trenches and pillbox. Total surprise was achieved and the German defenders, some still asleep, were bewildered and disorganised in the darkness. Some groups attacked and cleared the trenches and the pillbox but Brotheridge and his group headed for the bridge itself and charged across it. Halfway across they saw a German sentry about to fire a warning flare. He was instantly cut down in a hail of fire and fell dead as his flare burst above, intended as a warning to the defenders of the Orne bridge about ¼-mile away. It was a brave but futile action. The German troops there had already been overrun. Moments later the same situation applied to the Caen Canal bridge. Within 10 minutes of the landing both bridges had been captured.

After the crash of gliders, the firing of guns, the yelling of attackers and the general bedlam of the assault, an eerie silence descended as everyone recovered their breath, sorted themselves out and tried to bring some order back to the situation. The objectives had been achieved in an unbelievably short time but now the adrenalin had to be brought under control quickly. Bill Gray later recalled looking for his Platoon Leader in the disciplined calm that followed and then finding him lying outside the front of the Gondree café at the western end of the bridge he had so recently charged across. He had been shot in the throat and also hit by a phosphorous smoke grenade and his airborne smock was still burning. He died shortly afterwards, aged 29.

Lieutenant Brotheridge is buried in the Churchyard at Ranville, in Grave 43. Every year Major Howard, his Commander on the raid, returns to lay a wreath on 6th June in memory of his colleague. He wrote to Lieutenant Brotheridge's wife shortly after her husband's death:

"I am writing to tell you how badly the whole regiment feels the death of your husband. He was killed leading his men on the attack on the bridges, and it was very largely due to his dash and courage that the attack was successful. He was an officer we can ill afford to lose and was admired and respected by all the officers and men in the regiment."

The Canal bridge was later renamed "Pegasus Bridge" in honour of the shoulder flash of the 6th Airborne Division and in recognition of the courage and determination of those who had captured it that night. The precision of the landings at the bridge were recognised later by Air Chief Marshal Leigh-Mallory, Commander of Allied Air Forces, who said that in his opinion the event was the greatest feat of flying of World War II.

he Horsa gliders which landed at Pegasus Bridge. Gondree Café can be seen in left background.

I was on HMS "Scourge" at Portsmouth ready for D-Day and it was with pride, and delight, that we learned we would be escorting the minesweepers clearing the passage for the assault on one of the British sectors (which proved to be "Sword" sector on the extreme easterly flank of the overall invasion area). We would thus be in the vanguard of the British invasion forces.

The one great worry on that Monday afternoon was that we would be spotted by enemy forces and we wondered how well we would be able to protect the Army personnel and weapons in our care from a possible mass attack by dive bombers, or from the large fleet of U-Boats thought to be based in the area. Air attack seemed less likely as the night closed in and by 10.30 p.m. we had

Pilot Officer Adams with James Hinton.

reached the minefield. All crew members not working below decks were ordered to the upper deck and for the next hour and a half – at a speed of only three knots – we made our way through the minefield with the sweepers. For most of that time loose mines were clearly visible in the moonlight just a few yards from our beam.

During the minesweeping we saw and heard ghostly shapes in the sky and guessed (correctly) that these were our airborne forces in gliders towed by "tug" planes. Many silent prayers must have been said by the armada personnel as the men who would be the first to land in France passed overhead. Perhaps even now those who have survived may like to know that our thoughts and prayers were for their safety. Anyway, by midnight we had passed through the minefield and were not many miles from enemy territory. For an hour or two we guided some of the other warships through to their bombarding positions before taking up our own off Ouistreham.

As dawn broke on D-Day the sea around us was alive with ships of every description – it was the most amazing and wonderful experience. It seemed incredible that we had come across the Channel without attack. Not quite true. One of our sister destroyers – H.N.M.S. "Svenner" a Norwegian vessel manned by Norwegians – was torpedoed in the early hours by a German E-Boat in, apparently, their only attack of the day.

At 06.30 H.M.S. "Scourge" commenced the bombardment of her first target – a German gun emplacement. It was quickly demolished! By this time every type of craft imaginable was making its way to the "Sword" beach-head, perhaps the most impressive being the multi-rocket firing craft. Their rockets, and the shells from the bombarding warships, passed over the heads of the British troops attempting to get a foothold on the beaches. The noise was quite incredible. As well as shelling enemy positions from close to shore, during the early phase of the assault H.M.S. "Scourge" put down a mass of smoke screens to cover the troops landing ashore. For some reason it suddenly occurred to me that it was my grandfather's 74th birthday, and I wondered how he would consider this great event off France as a present!

After the initial landings had been established, seemingly successfully, our ship spent the last three hours of the morning patrolling the eastern flank to protect our bombarding battleships and cruisers from any marauding E-Boats and U-Boats that may have been about.

This was then followed by more bombarding of our own targets and giving assistance where needed such as shelling to set up "clearways" for the Allied tanks and infantry.

At 22.40 p.m. we resumed a patrol of the eastern flank, and within the next hour we twice became the target for enemy air attacks. The first sticks of bombs hit the water close to our stern, and the second string straddled our beam with three bombs falling on either side! No damage – but the bridge was drenched! I remember that at midnight I thought "Well, I don't know what's in store for you, but at least you've survived D-Day!"

On June 24th 1944 a second of our sister destroyers ("S" Class) was sunk by a mine just as she was about to come

MS Scourge.

alongside us off Ouistreham. H.M.S. "Swift" went down in minutes with heavy loss of life, less than a cable's length from our beam. A terrible tragedy. I was 21 at the time and an Electrical Artificer on "Scourge" which was awarded Battle Honours for her part in the D-Day action. At the end of June 1944 we returned to Scapa Flow in readiness to continue escort duties on the Russian convoys until the end of the war in Europe. My wife and I are now retired and in February 1994, four months before the 50th Anniversary of D-Day, we will be celebrating our own 50th Anniversary – of our Golden Wedding!

A note about the pilot in my 1944 photograph. He was Sergeant Pilot (later Pilot Officer) Ronald B. T. Adams. He was in 174 Squadron and spent D-Day above me flying a Typhoon! Early on D-Day his Squadron attacked gun positions in Normandy with rockets, all of which burst in the target area, and later that day it flew armed reconnaissances over the beach heads. There was so much bombardment coming up from the Royal Navy that Ronald later wrote to me to say their gunfire worried him more than the enemy's!

Ronald was shot down and killed in Typhoon MN977 on 24th February 1945 near Osnabruck after leading an armed reconnaissance in which a German train and railway tracks were successfully attacked. A wonderful and long missed friend.

James R. B. Hinton, 7 Miz Maze, Leigh, Sherborne, Dorset

I was a Signalman in the 6th Airborne Division and on 6th June 1944 I was just 23 years old, as were millions of others; just bairns really. Now as we crossed the French coast we were met by searchlights and a barrage of ack-ack fire. For most of us it was our first baptism of fire and tension was really high. Just when it was becoming almost unbearable an R.A. Officer in my glider undid his safety harness, stood up, placed his helmet upside down on the seat and sat on it. As he did so he hung on grimly to his safety harness as the Halifax towing plane and the Horsa glider "bumped" their way through the flak. We watched him in silent bewilderment as he rocked about on his upturned helmet. Eventually someone asked "Excuse me sir but why did you do that?" The Officer looked at him quite seriously and then said with a straight face "I don't know about you chaps but I'm getting married when I get back to England and I'm not going to have my bloody chances ruined!"

His reply broke the tension in an instant, and I can honestly say we became fairly relaxed, eager and ready on our way down to the fields of Normandy and, although we didn't realise it at the time, into the pages of history.

About two hours later, after getting the dead and wounded out of the crashed gliders, unloading jeeps, guns, stores and attending to the general organised chaos of a moonlit Airborne landing, I found myself digging a slit trench behind the Chateau in Ranville. Dawn wasn't very far away when a very "angry hornet" zipped past my ear, leaves flew off a nearby bush, and I heard the crack of a rifle. Frantically trying to stuff my body into the 6″ depression which I'd so far managed to dig, I realised a sniper had singled me out and that my war, barely two hours old, had suddenly become very personal! I was to find with experience that it remained so until V.E. Day!

I have returned to the cemetery at Ranville many times since then to pay my respects to those comrades we left behind who were not so lucky as me with "angry hornets". If God is willing I will be there on the 50th Anniversary, 6th June 1994 to pay my respects yet again because one thing is certain, I will never ever forget them.

Ted Hold, 18 Gillside Grove, Roker,
Sunderland, Tyne and Wear

ritish paratroopers, camouflaged and with blackened faces, ready for "take off".

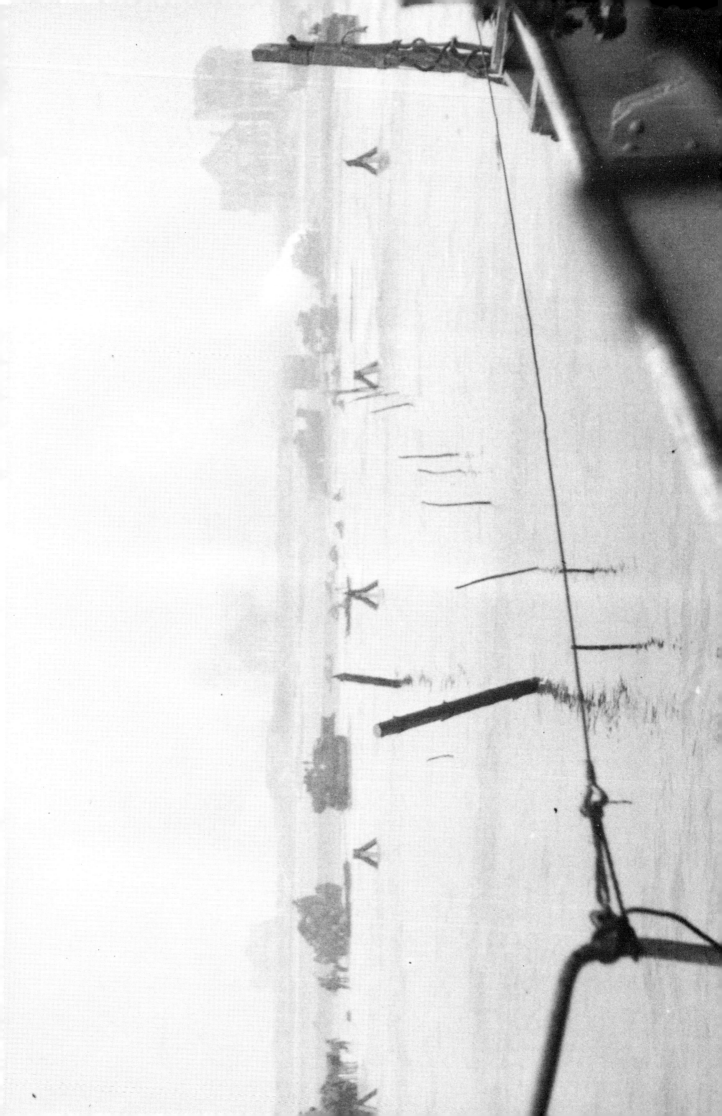

No. 3 Troop 6 Commando spearheaded No 1 Special Service Brigade on D-Day 6th of June 1944. Our landing craft leading the Brigade was hit twice on their run in to the beach, first on the bridge, then the water line, the troop having to disembark in deep water. The air resounded to the roar of the heavy naval guns, still pounding the defences. Planes roared overhead, and bullets churned the water as craft raced for the shore. Around them, bodies from other troops bobbed lifeless in the foaming angry now reddened sea.

Suddenly we came under attack from Moaning Minnies screaming just over our heads. Only seconds delay then the troop rushed forward again, each man carrying rucksacks containing approximately 60lbs in weight of equipment, as well as personal weapons. Within minutes the gun defences were reached and in minutes the area reported cleared for the loss of only one member killed by a sniper. The troop was doubling forward again, across fields, through hedgerows, along main roads as we raced for our next objective, Pegasus Bridge which we hoped had been held by the Airborne Troops who had dropped in the area during the night. No. 3 Troop's orders were to pass through the Airborne if the bridge was intact. If it had been blown and the Airborne wiped out, we were to attempt a river crossing in order to achieve the final objective of the day. On the outskirts of Benouville, spasmodic firing indicated that the battle for the bridge was still in progress. At the incline in the road the bridge was a welcome sight with the Airborne troops kneeling down either side of the bridge, engaged in a fierce sniping battle. We had been moving fast before, now in full flight we charged down the road and without a single pause thundered over the bridge to cheers, and shouts of "Snipers ahead" from the Airborne forces. Possibly taken by surprise by our sudden appearance, the German snipers melted away and we continued our advance.

Our next task was to attack the German Headquarters at the cross roads at Breville and hold this strategic position, in order to disrupt communications.

No. 3 Troop moved quickly through Amfreville enroute for Breville. Suddenly everywhere was quiet, a strange uneasiness, as we came in sight of the chateau which was the German headquarters. Captain Pymane led a section round the rear, whilst the rest of the troop made a rush through the gates of the chateau, across the orchard and into the large house. The Germans could not have anticipated our arrival. Steaming cups of coffee on the table, the radio still playing and the H.Q. was ours!

From the rear of the house heavy gunfire indicated that all was not well with our patrol section. We took up positions in and around the house to prepare for the anticipated counter attack which commenced immediately. At that moment a runner came in to report that Captain Pymane had been killed and the rest of the patrol had suffered heavy casualties and were pinned down by sniper fire. No. 3 Troop was now cut off; the Germans had managed to surround the chateau but were beginning to suffer heavy casualties from the determined attacks which they made time and time again as they attempted to retake their headquarters.

Soon the roadway around the Chateau was filled with the dead and wounded Germans,

but still they came on. Our heaviest retaliation weapon was a two inch mortar. The Germans retaliated with a battery of 88mm guns firing over open sights. Their shells crashing into the house and passing through the roof. Other shells crashing into the tops of the trees in the orchard; every salvo resulting in more and more casualties. Radio reports coming in indicated that the rest of the Brigade was involved in heavy fighting and no help was available. The orders were for Three Troop to hold out at all costs, nothing had to get past the chateau and cross roads at this stage.

Then came the order to cut all radio communication until we were contacted. No. 3 Troop's last request was to evacuate if possible the wounded and dead, a request answered by the sudden arrival of a lorry driven by two Airborne boys

5

...erman tanks of the 13/18th Hussars (27th Armoured Brigade) landing in France. Note the obstacles and infantry at waters '...ge. Flail Tank extreme left.

at high speed into the orchard. The wounded and dead were loaded as quickly as possible into the lorry which sped away at top speed as we gave it covering fire. The remainder of the troop then took advantage of a sudden lull in the attacks to gather together all the weapons and grenades left behind and prepared for the final assault as night began to creep in. The lull did not last for long, then the attack was on again this time without the heavy shelling so our casualties were light.

Evening was drawing in, the important position had been held against impossible odds. Suddenly the sky was filled with the roar of planes, flak, searchlights, and heavy ack-ack as the German defences went into action drowning the chatter of our own rifles and bren guns as we beat off further determined attacks. Then the attacks suddenly ceased as the illuminated sky was filled with gliders and planes of the Airborne forces. Our radio crackled into life ordering us to withdraw if possible and to rejoin the Brigade and No 6 Commando who were now dug in and had established a holding line with the other Commandos at Amfreville behind us. This order was carried out by a tactical withdrawal, the wounded and walking wounded being assisted by a covering Section bringing up the rear to ward off any sudden attack.

There was no jubilation as we arrived at Amfreville. Every other troop had suffered heavy casualties in carrying out their individual tasks but none more than No. 3 Troop. Their toll for taking and holding Breville on their own for that all important period and disrupting the German H.Q. had been a total of 22 killed, 12 wounded seriously. Others suffered slight wounds but still continued the fight to hold on to this vital and strategic position whatever the cost, knowing that they could not expect any assistance as the rest of the Commando Brigade were carrying out similar important tasks vital to the success of the Bridgehead.

Clifford Morris, Flat 1, Frencome House, Brighton Road, Lancing, Sussex

---

On D-Day I was a Prisoner of War in Stalag Luft 1 at Barth on the Baltic coast. I had been Flight Engineer of a Stirling of 196 Squadron which crashed in France whilst on an S.O.E. arms drop to the French Resistance.

We had a radio in the camp which obviously was concealed from the Germans, and the news which was received from British Stations was circulated daily very discreetly. The Germans certainly suspected that the radios existed but were never quite sure.

However on D-Day the news was much too important to be written out and passed around. It was relayed verbally to the first group of people and they simply exploded into a demonstration of joy which was repeated and repeated and went round the camp like a shock wave. Within minutes of the reception of the BBC morning news a "parade" of prisoners had been created and it started to move round the inner perimeter of the camp in a skipping, jumping, waving crocodile which lengthened continually as the news flashed from hut to hut. The men were banging cooking pots, tin plates, Red Cross boxes – anything that would make a noise!

Not unnaturally the German guards were quite astonished by this wild demonstration because the invasion had not been reported on German Radio. It was of course asking too much to expect the prisoners to keep their mouths shut and so with great glee they announced to the guards the news that the landings had taken place. This was at first treated with some scepticism by the guards, but as the demonstrations continued they came to accept that it was in fact genuine. Much later in the day German Radio did broadcast the news and confirmed what we had been saying for some hours! The result was that the Germans at last had actual proof of what they had long suspected – that we were in contact with Britain by radio. But who cared!

Gordon "Bert" Hemmings, 24 Elm Road North, Prenton, Birkenhead, Merseyside

The first German prisoners being marched along the beach. Landing craft marker flag flying.

our sight for an hour, and continually exchanging signals with the American tug, the frigate was eventually to sail away.

Reaching the Normandy coast, still listing badly, we saw through the rain and mist a mass of vessels, which would be at the half assembled harbour. Still in contact with the American tug by lamp we were made to understand from the Captain that it was not possible to land us owing to the weather and seas and that we were a danger to other shipping. We were to spend another night at sea and were towed up and down the coast well away and out of sight of any other craft. Morale was low, and everyone was getting frightened at this stage because of darkness falling. Tempers were frayed at the assumed attitude of the American tug's crew who seemed to have no interest in our plight. The water in the caissons chambers was deeper at one end than the other and the list was getting worse. There was nobody to communicate with and the tug crew were now ignoring us.

We had all worn our life jackets for the last 48 hours. Two of the lads were too scared to speak even and just sat huddled up in blankets. I was scared myself and most of us realised the strong possibility of the caisson going down during the night. A feeling of helplessness. Some of us took it in turns, in pairs, to walk the catwalk to the far end and check the water level by torch. It was always reported higher. By 3 a.m. in the morning I remember agreeing with Jack Crabtree that we 'jump together' as we were certain now that the caisson was doomed. Most of us thought that it was best to get down to the lower platform that ran the full length of the caisson and which was only eight feet above normal sea level. So we climbed down in turn that 27 feet of iron runged ladder and positioned ourselves on the highest corner. I remember that some of them must have been too scared to climb down such a ladder in those circumstances because I only remember being aware of about eight of us on the lower ledge. Sergeant Wally Newcombe was there, signalling to the last.

According to a letter that I wrote to my mother a few days hence the caisson actually went down at 3.30 a.m. At that particular time on the caisson I remember seeing in the distance the far end of our lower platform go under water, at the same time aware that our end was getting higher. It was obvious that the thing was going under so I jumped.

I seemed to go a long way down in the water for a long time and when I surfaced I remember thanking God for a large wooden beam that had appeared from nowhere. I slung my arm over it and called out to two bobbing heads nearby. It was Jack Crabtree and Alf Holmes and they joined me. I saw nothing of any caisson and no other heads in the water though there was still a heavy swell.

As the hours passed Jack's condition got worse. He was an older man and had swallowed too much water. I was determined to survive and trod the water continually to keep my blood circulating and to avoid any cramp.

At dawn a fishing trawler suddenly appeared and spotted us. It was commanded by a Sub-Lieutenant Brown and had been engaged in laying smoke screens off the beaches and was returning to its home port in England. I remember being pulled in by a boat hook and lifted aboard by the crew, and then nothing except drinking rum and put into a bunk with warm blankets below decks.

The first thing that I noted on waking up was a mess table top covered with our personal possessions that had been dried. The vessel was rolling and pitching but I couldn't have cared less. I was alive and safe. We had been picked up about six o'clock according to the crew, and were heading for Portland Bill and Weymouth Harbour. The Captain and crew were super and gave us all 50 cigarettes.

In dried clothes, with a meal inside us, and in the calm waters of Weymouth Bay, I went on deck with Alf Holmes and Arthur New to find the covered bodies of Jack Crabtree, Fitton, an Engineer and one other. I had survived the ordeal with only a very stiff shoulder and bruising.

Eventually I learned that my other close pal, Bob Beldon, had been picked up by a U.S. transport ship, downgraded and hospitalised, that Hannon, Martin, Fitton, both Engineers, one of the sailors, and two others had been drowned.

With Bill Farrell and Alf Holmes at Aldershot we luckily saw on the first day a truck bearing our Battery's colour and emblem, 416 Battery, 127 L.A.A. Regiment, R.A. It was learned that it was our rear party ready to leave for Normandy. Wishing to be reunited with our own unit we saw the C.O. and quickly found ourselves at Tilbury Docks, joining a small party of our Battery Headquarters, and boarded an American manned L.S.T. heading back for France, and Arromanches.

Mick Crossley, 10 Flower Haven, Haworth Road, Bradford, Yorkshire

---

I was a Flight Sergeant Engineer on a Halifax Bomber MZ513 LK-K. The pilot was Squadron Leader Geof Watson and the rest of the crew consisted of Flying Officer Hall the navigator, Flying Officer "Paddy" Hefferman the bomb aimer, Flying Officer Bert Onions and a Polish Flying Officer who's name I never knew who was the mid-upper gunner. Flight Sergeant Goode, or "Goody" was the rear-gunner. We were all second tour aircrew. I myself had done a "tour" of 30 ops with 76 Squadron with a crew that were all new to operational flying.

On the morning of 5th June Geof Watson caught me as I was going into the Sergeants Mess and told me we were on ops that night. "This is it – what we have been waiting for." "The Invasion?" I asked. "I'm pretty sure" he replied "although it's not official."

When we attended the briefing that night we knew he was right. The target was the Gun Battery at Mont Fleury. It didn't worry us. It was, so we thought, a case of nipping over the French coast, drop the bombs and get out again. We took off at 02.31 and were over the target two hours later without incident. I was in my position under the astro-dome from where I could see all that was going on all around us and above us. I remember I was watching an aircraft above us and slightly ahead and to port releasing its bombs. I was about to warn the skipper when I heard Paddy say "bombs gone" and almost immediately there was a terrific bang to port. Turning my head I saw lots of burning bits and pieces floating in the air. The aircraft rocked violently and we lost height. I looked out and saw a small hole in the port wing, out of which a flame was spurting, like a blow lamp flame. I reported this to the skipper who told the navigator to give him a course for home. When he had the course he told us "I'm going to dive to blow the fire out" which he did, but when we levelled out the flame was larger and more fierce. Soon the flames had spread and were coming from under the trailing edge of the wing. By this time we were well out into the English Channel and the skipper was holding the plane in a side slip to starboard to keep the flames away from the fuselage and the fuel tanks.

At last it was obvious that it was hopeless and the skipper suddenly told us to bale out. I clipped my chute on and picked up my dinghy in its pack and went down to the escape hatch by the bomb-aimers position. Bert, Paddy and the navigator had gone. I assumed "Goody" had gone as well because as rear gunner he could turn his turret 45 degrees and fall out backwards! I had noticed the Polish mid-upper gunner walking down towards the pilot when I left him.

I had baled out once before but that was from 11,000 feet and over the south coast of England. The aircraft had been severely damaged and almost impossible to land. This time it was over the sea, and it was very dark. I remembered a pal of mine from another aircraft just a few days earlier saying

that if you had to bale out over the sea you were as good as dead. However where there's life there's hope! With some difficulty, because of the dinghy pack I had clipped on to the back of my harness, I dropped through the hatch.

As soon as I could get my hand on it I pulled the rip-cord and looked up to see if it had opened. I could see the cords and the canopy at the end, but it hadn't opened and for a fleeting second I thought it had caught fire. And then it opened with a crack and a jerk which caused the dinghy pack to come away from my harness and disappear towards the water. As I looked down I was surprised to see the waves and realised that the aircraft must have been very low when I left it. It was the burning plane reflected in the silk chute that had made me think it was on fire. I remember thinking that the pilot would have no chance but in the next second I was in the water and the waves were breaking over my head. The chute dragged me through the water at quite a speed and I kept trying to release it by hitting the release mechanism with my hand but the pressure on it was too great. Then I managed to pull the cords towards me a little and tried again, this time with success.

Now I had a different problem! I was being buried under tons of water and then being shot to the surface with every wave. During one of these immersions I saw a light and realised it was the torch that switched on when hitting the water. I grabbed it from its pocket and held it above my head shouting, whenever I broke the surface, "Help, help". There was no- one to hear me, but it gave me hope, somehow. Just before I had hit the water I had seen a shadowy shape that could have been a ship of some sort and I kept looking around hoping. Whilst bobbing around and spitting out water I kept thinking about my parents and what they would think and how they would take it when I failed to turn up. As the thoughts churned through my mind suddenly there was the ship I had seen coming towards me.

Men were looking at me from over the rail and I remember one of them threw me a life-buoy but it was too far away. Then someone tried to grab me with a boathook as I bumped against the side of the ship and then I lost consciousness. When I came too it was daylight and I was lying in a bunk wrapped in a blanket. My mouth and tongue were as dry as a bone and I looked around for a drink. I called to a young man and told him what I wanted. He got an older man to bring me a drink and he told me I was on an L.C.T. (Landing Craft Tanks). It seems they were waiting in position to land men and transport on the second wave of the invasion. I asked him for my clothes. He told me there was only my battledress tunic and trousers left, but he brought them and I put them on and felt much better. I asked about my Mae West and torch attached to it but he hold me they had been lost in getting me aboard. I was disappointed. I owed my life to them as I was a non-swimmer! He told me I was very lucky to be picked up as the crew had been told not to stop to pick up survivors, but they were towing a rocket barge which had sprung a leak and had a crew of two and they had had to stop to take them on board. It was whilst doing that they had seen my chute being blown along with the wind and then my torch light. What a coincidence!

For some time I had heard distant bangs and also noises like stones hitting the side of the craft and then I found out they were mortar bombs being fired from the enemy. I went outside and saw an Officer standing on the deck and staring down at it. I went over and asked him what was happening. He told me the L.C.T.'s were bolted together in sections and it seemed this one was loose. He was worried how long it would hold! Then the engines started and before we could say anything we were heading for the beach at full speed. Fortunately it all went smoothly – I'd had quite an action packed night already! Vehicles and men were off-loaded rapidly and soon we were heading back to England. Having thanked them again for pulling me out of the "drink" I was transferred to another boat and after some food and another night's sleep I was transferred AGAIN to a Submarine Chaser and taken to Bognor Regis. After being questioned by a doctor I was taken to Nytimbre Transit Camp where I was delighted to meet Paddy and Bert. They were the only other survivors of our crew. They had been picked up by a French Destroyer. We all arrived back at 578 Squadron on 10th June where we were given 14 days leave which was very much appreciated – and needed!

All my family met at my brother's house. It was a very emotional meeting – lots of tears and lots of laughter. During my leave I received my Commission, and on 4th July Paddy Hefferman and Bert Onions joined me at 578 R.A.F. Burn where we went on to conclude our second tour of operations. I received the Distinguished Flying Cross in December 1944. I know that Bert Onions is dead now but I would love to hear from Paddy if he reads this.

Bill Middleton, DFC, Rose Cottage, Church Lane, Mareham-Le-Fen, Boston, Lincolnshire

D-Day – the memories come flooding back! I was 17 years old and doing voluntary work in the Y.M.C.A. in Duke Street, Woking in 1944. It was opposite the Astoria Cinema. All Service people could come in and get light snacks and drinks at very low cost – even for prices in those days! A Mrs Davies was in charge. Every Wednesday we had games, like dressing up from parcels of clothes and there were some great fashions! I won once – a bar of chocolate! I often worked cutting sandwiches – all sorts – with a Miss Cohen, a little old lady who I later found out was a J.P. But we worked well together. She seemed to like me with her and we changed places every now and then, or sometimes I had to go into the Muggery (washing up for hours). No nice washing up liquid in those days – only soda! But the mugs had to be kept coming.

I was on duty on the night of 5th June when we received instructions to start packing sandwiches in greaseproof paper. Amazingly no-one asked any questions or "Why". Then we noticed the doors were locked and a Policeman was stationed at the back entrance. But even then it didn't seem odd because we all knew him! We were just told to keep making the sandwiches.

Then! Then! The other doors were opened and the room was suddenly crowded with young Canadians, soldiers from all Regiments you could imagine. We were run off our feet. Everything was free – tea, coffee, cakes, even our sandwiches! I was put on the serving counter during that long long night and I was tired out when suddenly I saw a big tall soldier stood there – a Company Sergeant Major. It was my big brother from the Royal Engineers!

I just ran to Mrs Davies in wild excitement and she was very kind and told me to leave the counter to be with my brother. My brother cuddled me, held me tight to him and then playfully clipped me on the chin and said "keep your chin up love, I'll see you soon". It was the look on his face and the tone in his voice – I knew now something big was on but I daren't ask!

When they'd finished I was given permission to stand outside on Maybury Road which runs alongside the Station. A very very long road. As far as the eye could see there were trucks, armoured cars, jeeps, tanks – it seemed there was no end. But it was the SILENCE that struck me. All whispering – uneasy feelings. It's difficult to describe but its real.

Then the trucks began to move off, carrying my brother with them. I waved, I cried and I prayed for all those young men, some not much older than me, all moving off in the blackout. To where? Southampton is only 50 miles away but I didn't work that out. I was just numb, as if all thoughts had stopped forming.

Afterwards I joined the ATS and my brother came back 10 months later, wounded in action. He died in 1988. He was a peacetime soldier; saw service in India in 1935, went through Africa and then on to D-Day. I often wonder if we were the last to see, and talk to and serve those servicemen that night as they set off? I was near the Arch in Woking later when buses came through carrying sick and wounded servicemen. I ran alongside just touching hands that were hanging out from windows. The buses went very slow. They were returning Prisoners of War – just glad to be home and touch a loving friendly hand. God bless them all.

I've just remembered - those sandwiches were filled with dried egg, Bovril supplement, anything Mrs Davies could get her hands on! Funnily enough, after hours and hours of work, I don't remember ever being tired. The Y.M.C.A. building was pulled down years ago. The whole town has been ripped apart since. I'm glad I'm in my old age now – I don't like all these changes. Life was better as it was!

Mary T. Turner, 47 Sythwood, Horsell, Woking, Surrey

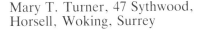

Mrs Turner's brother "Bobbie" Hill of the Royal Engineers.

I was in the Hampshire Regiment and I had not been on a ship before and had never been to another country when we set off to France shortly after D-Day.

The ship berthed alongside a floating timber platform; there had been nothing to eat or drink since we had left Aldershot the morning before but there was a huge cauldron of food on the forward deck and we discovered this contained a sort of salad mayonnaise – no one was interested! So each man was given five fruit drops and we went ashore to move inland in single file.

There were empty houses along the top of the beach with structural damage and doors and windows missing. This was Arromanches. Everyone assembled in a field surrounded by hedges and trees and here an officer gave us some advice. Not to make tracks which could be seen from the air and not to associate with ladies on the continent as they were different to English ladies and for ten minutes it wasn't worth the risk!

A water truck soon arrived and we made tea in our mess tins. The tea was a cube containing tea, sugar and milk heated by a white methylated tablet but it didn't really work. Gunfire could be heard constantly as we moved inland again to the outskirts of Bayeux. Buildings were damaged and an elderly Frenchman shook his fist as we passed. Our 25 pounder guns were firing constantly and the shells passing overhead could be clearly heard followed by explosions forward.

In a field there were many makeshift graves containing German soldiers; their bayonets had been fixed to rifles and thrust through the bodies with helmets hanging above. Boots and other parts of the bodies were still showing above the ground. We finally joined the 1st Battalion Hampshire Regiment in The 50th Division resting in a field. The field had high hedges around all sides. My pal Bill Muttitt and I were not too welcome as newcomers and rookies. This unit was from North Africa and there had been casualties.

We rested there overnight and next morning everyone assembled just to the edge of a wood of small trees. There appeared to be hundreds of chaps all milling around. To our front was a distant view with ground falling away down a hill and rising quite steeply to the skyline. There were trees in the distance and the fields were bound by neat hedges. We could hear gunfire to the right and left but here it was quiet and a beautiful day with blue sky and warm sunshine. A long single line was now forming right across the field and everyone began to move forward. A Sherman tank was moving forward to our left. Gun and mortar fire now began from forward of our position and there were explosions in the field. Some were quite near to us. We veered to the right to an opening in the hedge and at this point a soldier began to shout and run around in distress. An officer said to me to stay with him until he settled, then to follow. I persuaded him to sit by the hedge and talked for a minute and he was soon all right. A cow, bleeding from several shrapnel wounds, was still grazing.

We continued uphill along the side of the hedge and each time there was sound of a salvo we fell flat. There were more wounded cattle. At the top of the hill we went back through the hedge and I saw Bill with other lads assembled behind another hedge with a house and road just ahead. One of our chaps was rapidly firing his rifle at three German soldiers who were running from the house with heads down. Explosions were continuous with trees and branches splintering just behind our position. Everyone was lying down in the shelter of the hedge. Bill and I were talking to a Corporal Baker who was lying between us. He then said, "I've been hit," and two stretcher bearers immediately cut his trouser leg to reveal a severe shrapnel wound to his knee. A dressing was applied and the bearers carried him away sitting on their clasped hands. There were more casualties and others helped with field dressings and began to carry wounded back.

A Major now appeared; I believe his name was Anscombe. He told Bill and I to fire a piat bomb into the upper window of the house as this could be a German observation post. I loaded the bomb and Bill fired the shot right through the window. The Major now decided we should move left around the hedge corner and along another hedge leading to the road. He said: "I expect you chaps are scared, I am too". I now realised there were just five of us left here, the Major, two other lads and Bill and I. There had been no verbal instruction

15

to advance and we were unaware of everyone retracing their steps back down the hill! Perhaps battle experience had been a lesson to everyone if possible to move away from the bombardment area. We had expected the position to be held until a further advance was ordered. The Major now decided we should run down a small slope to the left to the shelter of a clump of trees; he would go first, then we would follow in twos. Shells and mortar bombs were still exploding and as the Major was running five explosions appeared to knock him flat. However, he regained his feet and ran on to the trees and signalled to follow. The other two lads ran down followed by Bill and me. This move had surely saved our lives because the next salvo blasted along the entire length of the hedge we had just left.

The Major now left to find a way back to our unit; he said we could follow or perhaps he would return. The bombardment continued and after about an hour the other two lads left. Bill and I decided to move out but it was difficult to know which direction to follow and we could have been wandering into front line troops of either side. After crossing fields, wading a stream and going through a wood we were pleased to arrive at a road. We went to the left and amazingly found our unit resting in a field. There had been no food and a Canadian Captain asked Bill and I if we would accompany him to find the cooks. We set off again and walked about an hour in the moonlight, as it was now dark. Everywhere was completely deserted. The Captain decided to go on alone and said to wait until he returned. We were beside a sort of rubbish tip at the side of the road. The Captain never returned and we eventually had a short sleep until dawn. Royal Engineers came along at first light clearing road mines and gave us a welcome mug of tea. We hurried back to the unit but breakfast had just finished and the cooks had packed away.

We moved forward to a new location and were proceeding in single file along a road with woods and just a few houses each side. Two British soldiers who had been killed were lying in a crawling position. A Padre was there and he had placed a gas cape over the bodies. I remember as we passed the sunlight reflecting on their boot studs and there were flies buzzing above. Somewhere the relatives back home would soon be informed. A little further on a dead German soldier was lying awkwardly in a roadside ditch and on the right were more dead German soldiers. Suddenly from the woods on the left came a burst of spandau fire. The bullets seemed to pass right through our column and two chaps dashed back down the road with the officer shouting for them to return but they kept going. Later we heard they had both been killed by a German shell. Bill noted that it could be safer from shelling when close to the front line as artillery from both sides did not fall in this forward area.

We now passed through the village of Villers Bocage and continued on to high ground with open country. At this point we were again under heavy bombardment and we were told to dig in as this was the objective. We were tired, dirty, unshaven, thirsty and hungry; we had been without food for two days. Shells were exploding everywhere; it was a very open position. Bill was angry but nevertheless we somehow managed to dig a trench through stones and rocks with the entrenching tools and prepared to spend the night. The following morning the Royal Engineers discovered a German mine inches from the edge of our trench! At this point we were each given a mess tin of water, a little to drink and the remainder to wash our faces as we were smothered with white chalk from the digging. We now moved forward

again and settled behind a hedge. This position was under shell and mortar fire and there were casualties in the field to our front. Stretcher bearers with white flags ventured out from both sides to recover wounded. Small arms fire had stopped. We heard later that our stretcher bearers had entered a house and met the German doctor.

Proceeding in file again next morning we entered a village which had possibly been strafed from the air. There were dead horses and abandoned carts. No doubt an attack on a retreating German column. There were also damaged houses each side of the road. I discovered a Sherman tank which had fallen into a deep concrete channel. The tank had come to rest on its nose and I wondered if the crew were still inside but we had to move on. That about sums up Normandy and what we had to do.

Ron Gladman, 6 Dairylands, Old Cleeve,
Minehead, Somerset

andoned and wrecked German guns and equipment at Breville. Heavy anti-aircraft machine gun, staff car and two tank-stroyers.

Sub.Lt. J. H. Warner, R.N.V.R.,
H.M.S. Rattlesnake.
Monday, 12th June, 1944.

Oh my darlings,

At last it can be told! No doubt you have already had strong suspicions as to my whereabouts, and now we're here we can tell you all – or nearly all. Little did I think, dad, that our ill-fated trip to Boulogne on the Brighton Belle, should turn into an invading cruise to Normandy in the Rattlesnake. Never did I think that my first glimpse of France would be at the unearthly hour of 05.30, watching little towns being bombed. I still can't quite believe I am able to tell you all this. It is so difficult to know where to start. I suppose I should start from exactly a week ago to the hour, to the day. It was about this time that I was thinking of you both, reading my longish letter, as we set sail in what I thought was an impossibly choppy sea. The little invasion craft seemed dwarfed in the troughs of the waves. I felt very sorry for the troops, as with all our size, we were rolling around, and they, poor things, in their tin-craft and no sea-time, must have been feeling far from offensive! I got several "bottles" for not keeping the ship in station, but I was so busy concentrating and praying that the weather would abate, I rather forgot about such mundane affairs as Mr. Stuart's Distance Metre!

It was an amazing sight. From all sides came big ships, little ships, tin-cans, landing craft, amphibious ducks, all converging on the rendezvous, where we had to alter course – alter course to France. There were low clouds o'erslipping the darkened seascape, the salt spray made white marks on my cap, and overall hung a silence and a steadfast hope.

At half past four we went to "action stations". I thought it was just a run through, so went up, ill prepared for the cold. That after-oerlikon is a very drafty place in a breeze. But I surreptitiously inveigled a steward to bring up my oilskin and seaboots, when he brought my cup of soup and a cheese sandwich for supper. Then, after this huge repast, I sat down, but became so cold, I had to rise again, and was still standing at one-thirty when he brought a cup of "kye" (basic English!) and another sandwich – this time tongue. By now, we were sweeping, and had left the landing-craft behind. All that could be made out was a flotilla just visible on each side of us, all bent on the same job. It was the silence that was so uncanny, broken only by reports of planes from the lookouts, who were kept very busy in that respect, and the thud of mines going off in the other ship's sweeps. There must have been much more tension on the bridge than down aft, for I didn't realise that mines had been cut, and that we had to keep a sharp lookout not to bump unexpectedly into one.

Expectancy grew round about three-thirty. We were still the leading ships – and now came the final and all important lap. The alteration of course order to sweep out the anchorage; the coast was not yet visible but I knew it was only eight miles away. We all knew it was close as we could see fires burning inshore from the heavy weight of our bombs – there was a continued roar overhead of our aircraft. Still we ploughed on, as daylight came inexorably nearer. Still no sound of gunfire from shore, save the "ack-ack" of small arms and machine

guns directed at our planes. Still no-one seemed to see us or our sweeping lights, or danbuoy lights which seemed higher than Picadilly Circus on Armistice night. Yet every flash of gun from shore made one expect a nearby splash, denoting a shell, and every falling flare seemed to illuminate us far better than the flares. The seconds ticked on, and the glimmer of a dull sun shyly peeped over the horizon. One's imagination ran away with one, and the Rattlesnake sounded like a runner all out for a speed record, who cannot become behind schedule, and however much out of breath must keep going. Now we could see the dim outline of coast. We must be visible. Never have I felt so conspicuous, not even as a veiled fairy in "The Merry Wives" at the Old Vic!

We could see the cruisers approaching for the first

19

"MS Holmes" drops a depth-charge on a suspected U-Boat.

covering bombardment. The last danbuoy was in sight, and up came our protecting destroyers, whom we hadn't seen all night, but had been close at hand and on the lookout for E-boats and U-boats. We felt rather like naughty dogs who having found their opponent rather bigger than expected, run up to their mistress and cower behind her skirts while she beats off the Alsatian. So behind the cruisers we went, and peeked out from between them as they started shelling. One felt very safe then, and with an air of complete detachment could survey the results of one's handiwork as the first Landing Craft Infantry crept forward. More and more ships were arriving, and it was funny to hear on the 8 o'clock news "The Germans report that cruisers and battleships are shelling the coast of Normandy" – and there was I on the spot saying "Yes, aren't they?" After the first landings, or "touch downs", my memory of what happened is rather vague – we just sailed happily up and down the anchorage, taking an interest in all the doings of various craft, peering with binoculars at them. It was difficult to see much owing to the smoke-screens of our landing barge.

At all the news bulletins I thought of you, and hoped you would not be worrying. It was nice to hear our kind of ship mentioned, and my chest did swell just a little. For the next few days we were kept pretty busy – but descriptions of these excitements will have to wait until I am home. At all there was invariably activity, when we returned to our anchorage. There were planes continuously falling, every one coming through endless tracers which were now well established shore battery. We saw them bring down two German planes in two minutes. In the area in which they were hit, there was hardly a space not covered by great balls of fire, and exploding onions. One night, when I was on watch, we had a nasty shock, when the sound of a shell – that ominous whine – passed right overhead, and seemed to fall very near the other side. At the time the Captain thought it was a splinter, until people down below came up on deck, as they had heard an explosion under water, which sounded too close for comfort. I think it was one of ours though, which had failed to explode in the air at the proper time.

We've only seen about four German planes, which were soon driven off by our gunfire. I am afraid I have to stop a minute, or rather for two hours, as I am due on the bridge for my watch. Will continue after lunch. It's a glorious day today, though droughty, so I hope it passes quickly and without event...

It's now nearly 6 p.m. and I've had a hectic day taking down shorthand notes of the Captain's Standing Orders, and having to type them out. So I am afraid I have no time to write more at the moment, so I hope to catch a post tonight. But I shall write tomorrow if at all possible. The one sonnet you already have I wrote two days before the invasion, and yesterday's one was written three miles off the French coast, with battleships firing at shore batteries, causing rather a disturbance. Here it is for what it's worth.

> Take care of yourselves,
>
> All my love,
>
> John.

The above letter was sent to his parents on 12th June 1944 by John "Onnar" Wurner, now of 16 Dolphin Street, Deal, Kent,

'You won't half cop it for being late for the invasion'
Acanthus, *Punch*, 2 August 1944

...anding craft passing USS Augusta and heading for the beaches.

I am a Captain in 22nd Dragoons, 30th Armoured Brigade. It's 07.15. We've landed and we're moving onto the wide sandy beach where Jock Stirling, my second troop sergeant, and the second flail are already beating up to the wall. I can see the Bridge AVRE moving through the beach obstacles behind them, when there is an explosion on the turret and the bridge falls uselessly. The AVRE tries Petarding the sea wall without success.

I move up to the foot of a concrete ramp leading to the top of the wall and blow my cordtex. Paddy Addis my gunner clears the barrel and I sight through it just as we did at Orford, and we fire HE at one corner of a railway-steel gate blocking the top of the ramp. Aim at another corner. Fire! Another joint. Fire! Several times until the gate is a wreck. I back off to let another AVRE climb the ramp to push the wreckage away, but it tips over on its side, one track off the ramp; another AVRE goes up the narrow ramp and pushes the wreckage to one side – and sets off a mine which halts it on top of the wall.

I move up to the foot of the ramp, dismount to attach the tow rope to the wreckage which we drag backwards towards the sea out of the way. The tide is coming in with the on-shore wind. I signal to Jock and the 2nd Flail to go up the ramp to start flailing inland. It takes a few minutes as they have to line up carefully on the ramp whose foot is already under water, but they're up, and just as we are about to follow the engine dies. We're flooded. "Bale out!" Almost before the words are out of my mouth, Dogger Butler, the co-driver, a tall gangling man, has come out through the turret past me!

We take pocketsful of grenades, the .3 Browning and ground mounting and several boxes of ammo, and cautiously, "walking the tightrope" along the jib, step off the rotor into deep water. It's almost up to my neck and cold as it trickles inside my clothes. There are some bodies, Chaudières, I expect, floating amongst the debris and flotsam already bumping against us. Some are not dead but we have strict orders not to deal with any wounded: a distasteful order which goes against one's instincts.

We struggle hard to help each other up and I leave my crew to set up the machine gun on top of the wall while I run to Jock's tanks which have halted about 50 yards down the path. They have struck so many mines that they've stopped to replace some damaged chains. There are marked minefields either side of us behind thick barbed wire with "Achtung! Minen" and the skull and crossbones notices hanging on the wire. The grass in these patches is burning fiercely and the smoke helps to screen us but makes us choke.

As I can't raise the other half of my troop under Sergeant Geoff Crew on Jock's wireless I run back to the sea wall and walk along the top cautiously in case of mines. I pass a Canadian soldier with no face left being comforted by a Padre, and see Geoff flailing merrily with his half troop past the now famous house and about to turn left along the "first lateral" road, which runs parallel to the sea. Relief that they too have made it safely to shore. Back to Jock who is once more flailing. I notice some German soldiers with their hands up near a house and a large Alsatian guard dog tied up outside it. The Infantry are dealing with them.

We get a short breather with some tins of self heating soup. Our first meal. But then I get a call from the Chaudières who have been held up by a minefield the other side of Bernières. I ride on the back of Jock's tank and we find a Bren carrier upside down, the crew killed by a mine. We flail a wide path round it. We finished about mid-night, utterly worn out.

Ian Hammerton, 65 Norfield Road, Dartford, Kent

I was a 14 year old Grammar School boy living at Chiswick in West London. I was mad about aircraft, and was a Corporal in the Air Training Corps. In the week of May 13th 1944 there were numbers of Air Training Corps Squadrons (boys between the ages of 14-17) sent to R.A.F. Brize Norton in Oxfordshire for the Spring Camp. Brize Norton was training Troop-Glider Pilots. There were seemingly dozens of these enormous Horsa gliders being towed by Albermarle bombers operating a perpetual cab-rank of towing the glider to altitude, releasing it, landing, hooking up behind another Albermarle, and going through the same routine again. As each glider passed a point on the Flight-Line a dozen A.T.C. cadets equipped with parachutes climbed aboard. Each flight took 20 minutes, and I logged 8

hours in the seven days I was there. It was called "Air Experience" but we were actually giving these student pilots their first taste of flying the gliders with passengers aboard. With hindsight, obviously they were not fully trained less than a month before they were required to be operational! Everyone that we spoke to was quite certain that the invasion was imminent, and even at 14 I felt that I was making a contribution to the War Effort, and proud that I was.

June 6th was a normal school day, and I had a paper round to do before I went to school. It was quite hazy at 7 a.m. and as I set off on my round I saw 16 Douglas Boston Day-bombers which were stationed at Heston flying in formation coming back to their airfield at low altitude through the morning mist. It was unusual to see them returning so early.

I got back home from my paper round just after 8 a.m. and my mother said that there'd been an announcement on the 8 o'clock news that General Eisenhower was going to make an important announcement on the wireless at 9 a.m. My father who was a policeman in the Mets. and had won the M.M. in the artillery in the First War, said, "There's no doubt about it, the Invasion has started, and there's a lot of poor boys not much older than you that have seen their last sunrise this morning." This was said at least partly for my benefit because all I dreamed of was becoming a member of R.A.F. Aircrew as soon as I could. At school I walked into my Form Room and "Ikey" Rees our Form Master told us that Assembly would be as usual, but we would be staying on to hear Eisenhower's announcement. The Head, Dr. Carran led us in the usual prayers, Miss Evans the Music Mistress played the piano whilst we sang, "O Valiant Hearts". Then came the prayer for the "Old Boys" serving with H.M. Forces. I was at the school for nearly five years, and I lost count of the number of times the Head had to announce that an "Old Boy" who had attended say between 1938-42 was reported, "Killed in Action," or "Missing on Operations," or was a Prisoner of War. My closest friend lost both his brothers who were "Old Boys", one before D-Day and one after. Then the Head said: "There is an announcement of extreme importance coming on the radio at 9 a.m. The school will wait." We waited in sombre silence. At 9 a.m. General Eisenhower made his announcement that the Invasion had begun. After he had finished, Dr. Carran said, "The School will now pray for the "Old Boys of the School", and all the other young men of Britain and the Allies who to-day are carrying the War to the gates of the enemy that God will keep them safe in the terrible days to come...Our Father..."

At mid-morning break we were all outside looking skyward. There were swarms of B17s, like

silver specks in the sky leaving white vapour trails behind them as they formed up, and as I watched "my" Bostons roared overhead going out again. This time I noticed that they had black and white stripes painted under the wings and around the fuselages. It was an aid to recognition which we soon learned to call Invasion stripes. Not long after D-Day the school was hit by a V1, and much of the roof went, then in September the first V2 to fall in England fell on Staveley Road, and the day after the Manager of Smiths made me redundant as my paper round was Staveley Road and I had no customers left! But if I live to be a hundred I'll never forget June 6th, 1944.
Derek W. F. Waters, 3 Garway Close,
Royal Leamington Spa, Warwickshire

I was in the 22nd Dragoons, 30th Armoured Brigade. At this time rumour was rife about preparing for the invasion of Europe. We were equipped with a variety of all sorts of weird looking AFVs (Armoured Fighting Vehicles) and they all had one theme in common, all were connected with the destruction of land-mines. We eventually ended up with the flail which consisted of a jib fastened to the front of the tank. A roller was fitted to the forward part of the jib. Fitted to the roller were a series of steel chains, with a steel ball at the end of each chain. The object being for the roller to revolve and cause the chains to beat the ground in front of the tank, thereby detonating any mines before the vehicle passed over. As the tank crept slowly forward a lane was being made to allow the faster tanks behind safe access through the minefield, and continue any advance. We were far from thrilled at the role we had been selected to play, but we trained on and by the start of 1944 we settled on the type of tank we were to use, which turned out to be the American Sherman, all purpose built and ready for the job of beating our way to the beaches at whichever place had been

chosen to attempt the landings on the continent. I myself was a tank commander and troop sergeant and second in command to Lt Allen who was my troop leader. Each troop consisted of five tanks. Each tank was equipped with two machine guns loose, and one 75mm gun co-axially mounted with a further machine gun in a rotating turret. There was a crew of five men to each tank, being tank commander, gunner, wireless operator/loader, driver and co-driver who manned one of the machine guns at the front of the tank. Each regiment had three squadrons each with four troops as above. Regimental HQ had just three tanks without flails.

On 3rd June we loaded as a troop on two landing craft myself and another flail on one, and my troop leader and another flail on the other. Myself in the front tank and would be first off. Also on the craft were four Churchill tanks manned by Royal Engineers and each equipped with a different contraption to combat the different obstacles we were likely to encounter after landing. Owing to wretched weather the crews of the tanks (five to each tank, making a total of 30 men) spent most of the time in a small cabin at the rear of the craft, passing the time telling the odd story and discussing the task ahead. I recall one of the engineers had a mouth organ and we joined in a few sing-songs. Rumours were afoot that the whole operation was being called off, but never the less at noon on the 5th June we sailed out of the Solent into the main channel and were maneouvered into the formation in which we were to land. The landings were scheduled to touch down at 0700 on the morning of 6th June 1944. We were familiar with it as H-Hour D-Day. This meant 19 hours in the most horrendous seas one could imagine. There was barely a man on our craft who wasn't suffering from violent sea-sickness from the word go. From what I learned later

all the other LCTs were afflicted in the same way. All the men were so eager to get on firm ground that the German reception was of secondary importance! Sleep was impossible and although rations were in lavish supply very little was consumed. I do recall that my gunner Johnnie Downs was one of the few who proved to be a good sailor, and he spent the time heating tins of soup and pushing them in front of the sick ones (myself included) and for thanks he was given a roar of army language or recipients running to the side of the craft to heave their hearts up. That more or less is the story of the crossing. We unshackled the tanks at about 0530 hours just as the rocket boats were delivering their deadly cargoes into what we hoped were the shore defences. We manned the tanks at 0600 hours ready to beach. I think it was about 0715 when we touched down on our return to France after almost four years to the date. The plan was that my troop on the two LCTs (Tank Landing Craft) were to sail into the beaches preceded by the amphibious tanks. Unfortunately the rough seas were too much for the DDs and all were sunk before they could make the

amps down! Infantry on an LCI ready to dash ashore. "DD" tanks on beach with R.E. Armoured vehicles.

I had volunteered for the Royal Navy in early 1940, before I was 18, and after training and experience in the Atlantic and the Mediterranean, I came back to Britain in a troopship which carried the hard core of those who were to go to Normandy.

I was drafted to "Scylla", in Portsmouth, the flagship for the invasion. This was a sister ship to "Naiad" which had gone down in the Mediterranean. Vice-Admiral Philip Vian had been rescued only after hours in the water. "Scylla" was a light cruiser, very fast, armed with 5.25 guns. She was fitted out with no less than 57 wireless lines, to control all events. We became very tired as time went on, with so much to do, so as to be ready for sea.

One event greatly feared was that Churchill or the King might come down to be part of the events – we didn't have the time for "show". It happened that the King did come, and we had to line ship as best we could. Vian walked as the last man of the inspecting "Top Brass" and he stopped at one tiny man who was very stout and bespectacled. Pointing to a large and colourful medal ribbon, the Admiral asked, "What on earth is *that?*" The little chap drew in a great gulp of air and said, "Metropolitan Police, Long Service and Good Conduct Medal...sir!" Vian said warmly, "Well that's one bugger I'll never get!" and he laughed his way on. This man was always popular, because he *knew* his ships, he bitterly regretted their loss, he knew on Malta convoys how much water, fuel, ammunition, gunpower, each had. He would work one ship to death, covering, searching, running errands on the convoy strays, etc. Then, when there was just time and fuel left, he simply ordered, "Go Home. Good Luck" – and off she went, while the rest of us were fresh for the fight to come. He inspired great trust and he got it. He also sought out action, he led by example.

After delays due to appalling weather, the choice was made to sail out. As I recall, it would have been perhaps late night on 5th June, 1944. Next morning, early, we heard a special broadcast from the General Commanding, Dwight Eisenhower, USA. It was very long, full of words like "Freedom", "Democracy", "Mankind" and so on, a full-blooded political speech. It eventually ended, and the voice of Vian came on with a typical piece of terse naval command. "You, hear me. When you are toothless old men, you'll want to be boasting about today – so Bloody Well, *get on with it!!!*" A great cheer went up round the Fleet. This was more like it!

It is not easy to set down the atmosphere aboard, but one *knew* what every man felt. They had seen London bombed, Portsmouth on fire, Malta juddering under the onslaughts, convoys butchered for lack of air power, some had lost their wives, all had lost relatives and friends – and here it was – the great chance...this time, instead of pulling soldiers out of the water, we were going to put them ashore, and there would be no retreat. It wasn't like a film, there were no memorable words, but you could *feel* the lively, excited way orders were given, taken, carried out smoothly, men trained by hard knocks for just this special day. Never was there a cross word, a moment of panic, irritation, excuses...it was like a great team of sportsmen – but it was not a game.

The command came to start the firing. The ships called up were H.M.S. Belfast and the old warhorse, "Warspite." The signal was sent in Plain Language to avoid all doubt – after all, the Germans were very well aware of our presence! Here is the signal which started it all: *"OPEN FIRE, FIRE AT WILL, DO NOT REPEAT DO NOT HIT THE WHITE HOTEL."* The White Hotel, near Le Havre, still stands. It was needed for the gunnery bearing.

The bombardment was deafening. I had been off the coast for the El Alamein artillery attack, but Arromanches, with the 16" shells of the Warspite, the rockets from barges, and all the other attacking guns, was unforgettable. It was as if every German soldier had his name on *something*.

We were always moving about. One young Boats Officer put up a life-long black when "he", Vian, wanted to go near the shore to see what was going on(!). The Admiral's boat was on the seaward side, with heavy waves thumping it against the stern. I was ordered to get it and bring it round, while the Boats Officer got the mother and father of a naval barrage...

Thousands of signals came in and went out. We had R.A.F. and Army signallers in our Radio Rooms, and a whole posse of recruited Policemen to assist with decoding after a short course of signals. They had their own "shop" and messages were rushed in and out for translation and sending off. The methods used were simply to paste signals which were "finished" into a vast book, page by page. For this, a huge pot of glue was set up above head height, and mugs were filled from it by the dozen...

Well, we overstayed our welcome, and one night, with the troops well inland and our work nearly done, we went too close to Le Havre and hit a huge land-mine set on the floor of the approaches. It took most of the stern off, but she steadied. We went to put on the emergency lighting, but the raw policemen, in the dark and with splitting heads, set off at a run to get above decks...dangerous, because it was a single-gangway ship. No-one knew what the true damage was, as yet. I remember bawling out at them, "Stand still! Go Back! The lights will be on soon. This is a warship! There's no halftime and no bloody oranges! Walk back slowly, do it." They did it and the lights came on; poor things, but our own!

At once, however, we heard a fearsome groaning...on and on..."Mary, forgive me, it was just the once...Mary, I'm dying..." I put my hand down to where the man was lying, under a bench and in the dark. My fingers were sticky. I asked him if he was bleeding? "Yes, 'course," he groaned, and I got hold of a torch. Near him was the old glue crock, smashed in the mishap, and glue was all over him. The gales of laughter released all our tension and I set about getting the whole Wireless Room cleaned up, using sea water. However, I had forgotten young Menzies, a Scot whose work was aft in the D.F. Room, a steel box on the quarterdeck. I rushed out there, suddenly cold at the sea air, but refreshed by its cleanliness. Menzies was calmly sitting in his steel chair, with no power and not much air. His deck was carrying sea water, but I had walked it well enough. He said, "Well, now, I knew you'd come, did you win the card game, then?" I told him shortly to bring out all code books for handing in, to bolt his door and return with me. He needed a hand once or twice, he must have had the headache of his lifetime! He had been sitting directly above the mine.

Next day, soon after dawn, a U.S.A. tugmaster sailed up to us and offered to tow us back to Chatham! The Admiral and some others had gone aboard a merchantman made out as copy for the "Scylla," also with 57 wireless lines aboard, so that the war went on. I think she was named the "Evesham" but I could have faltered in this respect. One event I do recall and this turned upon the Geordie accent. We had a very simple Call Sign so that small ships like MTBs and strangers could remember it. Soon after our drop-out, a call came from "Evesham" to take it over. In plain English the inquirer said, "Do you have a Call Sign?" How to tell it without telling every German around? The answer came from an astute Geordie, Norman Box. He said, in his heaviest accent, "Have we getten a Call Sign? Why Aye, man! O' Course we hev!" It worked. The wanted code was simply, "YI".

My abiding memory of D-Day was of a sea filled up with ships, all types, sizes, shapes, uses. All were represented. All were busy, bringing more troops, or more supplies. Men were there by the thousand, again, all busy. It was a marvellous naval operation, the key to the eventual victory. I remember the line of bullet or shell holes that ran along one side of "Scylla" when a single German 'plane attacked us as we lay still and helpless. It was soon seen off. And I remember the keen smell of the sea in the Channel that morning, after long days below deck. It was silent as we crept back to the white English cliffs, "like wrongs hushed up." I had never been to Chatham before, but I bought some red cherries there, to take home to a very special lady. They were bitter, she said...

The military cemeteries in Normandy speak out an eloquent testimony to the youth of many who lost their lives, especially in the Paratroop Regiment. Ages like 18, 19, 20, 21; on and on the slabs go in the serried ranks. I found one small cemetery in a tiny settlement where German, French, British and others are buried together, not separated by nationality. Each grave is tended by one family, the flowers are very beautiful and it is very moving to see such tenderness.

Norman Green, Windyhaugh, Skyreburn, Gatehouse of Fleet, By Castle Douglas

I had been hard at work for a fortnight getting our vehicles ready and waterproofed and also our radio equipment for our landing. Our unit was 65 strong; wireless operators, linesmen, signal office staff, despatch riders, and drivers. We were all attached to 147 Brigade of the 49th (West Riding) Infantry Division and our Battalions were the 1/6th and 1/7th Duke of Wellington's Regiments and the 11th Royal Scots Fusiliers.

On the 5th June, we cleared the camp of all equipment and set off. My wife was expecting our baby in early June but owing to restrictions I had not seen her since Christmas. We arrived at our concentration area and were promptly marshalled behind barbed wire with armed sentries patrolling outside. After a briefing by the Brigade Major about our landing area (King Sector of Gold Beach) I sought out the Army Chaplain and explained about my wife's imminent prospect of becoming a mother. He was extremely sympathetic and obtained a priority call to my wife's home for me. As the phone rang my heart was pounding and then my wife's mother answered. "Harry, you've got a bonny baby girl. She was born ½ hour ago and weighs 7lb 8 ounces. When will you be home?"

I stammered an excuse and said I would ring later. My heart sank as I knew that in a short while I would be on my way to Normandy. I wrote a hasty letter and to save my wife worrying I dated it a few days later, knowing that the green envelope wouldn't have a date stamp.

We sailed down the Thames and headed towards the Isle of Wight. As night fell I fell into a deep sleep. My only thoughts were still of my wife and our baby daughter.

A huge thump on the metal deck woke me instantly, even though I was still in a daze. Bill Sinclair, a fellow wireless operator, shook me fully awake and in his Glaswegian accent shouted "Come on Corp, we've been hit by a bomb; let's get on deck". As we scrambled out bullets zipped off the deck from the Heinkel above and so we promptly dashed below again for cover! We had been hit by a radio-controlled "Glider bomb" which had cut through a steel cabin and now lay in the coal bunkers in the bowels of the ship. Would it explode? Did it have a time fuse?

It was still there in the cold light of early dawn off Arromanches. All we could hear now was the thunderous roar of the guns from the battleships, cruisers and destroyers which surrounded us. It was deafening, and added to it was the belching fire of a rocket firing ship a few hundred yards away to our left. Enemy artillery fire was falling erratically around the fleet. I picked up a small metal plate from the wreckage of the bomb and slipped it automatically into my pocket, and gazed sullenly at the unwelcome monster as it lay amongst the coals.

Fortunately we had a small detachment of Royal Engineers aboard and as daylight came we watched fascinated as they defused the bomb and swung it over the side on a gantry. A fussy destroyer saw us. "Keep for inspection" it signalled. "Not bloody likely" our Aldis lamp flashed in reply as it was released into the depths of the sea! Later as I climbed down into our Landing Craft to oversee our radio vehicle ashore, I made a stupid mistake and realised I should have stayed on the vehicle. I found that out as I walked down the ramp until the sea reached my chin! So what – I was ashore, alive and the father of a day old baby!

But it wasn't all over. I should have realised that. By the end of June the 1/6th Duke of Wellington's took a terrible mauling in the area of Fontenay, Cristot, Rauray and Hottot and had to be replaced by the 1st Leicestershire Regiment. They stayed with us until the final defeat of Germany. The metal plate from the Glider bomb became my mascot – and it still is! I was lucky – I came through it all, and I am writing this on my 76th birthday. But it is really for my pals who didn't come through it and who are still in Normandy:

    Signalman William Sinclair, the Wireless Operator who woke me, Signalman Reg. Thomas and L/Cpl's Hartley, Eric Dale-Thompson – all wireless operators,
    and L/Cpl. Fred Sillitoe, Despatch Rider.
God bless them all – I never forget them.

Harry A. Teale, 26 Hill Crescent,
Rawdon, Leeds, Yorkshire

th S.S. Brigade at St. Aubin sur Mer. Note mine detection being carried out and "white marker" lane. Contour mounted owitzer in foreground.

It was approximately 01.30 hours on June 6th, 1944 when I stepped out of the belly of a Stirling bomber.

I felt the tug on my shoulders as my 'chute opened and my kit bag, which was strapped to my leg and was grossly over-weight, fell off and vanished into what was obviously an orchard below me. I then realised that something was wrong. There wasn't supposed to be an orchard below me and I was apparently going down in the wrong place! I managed to steer myself towards the corner of the orchard, as past experience had taught me that landing in trees by parachute can be quite painful.

I was at this moment oblivious to the sound of gun fire all around me, but on landing the sudden realisation of where I was and what was going on around me sent a short, sharp stab of terror up my spine. Here I was laying on my back in a field in Normandy, taking part in the liberation of Europe from the Nazi's, with only a couple of hand grenades in my belt. All my equipment, including my rifle and ammunition, my P.I.A.T., and food, were somewhere in the orchard and I was lost!

I had joined the 12th Battalion Para's in September 1943, having volunteered from the Royal Armoured Corps., where I had been engaged in demonstrating flame throwers mounted in Bren carriers. But I was not happy with the idea of running around in a Bren carrier loaded with highly inflammable jelly. I was 20 years old and looking for some adventure and a bit of excitement, but did not fancy the idea of being blown sky high in a Bren carrier and the prospect of parachuting appealed to me.

The training was hard and rigorous but very thorough. We had been well briefed on the D-Day landings and knew exactly what we had to do.

I scrambled out of my harness, got to my feet, and took stock of my surroundings. Although it was dark the sky was aglow with light from the fires in the coastal towns that were being bombed by the R.A.F. in preparation for the main landing force due to assault the beaches at daybreak.

I could see the orchard a short distance away and thought of my kit bag. I could see figures all around me and they all seemed to be going in the same direction, so I joined them hoping that I would eventually reach my alloted position. It was just breaking daylight when we approached Ranville, having been dropped some four miles from the D.Z.

I was re-equipped, given a P.I.A.T., and had been joined by the other two members of my section. So fully equipped we made our way to "Le Bas de Ranville" and took up our positions in the corner of a wood.

A P.I.A.T. and three men may not seem much of a deterrent to German Tiger and Leopard tanks but on the contrary is quite capable of disabling a tank when used efficiently. However the main object was for the three of us to make contact with the pilot and co-pilot of a glider which contained a Jeep, five pounder anti-tank gun and limber, and within an hour of us setting up our position a Jeep, gun, and limber joined us and as a crew of five we became an even more efficient anti-tank section. In fact after a while a Tiger tank came down the field in front of us and promptly received two shells from us. One in the belly and one in the turret.

Things were pretty hot up until then with machine gun fire and mortar shells landing all around. A great many lads had

parachutist who didn't make it.

been killed or wounded but so far we had been lucky and in the early afternoon we had been called back to base for a short rest period.

We spent the next few days taking up various positions. All the time under mortar and machine gun fire, but our defences were sound and we held our ground, thus preventing the enemy getting through to the main assault taking place on the coast.

On the 5th day, during a heavy mortar attack, the young lad, who had joined us just a few days before D-Day, was killed. This upset my mate and I considerably as we were just getting to know the lad. He was only 18 and quite a jolly little bloke.

We assembled in the church at Amfreville and shortly after were ordered to take up positions outside. There were just the two of us at this time as no replacements were available. I carried the P.I.A.T. and my pal Bill carried the shells. We left the church and immediately came under extremely heavy shell fire. We got across the road when Bill took a lump of shrapnel in his leg and went down in a ditch. I could see he was out of action so I took the shells from him, saw that the medics were with him, and went through into an orchard. I explained the situation to a nearby Sgt. who told me to stand by while he tried to get me some replacement. I was standing under a tree in the orchard when suddenly there was a great bang, a huge red flash, and a great cloud of dust.

I knew no more until three days later when I came too. I was at Portsmouth Dock on board a train heading for Shotley Bridge Hospital. My small part in the liberation of Europe was over, but I was proud to have been part of it all.

George Price, 31 Sussex Walk, Norton, Stockton-on-Tees

I was in the 79th Assault Squadron. We were the first wave in on D-Day and the first to land on the beach.

Our Churchill tanks were fitted with special guns for putting out pillboxes, and the hatches were sealed so that we could go in the sea. We were supplied with survival packs and French money. We were in the leading landing crafts and when we left England the sea was rough and nearly all of us were sea sick. As we neared the French coast there was gun fire and two of the ships went up in smoke.

The rocket firing landing craft fired their rockets. As we were the next to go all the crew got in the tank through the gun turret, I was the first in to start the engine.

The first two tanks that went down the ramp off the landing craft were flail tanks. They went up in flames. It was not a very good sight to see your mates on fire trying to get out of their tanks. The flail tanks were to clear the mines. I was driving the third tank which was an officer's tank. When we came down the ramp you could see mines everywhere on cross pieces about 2' off the ground, and pillboxes further up the beach. The officer told me to pick my way through the mines as best I could. That was alright for the ones you could see. Just before I made it up the beach we hit a mine and it blew the bogey off, but the track held. One of the crew put the wind-sock up. The officer and sergeant in our crew had been killed. Over half of the squadron had been wiped out. I drove the tank behind a sand dune, there we unsealed the driver and co-driver hatches. By then the Commandoes were with

us. Then the Major came and took charge of our tank as his had been knocked out.

We then went along the road and came under some small arms fire which our gunners returned. We came to a bridge over a canal, there was a pillbox and Germans on the other side. As our gun had only a short range the Major decided to cross the bridge. We had just started to cross when the Germans blew the bridge, the section we were on held so I was able to reverse off. The Commandoes took charge over the bridge.

The Major told me to drive the tank into an open space so that we were clear of the houses, and to stay there as he had to go. The tank engine was running warm so I got on the back of the tank to unseal the engine covers. I had just started when I heard an aeroplane. I thought it was a Mustang until I saw it release a bomb. The bomb was coming straight at the tank. There was nothing I could do but to lay down on the tank covers. All my strength went and a funny feeling went all over me, but the bomb just cleared the tank and exploded in front of it. I had to lay there for some time until my strength returned. I then got back into the driver's seat and we stayed there all night. There were bombs and shells exploding, small arms fire and houses on fire all night. We pulled back next day to get repairs done and re-group. That's how it was for me the first 24 hours of D-Day.

Eddie W. D. Beeton, 2 Church Close, Great Wilbraham, Cambridge

wrecked Sherman flail tank on Gold Beach. 2nd County of London Yeomanry (Westminster Dragoons), 30 Armoured Brigade. Note balloons.

For us D-Day came too late, my brother, nicknamed Loulou, had been arrested on the 25th of May, 1944. As he was taken away by the Gestapo, he whispered "mauvais" or "Anglais" to his wife Christiane. She did not know for sure.

We had been involved with the Resistance from the earliest days. Loulou who was a Belgian officer like my father had been taken prisoner of war on May 10th, 1940. Mother had been a Belgian refugee in Britain during WW1 and had delayed leaving for London to the last moment as she wanted to know where he was, and by the time we decided to go it was too late. So we stayed in Brussels. German planes laden with bombs and flying low were on their way to Britain. As a ploy to divide Belgium, the Germans released the Flemish prisoners and as Father was Flemish, Loulou came home in September, having joked with the Camp Officer about his place of birth being Bexhill-on-Sea. Both Father and Loulou decided that it was their duty to resist and in order to do so efficiently my brother joined the "Flying Brigade" of the Rationing Control Authorities. That way he had access to the various places forbidden to Belgians. We were working with Edith Bagshaw, a British lady who had married a Belgian and who was a member of Secret Intelligence Service (SIS).

By November 1940 we had began a life of danger. We lived in Brussels in a large house which was a "safe house" as there were plenty of young people coming and going. Loulou had his work as a British Agent and Father directed the Provincial Department of Food. We worked at home helping both with various nitty gritty tasks required by their work, writing on false identity papers, degluing and re-gluing rationing stamps, preparing bandages and parcels for the "refractaires" and generally helping doing the dull part of their Resistance work. Loulou's specific job was to liaise with the various groups within the Resistance: collecting money and arms dropped by parachute, organising the many informations required and deciding upon how to best inform SIS. Altogether his task was to smooth the relationship between the many factions of the Resistance so as to facilitate and establish a sound working state for when the Landing would take place. As a sideline we harboured Jews, Forced Labour evaders, wanted killers, etc. In July 1943 William Alan Poulton of the R.A.F. came to the house, proudly brought to our safety by a non-English speaking Loulou. We collected another two: Vincent Horn R.A.F., and Robert J. Hoke, U.S. Air Force. There were no safe "Routes" to send them back. In January 1944 we were contacted by a man who said, and proved, he had a "line" to get the boys back. He was the 'infamous' "de Zitter" a German agent, and the creator of the infamous "ligne Zero".

Edith was arrested at the end of January. Loulou was offered to be taken to Britain but felt the end was near and wanted to be there then. When the Gestapo came it was very quick. None of the leisurely and thorough searching as they had done before. They simply took his valuable stamp collection as they always took what they fancied, and left with him.

We learnt of his arrest the same afternoon. All we could do was to hide everything possible. We had dynamite, we buried it in the garden. We stopped having anyone visiting. We spoke to no one. We were in terror of my sister's children being interrogated as more of our work would be known. We were still in a state of shock when we learnt of the Allied Landing through the German-controlled radio – we did not even dare to listen to the B.B.C. so D-Day found us not only devastated but powerless.

Louis Thyrin

I remember making my way that day to the hospital where I worked as an auxiliary nurse to avoid deportation to Germany. I had been so distressed by Loulou's arrest. Then suddenly a feeling of utter joy overcame me. At last there was a tangible end, we would be free and together soon. Mother took the whole day to understand the full implication of the events in Normandy. She found a great calm and proud hope restored her spirit: we all knew Loulou had had a hand in the Landing and she rejoiced in the anticipation that he would soon be there to triumph when four years of oppression would end and our reward would come with freedom.

'lider troops with 3 "trophies", a very happy French girl, a captured German motor-cycle, and (man on left), a German ːhmeisser machine-pistol.

Mother received a typed card from a place called Buchenwald, telling us that Louis Thiryn had arrived there. The simplicity of the printed form reassured us as we knew where he was. We did not understand its awfulness. We learned of Loulou's death in the cruel shifting operated by the Nazis on their slave-labourers. He had been used to work at the V1 and V2 plant at Dora-Mittelswerk and the S.S. had not wanted them to be alive when the Allied Troops finally reached them.

What must be quite understood is what we endured – and we were privileged – must never be allowed to happen again. Even if my brother had survived the message should be the same. It took great emotional stress to write my story, as even after 50 years I mourn my brother.

Claire Keen, Pen-y-Borfa Fawr, Caersws, Powys.

I was in the United States 29th Infantry Division from its induction into federal service. If you've read Joseph Balkoski's account of the Division in Normandy – Beyond The Beachhead – you know that I figured prominently in that decisive World War II campaign.

I was then Captain King, 175th Infantry Regiment, Maryland National Guard, and the Commanding Officer of K Company, the leading unit, or "point", for the 29th Infantry Division. And, as Balkoski noted, "Company K seemed to get all the dangerous assignments." Not the least of these was the crossing of the Vire River and the capture of Auville, a critical linking point for the widely separated Utah and Omaha beachheads.

I had led Company K in the final assault on Omaha Beach on D-Day+1. I then moved my troops up the coast road, marching for 14 hours, and captured the port city of Isigny. While in the city's main square rounding up prisoners – Cossacks who fought for the Germans in exchange for rations and keeping their horses – I was handed a special assignment from the Division Commander, Major General Charles "Uncle Charlie" Gerhardt. He ordered Company K to advance three miles to the River Vire, secure its bridge and seize the town beyond: Auville-Sur-Mer.

Capt. King being decorated by Field Marshal Montgomery.

I remember nobody had the faintest idea what we were up against. We owned the air, but intelligence reports on ground forces were nil. For all we knew, the Germans could be preparing to counterattack with several armoured divisions.

When we arrived at the Vire just before dawn, we found the Germans had blown the bridge. We had no boats or bridging equipment and we were down to 150 effective troops. So we moved to high ground, organised a perimeter defence and waited for reinforcements.

We didn't have to wait long. But instead of additional support, we were handed a new order by General Gerhardt himself: Cross the Vire in broad daylight and storm Auville!

It seemed like Balaclava and the 'Charge of the Light Brigade' all over again! We would be completely in the open, no cover for our flanks and no protection at the rear, facing an enemy of equal force occupying high ground. It was obvious it should have been a night operation, but my orders were to attack at 1600 hours!

My maps gave no indication of the depth of the Vire. Even worse, the only approach to the river was across 200 yards of open field strung in barbed wire!

Calling for a mortar barrage and fire support from four light tanks, I deployed my troops in a single skirmish line to make the Germans think I was leading the entire U.S. Field Army. To suppress enemy fire, I ordered my men to deliver rapid fire from the hip without selecting a target! Gerhardt had said to simply "walk across the river," and I tell you I was relieved to find that "Uncle Charlie" was right. The Vire was only knee-deep!

Halfway across the river, I called for a signal flare to move friendly overhead fire to my flanks and it was then a German machine gun nest opened up and I took a bullet in both thighs. The men of Company K went on to seize Auville. I recuperated from my wounds and returned to active service, serving in the Rhineland and Central Europe.

After advancing to the rank of Major, I left active service in 1945, having earned the Silver Star, Bronze Star and Cluster, Military Cross (British) and the Purple Heart. The latter two were for our crossing of the River Vire. All those who participated in that invasion, whether Army, Navy, Air Force, Coast Guard, Marine or Merchant Seamen, officer or non-com or in the ranks, are part of a noble brotherhood from whom no other event nor time itself can take away the everlasting association. It was, indeed, one of those rare happenings that did and will forever stir the hearts of men.

John T. King III, 27 Warrenton Road, Baltimore, U.S.A.

...maha Beach – soldiers of 5th U.S. Engineers Brigade helping a wounded infantryman of 116th Regiment U.S. Army.

Not many 20 year olds were lucky enough to land on Sword beach, at H hour on D-Day, 6th June 1944 without getting their feet wet. The 13/18th Royal Hussars in Sherman tanks and the Commandos on Shanks's Pony were among the first ashore. The 13/18th Queen Mary's Own, were part of the 27th Armoured Brigade. The flash on our uniforms was of a sea horse, more commonly known as the Pregnant Prawn! It was expected that on landing the 27th Armoured would receive so many casualties that we would have to be disbanded soon afterwards. We were disbanded all right but fortunately without too many casualties at this point.

A and B Squadrons were in "DD tanks", which had to swim ashore. C and H.Q. Squadrons were the lucky ones. They waded ashore! For the uninitiated the DD stands for duplex drive. Each Sherman tank was fitted with a propellor between the rear sprockets which drive the tracks forward, a canvas screen all the way round the outside of the tank. The bottom was also sealed to keep out the sea water. These Heath Robinson modifications turned a conventional tank into a floating vehicle.

A and B Squadrons had to drop off the Tank Landing Craft into deep water, well away from the beach. They looked tiny in the water and very vulnerable in the rough seas. It was only when their tracks touched bottom and the screen was dropped that the enemy found they had to contend with a tank.

But now our years of training were over, no more firing on the ranges, no more cruising in an L.C.T. around the North of Scotland in mid winter, no more paddling on the Norfolk Broads in a DD tank, learning the intricacies of the Davis Escape Apparatus. Had I volunteered for the tanks or the submarines?

As soon as we left Gosport, knowing this was no exercise, this time it was for real, out came the spanners, and the guard around the 75mm gun was thrown overboard. Let me explain. The gun recoils when it is fired and the guard is there to protect the crew from sustaining broken bones. On the practice range this is fine but in action if the three men in the turret had to make a quick exit the poor wireless operator, who also loaded the gun would have difficulty getting out, so the guard was fed to the fishes.

As most of us know D-Day had been postponed for 24 hours because of the weather, but some poor sods were already at sea and were left sitting it out, somewhere in the Manche. Sea sickness was our main concern. Even the sailors were malade. But on seeing land at first light our spirits picked up. The adrenalin was flowing and we wondered with some apprehension what was awaiting us. Our main aim was to get ashore and off the beach as soon as possible. If only we could get our tracks on dry land. The enemy were of secondary consideration. H.M.S. Warspite was alongside us sending broadside after broadside on to the enemy positions and as we passed the Warspite I thought "now it's our turn. God help us!"

A few kilometres inland – let's forget about the killing which was what we had been trained to do – our tank found its way to a small farmhouse. The farmer was pleased to see us. He was free and we had not damaged his property – not yet anyway. He produced a bottle of home brew and five thick glass tumblers. All the contents of this bottle were divided equally among the tank crew. This clear liquid may have looked like water but it turned out to be Calvados. It put fire in the belly as it worked its way down! In my best schoolboy French all I could say was "Sante, Monsieur, Vive la France". For the remainder of D-Day this tank crew felt remarkably brave! We learned the meaning of Dutch courage.

Fifty years later, now an O.A.P., not quite so young and innocent, I know that Calvados with age takes on a slight brownish tinge and can become quite smooth and pleasant. Our arrival on D-Day must have been rather premature. This bottle had not had time to mature. Perhaps it had only been distilled the week before! But as far as our tank crew was concerned it settled our stomachs and was much appreciated.

Matt 'Jock' Lamont, 1C Monkton Court, Prestwick, Ayrshire

In 1941 I joined the railway and started work at the L.M.S. Locomotive Depot at Royston, Yorkshire. I was 16 years old but because of the war new entrants were under pressure to learn the railway rules and regulations and work on the footplate earlier than would have been under normal circumstances. Consequently boys of 17½ were finding themselves firing the engines of main line trains.

So in 1944 at the age of 20 I had become an experienced fireman, and shortly before 5.00 a.m. on the morning of 6th June I was walking across the fields from Cudworth where I lived to the depot at Royston. On that day our job was to take an engine to Barnsley, and pick up coaches there to work a passenger train via Sheffield to Chinley in Derbyshire and back, stopping at all stations on the way. It was a beautiful sunny morning, all quiet and peaceful as I walked along the path, when I heard the sound of heavy planes. Looking up I saw about 20 planes overhead with many more in the distance. I took them to be bombers returning from a raid. But then I noticed there were broad white stripes on the wings of those nearest to me, markings I had never seen before.

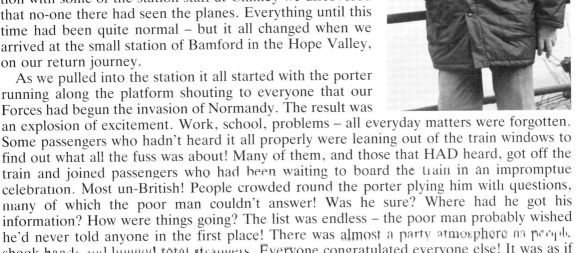

On arriving at the engine shed I found a discussion going on about the planes and my driver asked if I had seen them and whether I had noticed the unfamiliar markings. There were several theories put forward, but the general view was that there must have been a special raid of some sort. My driver and I set off with the engine to Barnsley where we found more discussion going on about the planes with the unusual markings. We then attached the coaches and drew into the station where we picked up our passengers and left at our scheduled time of 6.15 a.m. We then did our usual run to Chinley via Sheffield and the Hope Valley. In conversation with some of the station staff at Chinley we discovered that no-one there had seen the planes. Everything until this time had been quite normal – but it all changed when we arrived at the small station of Bamford in the Hope Valley, on our return journey.

As we pulled into the station it all started with the porter running along the platform shouting to everyone that our Forces had begun the invasion of Normandy. The result was an explosion of excitement. Work, school, problems – all everyday matters were forgotten. Some passengers who hadn't heard it all properly were leaning out of the train windows to find out what all the fuss was about! Many of them, and those that HAD heard, got off the train and joined passengers who had been waiting to board the train in an impromptue celebration. Most un-British! People crowded round the porter plying him with questions, many of which the poor man couldn't answer! Was he sure? Where had he got his information? How were things going? The list was endless – the poor man probably wished he'd never told anyone in the first place! There was almost a party atmosphere as people shook hands and hugged total strangers. Everyone congratulated everyone else! It was as if everyone realised that at long last this was the beginning of the end of the war and that peace really was in sight at last.

But the British stiff upper lip was not totally dead! In the middle of the celebrations the guard came down the platform blowing his whistle to get attention. He had to blow it very loudly several times! He then announced in dignified tones that he was very sorry but the train was now already late and that it really would have to resume its journey! If passengers wanted to go with it they would have to board at once. They did – very reluctantly. Between us the guard and I managed to persuade the passengers to get back on the train and then with a wave of the green flag, we set off for Barnsley.

I remember that on our way the driver and I talked about what we would do when the war was over, when rationing finished and when things were back to normal. After years of war and shortages, with bad news so often the order of the day, the tide had at last turned and we could already look forward to better times ahead. The driver said that when it was all over he would buy a whole leg of lamb and eat it all himself! When we finally arrived back at the locomotive depot we found the same atmosphere as at Bamford. Everyone was talking at once about when the war would be over and what they would do. The foreman,

who after all still had a depot to run, had been making sterling efforts for the last couple of hours to chivvy the men into stopping talking and getting on with their jobs. When we arrived he'd obviously given up!

As I walked home that day after the shift people I met or passed on the way, whether I knew them or not, called out a cherry greeting or added "Not long now" or some such remark. My memory of D-Day is the tremendous boost in confidence that it gave to everyone, the lift in morale, but most of all seeing British "reserve" abandoned when the wonderful news was received!

Jack Allen, 5 Berkeley Croft, Royston, Barnsley, Yorkshire

I was 18 and a student at London University, but Queen Mary College had been evacuated to Cambridge, so at 9 a.m. on the morning of June 6th, 1944, I was at King's College and trying to get absorbed in a heavy French classic. I was sitting on a window-seat in a room of the Fellows' Building, where Miss Aitken – Q.M.C. Librarian – had been allowed to set out essential books. There wasn't much room for readers, so the window-seat was much in demand – peace and quiet, and possibly bringing its occupant a cup of weak wartime tea from Miss Aitken.

There was another reason for wanting a good place to work. Call-up regulations put the pressure on all students – girl entrants of 18 were only allowed two years for their degree course instead of three, and were called up immediately after their final exams, I was lucky in that I was an under-age student, of just 17, when I started, and would be allowed the full three years. But to work hard was the "in thing". Failure in intermediate examinations meant instant call-up. There was a staggering imbalance of the sexes. In the schools of Medicine, Dentistry and Theology, hardly a woman was to be found among those hearty and healthy young men. But elsewhere, most of the men were either medically unfit for service or were not British. Our French Department of about fifty had just six men, four Belgians, a noisy and self-opinionated Dutchman and a quiet, witty Englishman with a weak heart.

The spring of 1944 buzzed with rumours in Cambridge – our Belgians became reticent and mysterious for no clear reason. The town was full of American G.I.'s and airmen. They were friendly and known for their generosity, but at night they terrified us girls in the blackout. They could come upon us silently in their rubber-soled boots and try to start up an acquaintance with the invisible females! We never walked alone, but then, they usually roved in twos and threes. (On the other hand the tramp of British Army boots was a wonderfully reassuring sound!)

Just after 10 a.m. that morning Miss Aitken's cup of tea appeared beside me. Almost at once the Library door flew open and an excited male voice called, "We've landed! It was on the News!" For a few minutes there was a babble of raised voices, then normal silence returned. A few students had rushed out to find out more, if they could. I went on with the "heavy classic", but it was impossible to concentrate. Instead of the students in the hot sunshine of the quadrangle, I saw men in battle-dress storming up the hot sands of the French Beaches.

I was facing in exactly the right direction to see what was going on in Normandy, could I have moved away all the buildings and hills between myself and France. So I sat and tried to use a mental telescope.

With youthful optimism I discounted failure of the plan, and danger to the troops. Surely all possible safety measures had been put in place? This was, we all felt, the beginning of Germany's downfall. We were quite sure that all would be well, but we wanted every scrap of news about progress.

It happened that this was one of my two weekdays for having a meal at my digs rather than at the British Restaurant. Rations were tight. I suspect that the food saved by my three days out was redirected to help feed the man of the house. There were

45

three in the family, Father (mid 60's), daughter Joan (12), and the lady (early 50's), who was excessively house-proud. She would cover the kitchen linoleum with newspapers, even though our slippers stood just inside the back door, and she counted the number of times that her students went up and down the stairs. She usually had two girls at a time, but she had complained that two were too much to cope with, so I was 'sent as a lamb to the slaughter'. I heard of this only when I myself complained – on D-Day! – and asked for a change of lodgings. (I got the change and went to a proper study-bedroom in a luxury home on Grantchester Road).

Meals were served punctually, ferociously so. We, Father, Joan and I, always hoped that we would have finished eating by the Radio News time as Mother insisted that we stand to attention while the National Anthem was being played. We were allowed to sit down again while the band went through the Anthems of the Allies, which was just as well. I believe it eventually took something like twenty minutes to get through them all.

At the end of the morning lectures, I cycled back up Hills Road to my digs, hoping to hear the 1 o'clock news, but when I arrived home, my excitable landlady was sitting on a stool in the kitchen, very flushed. "You haven't got any dinner today! I couldn't bother with it. I keep thinking about all those poor boys in France!" The daughter came in. Same reply; and we both felt *very* hungry. Then Father appeared. He was unflappable. In his hand he held a bright new galvanized pail. "Look dear! I've managed to get you one at last!" Mother glared at him. "Damn you and your pail!", flung her apron over her face, burst into tears and left the room.

Unperturbed, Father enquired about dinner, then calmly made a fry-up, chips, an egg each, and a single sausage shared between the three of us. For all of us quiet prevailed for once on D-Day!

Phyllis S. Bowles, "Covertside", Filby Lane, Ormesby St. Margaret,
Great Yarmouth, Norfolk

Len Horsfall 2nd from left.

This is a letter written by my sister on the morning of June 6th 1944 which I received some 10 days later in France. I am sure you will find the sentiments interesting.

Dear Leonard,   Tuesday

So the great and awful day has come at last!

As we listen to the news it is impossible to put our feelings into words. With what eagerness and anxiety do we await the reports on the wireless. Since the announcement was made, we have thought of you constantly, and there hasn't been a moment when you have not been in our minds.

It is with a new and dreadful thrill that we listen to the recordings of the embarkations etc., given by the BBC, conscious as we are that you are a part of that bustle and turmoil.

It seems all wrong somehow that things should just be going on the same here.

Mother is trying hard to keep a stiff upper lip – we realise now the truth of the statement that they also serve who only stand and wait. We know that you will let us have news of you as soon as possible.

We are thinking & praying for you always and trust that God will have you in His keeping and shield you from danger.

God bless you – keep your chin up.

Love from all, Ivy

Leonard Horsfall, 13 Fieldhead Drive, Guiseley, Leeds
(Sadly Leonard Horsfall died in January, 1993, shortly after sending this in).

47

I had returned with my Brigade from the Middle East to train on specialist tanks in Suffolk. All the tanks had peculiar names and were called 'Hobarts Funnies' after General Hobart, the Divisional Commander. I had around three months intensive training on this equipment and, when it was finished, I was declared proficient on the Flails and Flamethrowers. We were moved to Worthing. The town had been evacuated and was almost all military. We were then engaged on stripping down every bolt and screw, access plates etc. on our tanks and refitting them after they had been coated in a special waterproofing compound. The tank tracks were modified with fabricated scoop extensions to assist in obtaining a better grip in sand.

Then we had word to move again, "another exercise" we thought, but not this time. This was different. We went into a large wooded area, with more Military Police than we had seen in our lives. Bell tents, equipment and men were everywhere. Loud speakers were giving out instructions, "no-one allowed out", "no letters". All night long there was one long procession of units moving out with full kit. Then it was our turn. We were given our pay, which was all in French money specially made for the occasion, and an extra blanket, shaped like a sleeping bag, but in effect, a burial blanket – lovely thought – and a stock of paper bags for sea sickness!

Off we went, and in a short time we suddenly arrived at the seaside!!! There were boats as far as the eye could see, troops, tanks, lorries all embarking and moving out. I learned later this was Gosport and we were to be Strike Force 'J'. We loaded up and secured the tanks and moved out of harbour and lay off the Isle of Wight for 48 hours. We were all very, very sea sick. The flat bottomed craft and the corned beef sandwiches, given to us by someone who had a sadistic streak in them, had taken its toll!

On the late afternoon of June 5th, we set sail. I was in 'B' Squadron 3rd County of London Yeomanry. Our sea sickness got worse and we felt that anywhere would be nice as long as it was dry land. Then, at first light, we were called together by our Squadron Leader, who said "well lads, there is the coast of France, this is IT. Tank commanders will collect their orders, crews mount. God bless you all and a safe landing." I can never forget these words. It was then that I knew fear. My sea sickness had gone and my whole inside seemed knotted up.

We climbed into our tank, the navy lads wished us well and then we felt suddenly very alone. The hatches were shut, and the spare crews busied themselves putting the final seal on the hatches. We were now virtually in a steel tomb. No-one spoke as the tank commander read out our orders, but thoughts were passing through our minds, "will the waterproofing hold", "have the spare crews done the job right after we closed the hatches", "would we sink too far in when the ramp was dropped", "what was waiting for us when we landed". Our minds were in turmoil.

Then, as if he knew what we were thinking, the tank commander tapped me on the shoulder and offered his hand. We all shook hands in turn, but no-one spoke. We knew that, whatever happened, we had a bond of friendship and we would support each other. It was a unique but calming feeling. Then radio silence was broken, the ramp was lowered and it was "GO! GO! GO!" Into the sea we went. It seemed an age before we hit the bottom, which gave us an almighty shaking up. Had the bump dis-lodged anything? We had no means of knowing.

The lack of noise was eerie as the engine exhaust was above sea level, but we could tell the engine was still going and we were making slow but steady progress. Then, through the periscopes, we saw daylight. It was 7.30 a.m. and the beach was "Juno", Courseulles sur Mer. I fired the electric detonators to blow away all the waterproofing on the hatches and guns. June 6th had begun, an event I will never forget as long as I live. Out of four tanks in my troop, two never came out of the sea.

Charlie Salt, 81 Matlock Road, Chaddesden, Derby

49

casualty of war at Hermanville. A "DD" tank – note wrecked "skirting".

Leaning against the rail on that bleak morning of 6th June, 1944, my eyes were riveted to the spectacle which had started to unfold bit by bit as the dawn broke, like the lights going up in a theatre. It was only half light when the first bright flashes could be seen, followed by the swish of 16-inch shells passing high over our heads to land ten miles inland. On the skyline, we could see the dark silhouettes of the great warships. As the landing beaches came into focus I thought of my comrades in the 1st Bucks Battalion (Oxs. and Bucks. Light Infantry) we had lost at Hazebrouck on 28th May, 1940. They had fought with such doggedness that according to at least one report 100,000 men had got away at Dunkirk who perhaps wouldn't have made it. Only 10 officers and 200 men got back from the Hazebrouck action, and they received a rare compliment from the enemy themselves. A German broadcast stated "The defenders of Hazebrouck resisted in a manner truly worthy of the British Army." It had been a sad day for

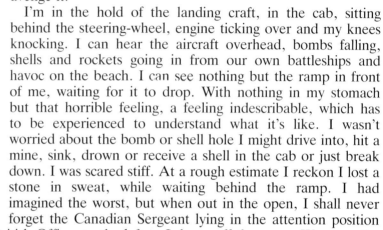

many Buckinghamshire families – now we're going back to avenge it.

I'm in the hold of the landing craft, in the cab, sitting behind the steering-wheel, engine ticking over and my knees knocking. I can hear the aircraft overhead, bombs falling, shells and rockets going in from our own battleships and havoc on the beach. I can see nothing but the ramp in front of me, waiting for it to drop. With nothing in my stomach but that horrible feeling, a feeling indescribable, which has to be experienced to understand what it's like. I wasn't worried about the bomb or shell hole I might drive into, hit a mine, sink, drown or receive a shell in the cab or just break down. I was scared stiff. At a rough estimate I reckon I lost a stone in sweat, while waiting behind the ramp. I had imagined the worst, but when out in the open, I shall never forget the Canadian Sergeant lying in the attention position to the right, and the headless British Officer to the left as I drove off the ramp. We were the lucky ones. Many in more unwieldy craft had no alternative but to jump for it and get very wet – or worse, many were off loaded well out of depth and never made it to the beach, with the loads the infantryman was carrying holding them under.

On the beach were a lot of people on stretchers waiting for a return passage and also a lot of people who would not be needing stretchers. The dead for most part had been laid out in neat rows, as if still on parade. This was a practice which the British seemed to adopt even at the height of conflict, unlike the Germans who were apt to leave their dead where they fell. Worse, sometimes they are wired to booby-traps so the tidy-minded medical orderlies, surely among the bravest of all, were liable to get blown up for their trouble.

My contact on the beach was the pioneer platoon, who were responsible for lifting mines and keeping a beach exit free from obstruction. I had with my load the tools to do the job, mine detectors and explosive charges to clear obstructions.

Battalion bren-gun carriers and anti-tank guns went in support of the 6th Airborne, while the remainder of the battalion prepared the supply dumps.

D1. 7th June.

At 1200 hrs, a single German aircraft chased by Spitfires flew low over the main lateral, which was crowded with traffic, and dropped a bomb. A Dukw carrying petrol was hit and the burning petrol flowed down into an ammunition dump, which began to explode. Stack after stack blew up with deafening reverberations and pieces of shell started to fall all over the beaches. Soon blazing petrol added a huge column of smoke and flame which roared skywards with a mushroom of smoke. The explosions and fire were fully visible to our own troops and the enemy in the line and must have been as disturbing to the former, (who saw the ammunition vital for their attacks exploding in their rear), as they must have been gratifying to the latter.

Many ordnance experts hold the opinion that once an ammunition dump catches fire the only practicable thing to

50

do is let it burn out and then to start stacking elsewhere. In this case they were strongly of this opinion, as the stacks were placed so close together. But anyone with even a nodding acquaintance with Lieutenant-Colonel Sale knew that such counsels of despair were not good enough for him. Soon after the first explosion had taken place he was in the dump rallying the staff.

The stacks had been covered with camouflage netting, which caught alight easily, the grass was so dry it burst into flame whenever red-hot fragments of metal landed and the result was that every stack that exploded started up a succession of new fires. Helped by a small band of officers which included Major Geoffrey Pepper, the D.A.D.O.S., Captain Erdle of the petrol depot (who was very soon fatally wounded) and Major T. W. Butcher of No. 12 Ordnance Beach Detachment, and by a handful of pioneers, the Commanding Officer started to drag the nets from the stacks, beat out the blazing grass, drive out vehicles which had been abandoned by their drivers, and eventually, as more men were rallied, to demolish the stacks nearest to the seat of the fire so as to create a fire-break. For nearly an hour the party worked in this blazing inferno until Colonel Sale was hit in the stomach by a piece of flying shell and carried off unconscious to the nearest Field Dressing Station. His place was taken by the second-in-command, Major Carse, and after a further two hours' hazardous work the seemingly impossible was achieved. The fire burned itself out and half the dump was saved, with the result that when an urgent call for anti-tank ammunition was received that evening from the 3rd British Division the call was answered and the ammunition supplied. But 400 tons of precious ammunition and 60,000 gallons of petrol had been lost.

No. 6 Beach Group – 1st Bucks Battalion

The following vehicles were to be landed on the first four tides:

D-Day	Tide 1	1,510 vehicles
D-Day	Tide 2	720 vehicles
D plus 1	Tide 3	532 vehicles
D plus 1	Tide 4	118 vehicles

1. It was planned to land 2,200 troops and 1,500 vehicles in the first nine hours.
2. An average of 3,000 tons of stores was to be unloaded daily in addition to the troops and vehicles.
3. This was all *double* the highest tonnage ever previously landed by this method and if a proper beach maintenance area was not established, chaos would result.

Les Root, 16 Absalom Court, Wright Close, Twydall, Gillingham, Kent

---

I was a (very) Ordinary Seaman at the time, a member of the crew of a Fleet Minesweeper, H.M.S. "Selkirk" of about 700 tons displacement. The armament of each ship was minimal, I think only a twelve pounder gun on the forecastle and Lewis guns at the Bridge extremities. So, they were no match, especially when sweeping with wires etc. streaming, with their top speed around twelve knots, to the enemy 'E' boats which were heavily armed and with a speed of over forty knots.

Some two months before D-Day, it was confirmed that we would (as expected) be required to take part in that huge Operation, sweeping a channel for the ships and craft of the U.S. First Army, I think the Fifth Corps. It meant we would be out ahead all the way, and the first ships to cross to the 'Other Side' on that Day. Now, sweeping essentially was (and probably still is) a day-time occupation, not only for accurate fixes in connection with navigation, but also because a mine that has had it's mooring wire cut by a sweep, bobs to the surface where it is still lethal until it is either sunk or blown up.

But since the D-Day landings were planned for the hour of dawn or thereabouts, the sweepers had to accept the enormous risk of sweeping at night if surprise was to be achieved. So, we practised night sweeping, culminating one night in May, 1943 when we swept a channel right across Lyme Bay ahead of a large number of American landing ships for their rehearsal landing at Slapton Sands in Devon.

Unfortunately during the night, 'E' boats found the convoy astern of us and torpedoed three large landing ships with the loss of over 700 men. Our daylight hours following this grim night found us searching the seas for any survivors, and when we didn't find any, for the bodies of those who had drowned. That was a ghastly day!

We arrived back at Portland long after dark to discharge our sad cargo at the jetty. In those days of strict blackout, only an emergency such as this could cause restrictions to be lifted. And they were! The jetties were bright with lights as probably they had not been for over four years. So far as we could see was a queue of military ambulances waiting for the dead Americans who were carefully carried ashore.

A day or two later, we received a signal from the American Officer Commanding, of grateful thanks. We and others who had taken part were enjoined to especial secrecy. Sir Winston Churchill judged that news of the disaster would be so bad for the morale of the nation(s) at the time, that complete silence was observed officially and details did not begin to leak out until some thirty or more years later when those delving into the old records at the Official Records Office were able to read some of the signals and edicts which had passed.

About a fortnight before D-Day, our Captain, a Royal Naval Reserve Lieutenant Commander, Lt. Cdr. Goff RNR, informally came to the messdecks to tell us of our role in the then forthcoming invasion. As known, we had to sweep the passage across the English Channel for the American landings; it would be at night and would be extremely hazardous. We would have to sweep through at least three known minefields laid in the early years of the War, where because of age the mines would be more volatile than usual. Further, there were always fresh minefields being laid, and our course might take us through such as well. Although some American craft were to have rescue cutters following them, we would have no such assistance. A destroyer was detailed to protect us, but because of the possible danger from floating mines would be one mile astern of us instead of with the flotilla. 'E' boats were to be expected. If we were hit by torpedo or mine, we had to put our steering wheel hard over so that we would sink in the unswept seas, out of the way of the following ships; and the Flotilla would close up. Once that happened, we were to fend for ourselves, but no one thought much of our chances of survival!

As June arrived, the Americans started loading their huge tank landing ships, and the town and 'hards' became clogged with heavy traffic, lorries and tanks, each one reversing into the gaping interiors of the landing ships. As a ship was made ready, she would move out to anchor in Weymouth Bay, the harbour being packed.

Immediately before D-Day there was much activity on board! The ship bustled with life as guns, equipment and engines were cleaned and checked. The sweeping gear and winch were overhauled, and the ship's boat and carley rafts were re-stocked with fresh water and provisions etc. ready for immediate use should we hit a mine...It became known that this was 'it', and I am sure that many a prayer was offered up!

Towards late afternoon, on the 5th (my 20th birthday, and what a birthday!) we weighed anchor, hoisted our 'battle ensign', and in company with the remainder of the Flotilla (by then, I think, depleted – whilst on lookout duty a few weeks previously, I had seen the explosion from a mine under one of our sweepers; and it could well have been that another was unseaworthy at that time because of damage), we left the Bay. This was a repeat of the previous days activities when D-Day had been set 24 hours earlier. Then we had steamed well into the early hours before being recalled when we were about half-way across the English Channel!

At some point, I do not remember where, we reformed from 'line ahead' to our usual echelon formation for sweeping and would have had the usual signal 'out sweeps, speed 8 knots'. We set course for the point south of the Isle of Wight for the purposes of the Operation known as 'Piccadilly Circus' where a change of course was necessary to take us directly across the English Channel. Here was the area where all our shipping and invasion craft would come in the next 24 hours and for some weeks, to pass to the 'Other Side' through about eight separate swept lanes.

When sweeping normally, the only guns manned would be those needed to fire at and to sink or explode floating mines. We even had an elephant rifle donated by a loyal citizen!. However, for this Operation where attack was expected, we had to man our twelve pounder gun and for the first and only time in my naval 'career' my action station was manning a gun. It was just as well we did not meet any 'E' boats!

We plodded on and on through the night. I cannot remember the state of the moon, but there was a degree of visibility to enable us to do our work. Nevertheless, we were constantly on the forecastle straining our eyes for the tell-tale wake of 'E' boats, and more importantly for any floating mines cut adrift by our sister ships ahead. A bobbing mine in the swell prevailing, at night, was difficult to see, and despite the lack of sleep in the previous 48 hours, we were all wide awake, for obvious reasons!

As usual when sweeping, we were each wearing cork lifejackets (similar to those worn by lifeboatmen – and better than our standard issue), and on the forecastle we consoled ourselves with the thought that if we hit a mine, it would be almost under our feet and that the explosion would probably fling us into the sea where hopefully we would float until a returning ship could pick us up. (The Orders were that no ship was to deviate from the outward course for any reason, unless sinking! The invasion was not to be held up).

Amazingly, I think for us all, as the dawn began to break, we had had few alarms, but were still alive and well! We had survived! What is more our Flotilla was still afloat and on station!

It has been said that there are no atheists who serve at sea; my distinct feeling was that there were none on board that night! I cannot describe the feeling of thankfulness that appeared to come over everyone on board. I am sure it was not my imagination! The wonder of that morning those years ago, is still with me! I was in no doubt that the Good Lord had watched over us! And I suspect, others felt similarly!

It was not long before ships and landing craft anchored in the area we had swept. From there, they dropped their smaller landing craft, which embarked their troops, and proceeded towards the beaches. At that stage, I think we were off Omaha beach and Vierville, though once, I was called onto the Bridge and shown our position on the chart with Arromaches in the distance. It was probably Vierville, but the coastal town we saw from a distance through the haze and smoke looked just as one might have expected a small seaside place to look with buildings onto the front, some white. Some were obviously damaged or on fire.

Our own landing craft and ships were firing at the shore defences; there was much confusion and noise and fireworks! To our mind, the most fearsome craft from a defender's point of view, were the rocket landing ships which had batteries of rockets mounted where troops would normally be carried. The rockets were fired in awe-inspiring broadsides of fifty or more at the same instant, horizontally at the beach defences. A general view on board was that *we* would not wish to be facing such an armada!

Although our Flotilla was to return time and again to the French coastline, our job for the present had been completed, and at some stage in the morning, we reformed into line ahead and turned northwards, back along the swept channel we had so fearfully made in the dark!

As we returned, we saw more ships and landing craft than we had ever seen together previously! Convoy after convoy of ships and craft of all sorts were heading towards the 'Other Side' – all of them in the swept lanes from 'Picadilly Circus' – and many of them making heavy weather of progressing through the rough seas!

So, we steamed back to Portland, still flying our 'battle ensign', so that ALL could see we had done our work! We all felt highly relieved, elated, proud, and thankful indeed!

Needless to say, Weymouth Bay was all but clear of ships at anchor, and Portland Harbour was now easily navigable after the congestion of the previous day(s) and weeks. On many of those ships and craft still there, frantic activity was in progress, with loading of landing ships continuing from the 'hards'.

We felt for the soldiers who soon would be on their way to the 'Other Side' in crowded ships or craft. They were going to have an uncomfortable voyage, and many of them would be seasick! For them it indeed would be 'the longest day'; for us it had been not only the longest day but the longest three days in our lives!

As I reflect back over the years I feel a deep sense of indebtedness to ALL my shipmates of the "Selkirk" with whom I had the honour to serve for they taught me what true comradeship was! Further I am even more grateful to the Lord who brought me through D-Day and life's experiences since!

Derrick L. Willcocks, "Hildenborough," 63 Cowdray Park Road, Little Common, Bexhill on Sea, East Sussex

I was with Coastal Command, 59 Squadron Head-quarters at Ballykelly when we were told that the invasion had commenced. Soon our 16 aircraft took to the air to carry out 'Stopper' patrols at the entrance to the English Channel and over the narrow seas. The aim was to prevent a large expected force of German U-Boats attacking damaging and sinking the vital ships of the Allied Invasion Forces.

Our duty was to fly on parallel courses back and forward covering the designated sea area once every hour by day and by night. All told we flew in Liberator FL990, 59 Squadron for 10 hours of day-light and six hours and ten minutes by night keeping watch with all the other anti-submarine aircraft visually by day and with our modern ten centimetric Radar by night. Neither directly with our eyes, nor on the Radar Screen had any of us seen such a sight. By day we saw ships everywhere sailing in regular lines shown up through the mist and cloud by the white foam of their wakes: by night the usually empty cathode ray tube was a mass of orange blips – ship echoes from which we attempted to sort out any small splinter-like blips indicative of likely submarines. On the whole the weather was dreadful. High winds, mist and low clouds. A very bumpy flight for the nine man crew as we nosed along at about 140 knots at our normal patrol height of between 500 to 1000 feet.

We did not see a U-boat. Firstly the Germans had been caught totally by surprise and the orders for U-boats to attack the invasion forces were not issued until the small hours of D-Day. A week too late! "Wolf-packs" of U-boats ought to have been lurking in the Armada path, and not at their bases. The density of the air patrols together with the naval submarine attack groups gave the U-boats little chance. Apart from the loss of the Frigate Mourne and the Destroyer Blackwood and one tank landing craft the only success U-Boat Command could claim was the sinking of three Liberty ships and the damaging of another by torpedoes off Selsey Bill on June 29th. In one month Coastal Command in co-operation with the naval forces, had sunk 18 U-boats of the 43 found and rendered harmless the others by being kept away from the convoys or by being driven back to their bases.

All told my squadron put in 96 sorties as part of the invasion protective air screen. It was a memorable task in the squadron history. Congested was indeed the right word for the sky. On that day the full strength of 171 Squadrons was in the air above the short stretch of French coast and the narrow channel.

And that brought about for my crew one of the most unforgettable incidents of their operational tour. When aircraft collide there is no escape and collide we nearly did. Flying so low in darkened aircraft in such demanding weather conditions amongst so many other aircraft keenly searching for enemy targets we had to keep alert. It was possible to mistake a low flying aircraft for a U-Boat. The Radar blips were small and very much alike. In any case collision even without such mistaken identity could have easily taken place. Whatever the reason on this night an aircraft of a sister squadron thought we were undesirable and not only nearly ran us down but switched on the powerful Leigh Light (anti-submarine searchlight) and possibly prepared to attack. Nearly blinded we weaved from the area at maximum knots! Worse, when we met later at the Intelligence interrogations on our return to base the culprits did not even apologise!

So if any members of B-120 flying at that time read this perhaps they will recall what was possibly a mutually lucky escape.

Dr. Joseph E. Collins, 12a Charmouth Grove, Parkstone, Poole, Dorset

That was suffered! Photo by Coastal Command aircraft showing the Queen Mary in mid-Atlantic bringing U.S. troops to Britain. Photo kindly supplied.

I served with the 1st Battalion, the South Lancashire Regiment in the 8th Brigade of the 3rd British Infantry Division. After 2½ years of tough and intensive training in Scotland, we were moved south to a wooded area in a place called Cowplain just north of Portsmouth in April 1944. We were all sealed in the camp with barbed wire all around the perimeter and the outside patrolled by security troops who wore green armbands to distinguish them from the assault troops. Later we were taken into a huge marquee and inside on the floor was a huge model of the beach we were to attack. It was codenamed "Queen White" a Sector of Sword beach. There was also a strong point code named COD and a small village about one mile inland.

At 4.30 a.m. on Saturday 3rd June we left our camp and joined the massive convoys all making their way to the docks for loading on to the Assault Craft. There were security troops lining the roads and streets to make sure we couldn't talk to the civilians but very often trays of beer were brought out from pubs for the convoys which the security troops couldn't do much about, and we also spent the last of our English money. At about 5.00 p.m. we eventually loaded onto our LCT (Landing Craft Tank).

The docks and harbour at Portsmouth and Gosport were a sight to behold. Just one seething mass of Assault Craft all being loaded with young men and their machines of war to be then transported to their Day of Destiny. We were on board until we finally set sail at about 5.00 p.m. in the early evening of Monday 5th June into a rough and unkindly sea. Our LCT, being a flatbottomed craft, shuddered violently at every wave it encountered – and there were plenty! The voyage was a nightmare in itself. As we crossed the Channel in the fading light everyone appeared to be quietly having a long last look at dear old England, and wondering to themselves what tomorrows H-Hour would bring for them.

Conversation on board was very hard to make. Your mouth was so dry and you felt very self-conscious trying to hide your fears from one another. Most of the men in our Battalion were conscripts, in their early 20's, and going into battle for the first time. And what a daunting task we had been given. We were to lead the assault. The two sacrificial Infantry Battalions assaulting "Queen White" and "Queen Red" were both north country Regiments – 1st South Lancs and the 2nd East Yorks. They'd obviously chosen the dour men from the North! As we continued to plough our way through the heavy sea the senior Officer on board our craft called us all together on the open deck and told us the named destination of our assault. Normandy! We would be on the extreme left hand flank of the whole invasion force.

Overhead we could now hear the drone of a large number of aircraft. The Officer told us it was the Paras. going in to capture and hold the bridges on our left flank. We all wished them God Speed with all our hearts. About an hour or so later the same Officer called us all together again for an impromptu Church Service of sorts – I can remember we sang the hymns "Abide with me" and "O God our Help in Ages Past" and that it was so very emotional for us all. Fleetingly the moon would appear and lighten the heaving sea, and I remember seeing the battleships Warspite and Rodney steaming past us in preparation for the bombardment of the beaches.

The streaks of dawn began to appear in the east. This was it! Looking to our right we could clearly see the vast invasion Armada and I remember that our hearts were really filled with joy. In our briefing we had only been informed about our Sector – now we saw all this support! Suddenly there were huge flashes and an unbearable noise as the whole Fleet opened up, firing onto the landing beaches. It was a terrifying spectacle and one I have never seen repeated. We sat in our Bren Carrier with our heads well down! After about an hour of this bombardment I ventured a look over the top of our vehicle in the direction of France and for the first time I could just make out the coastline. But even then it was obvious that our craft was making its way steadily to a blazing inferno, which was our alloted beach.

Most of the troops on our LCT had suffered seasickness very badly but we were now making full speed ahead to the beach which was shrouded in smoke and fire. Suddenly there was a violent explosion underneath the craft, stunning me. We stopped in an instant about 100 yards from the beach. The Naval Commander immediately lowered the ramp and in no uncertain manner ordered the vehicles off. Not knowing how deep the sea was at this point a Sherman Tank moved down the ramp into the sea and disappeared beneath the waves in seconds. Only two men escaped – the others drowned. Next off was our Bren Carrier with its gun in tow, and urged on by the Naval Officer. The tracks of our Bren Carrier stuck on top of the submerged tank and couldn't move at all. The sea at that point must have been some 20ft deep.

Being good swimmers my four pals launched themselves into the sea, but me not being able to swim at all stood at the barrier with ice-cold water up to my chest. I tore off all my equipment, including steel helmet and rifle, blew up my life-belt to the full, and urged on by a burst of machine gun fire from the beach striking the water just in front of me, a silent prayer and into the water I went! No words can ever possibly describe my feelings at this moment. The landings having been planned for low tide, I remember thinking that if my lifebelt holds out then the tide will eventually bring me onto the beach!

On the way in, an Assault Craft having discharged its cargo of troops was pulling away full speed astern to get away from the hell on the beach. One of the crew leaned over the side. I thought he was going to help me, but all I got was "Good luck mate". Thanks a lot! I suppose I was in the sea for 15 or 20 minutes before my feet suddenly touched the ground. So I waded through the heavy breakers and could see a number of men laid on the sand clear of the sea. I stumbled to the one nearest to me and was shocked when I got to him to see that his chest had been torn wide open. He had paid the full price without even firing a shot.

Having no weapon I took his rifle and bayonet together with his bandolier of 50 rounds of ammunition and his steel helmet and ran like hell to the cover of the dunes at the top of the beach. In these early minutes of the assault both the dead and wounded lay scattered about the beach, with no apparent sign of anyone attending to them. It proved to be an awful baptism of fire for us all. I lay on the sand dunes for a while, recovering myself and my thoughts – I had also swallowed a fair amount of sea water and was now violently sick.

A War Photographer saw me and came over. He gave me a packet of cigarettes and told me he had got some wonderful film of the landings if only he lived long enough to get it back to England! I assume he did so as he shot the world famous photograph of the landings taken on "Queen White" during the early assault. I understood his worry at the time though – snipers were still taking pot shots from the houses on the sea front and the beach itself was still being heavily shelled and mortared by the Germans.

When I had recovered I moved off the beach into the side streets of a sea-side village in search of my unit. Going along a narrow country track with hedgerows on either side, all alone, and not knowing whether or not I was walking into the enemy lines, there was suddenly a burst of machine gun fire through the hedge just in front of me. I fell flat on my stomach and as I lay in the ditch I spotted one of our tanks in the field. He immediately opened fire and silenced the enemy gun. As I looked along the track I could also see troop movements in the grass. Moving closer I suddenly realised it was my Unit preparing for an attack on a small village so I rejoined them and within the hour the village had been taken.

By mid-day we had cleared the beach, destroyed the strong point codenumed COD and liberated the village of what I now know was Hermanville. But we had paid an awful price. 107 Officers and men killed and wounded in those first few mad hours. The German 21st Panzer Division counter attacked about 4.00 p.m. in the afternoon and at one stage reached the sea between us and the Canadians. They later withdrew after seeing the glider-borne troops coming in about 7.00 or 8.00 p.m. in the evening. What a wonderful sight they presented. The sky was full of planes towing gliders carrying troops to reinforce the Paras. Then came darkness and the German bombers came over instead, dropping hundreds of anti-personnel bombs.

No sleep at all that night! Weary – still wearing my sodding-wet battle dress uniform – I was still reasonably happy. I was alive! God only knew why, but I was, and that was enough to keep *me* happy!

Tommy Platt, "Le Londel", 3 Banbury Road,
Billinge, Wigan, Lancashire

My ship, of which I was the Navigating and Gunnery Officer, was the S/S "Empire Moorhen", an American 'hog-backed' cargo vessel of the First World War, at this stage having completed her life as a cargo-carrying ship now displaying, in very large figures, on either side of her bridge, the Identification Numbers "307".

She had previously been divested, at Glasgow, of all her cargo winches, derricks, and of everything else that would be of no further use to her during what was to be her future task, which, at this time, was not known to us. Explosive charges had been laid in two corners of each of her five cargo holds, and electric cables had been 'run up' to her bridge, each one having been connected to the respective charges.

We set sail, in Convoy, together with many other Merchant, Royal Naval and Fleet Auxiliary ships, towards the coast of Normandy, having very little idea as to what was in store for us. We arrived off Arromanches on the morning of D-Day, and dropped our anchor, in line-astern of some dozen or so other 'Block Ships' (as had been designated in our sealed orders). Many others followed us, to their respective charted positions.

After a short while, we were boarded by the 'Wrecking Officer' and his party, and, without further ado, the aforementioned cables running to the Bridge, were connected to a 'plunger', the trigger was pressed and "Number 307" sank gently onto the bed of the English Channel, in about 2½ fathoms of water, close inshore at Arromanches Beach.

I noticed flashes coming from the spire of a Church just behind the beachhead, and then I noticed shells or bullets falling into the water close to my ship. By this time, several small oil-tankers and other supply ships for the troops, had entered the Artificial Harbour made by the 'Block Ships', and they, also, were in line of fire from the snipers. The missiles were getting too close for comfort.

On our starboard quarter, there was a large Royal Naval Landing Craft – apparently doing nothing at that moment of any vital importance. I signalled to her, on the 'Aldis' (daylight signalling) Lamp, and told her what I had seen. Within a very few moments, she had manoeuvred onto the beach to get as close as possible to the Church (which was out of range of my 4 Oerlikon guns). Then she fired! Only two or three rounds, as I remember. Then it was all over! The spire disintegrated, and, of course, the firing ceased.

I, and some 30 of my crew members, remained on board "Number 307", the two upper decks of which were clear of the water, for a further two weeks, during which time, in addition to being on continuous action stations, we had several encounters with attacks by German planes. I had a grandstand view of the two-way journeys of the 'Thousand Bomber' raids. I was also able to watch the flashes and hear the guns during the Battle of Caen, watch our Paratroopers landing behind the beach-heads and watch (with pride and concern) the embarkation of our brave soldiers and marines on to the beach. I think that this latter sight was the most moving of all my war-time experiences (which were many!). I felt proud to be British, and my prayers went out for all those brave men and women (for very little praise has been publicised for the forces' Nurses and other female participants who were very much involved in the landings) who were fighting for peace.

When I eventually arrived home (in Higher Tranmere, Birkenhead) – we were taken from "Number 307" to Southampton on a returning Landing Craft – my father, whose interest was to keep press-cuttings concerning anything in which he thought I may have been involved, produced, amongst other things, a Press photograph depicting a woman prisoner being escorted ashore at Southampton. The caption read that she, and others, had been captured whilst trying to escape from a Church at Arromanches, which, some two weeks previously had been shelled by the Royal Navy, as it was believed that the said Church was harbouring the enemy or its agents.

I still have the (rather tattered) Red Ensign which I 'acquired' from the flag-staff of "Number 307" as the landing craft came alongside to bring us back to England.

Just a note about the block ships at Arromanches. Virtually, it was a man-made breakwater, consisting of thirty-one Merchant and other vessels (five more were added at a later date) manned by volunteer crews and scuttled in the approaches to Arromanches.

These vessels were of various categories – cargo, passenger and intermediate type ships which had been converted. Each vessel was armed with Oerlikons and/or other types of guns, for their own defence, should that be necessary.

The conversion consisted of the stripping-off of all unnecessary deck and engine-room equipment – derricks, some winches, capstans etc., mainly to reduce their respective draughts, but also to swell the country's supplies of scrap metal. Into each corner (bilges) of each hold of each vessel an explosive charge was fitted (by Admiralty personnel) and these charges were connected to the bridges of each respective ship by twin electric cables.

Lester Everett, "Angorfa", 86 Franklands, Longton, Preston, Lancashire

---

Recollections of the War years remain very vividly in my memory – especially D-Day. I, with many girls of my age group, was called up in 1942 for National Service, for the duration of hostilities. Having completed my initial training at Glen Parva Barracks in Leicester, I was duly sent to a Signal Training School at Kingston-on-Thames, for an intensive six weeks, at the end of which I proudly wore my badge of the Royal Corps of Signals.

I was then posted, with five other girls, to R.A.F. Fighter Command H.Q. at Exeter, where I worked underground in the 'Ops' Room for three and a half years. It was a most interesting and exciting job, being in control of all guns and searchlight units in the south west of England. We worked in close co-operation with the R.A.F. in bringing down enemy aircraft. There were many raids during that time.

As time passed, we knew D-Day was imminent. We all hoped we would be the lucky ones to be on duty when the time came! As tension grew, we knew it wouldn't be long. Day and night, from our camp, we heard the continual noise of American transport tanks, jeeps and landing crafts, one continual stream all heading for the coast of the south west of England. I remember going to Torquay on my day off and seeing the harbour completely filled with all kinds of these craft all waiting for that eventful day! Americans took over our aerodrome with their troop carrying Dakotas. We waited and waited knowing it could be any time.

Then one very clear moonlight night I, with five signal girls, along with W.R.A.F. plotters went on duty at 11 p.m. When we arrived at the 'Ops' Room, we realised something was happening. All the plotting tables were fully manned and all our searchlights and guns were at readiness. As I took over our Colonel in charge came up to us looking very excited saying: "Now then girls, this is what we have been waiting for. You are going to see history in the making;" and we did!

From our glass gallery, looking down on the 'Ops' tables which were fully manned with W.R.A.F. personnel, we watched the whole operation being plotted across the Channel to the landing beaches of Normandy – the boats and landing crafts and those wonderful squadrons of our fighter planes which accompanied them. We expected terrific retaliation from the Germans, but strangely only two hostile aircraft left the coast of France that night. We had certainly caught them on the hop. We did not need our searchlights and guns after all!! I came off duty at 8 a.m. the next morning feeling very tired, but proud that I had played a part in that wonderful historic event, D-Day.

Mrs Kathleen M. Thompson, (nee Fisher), 2 The Rise,
Elmswood Gardens, Sherwood, Nottingham

I was in the 83rd Welsh Field Regiment and what I remember most about D-Day was the noise, the feeling of unreality and inevitability of it all. There we were, about two hundred in my unit, facing the most terrible ordeal in our lives and we were standing on the deck of an American ship, the S.S. Frank Lever watching the historic battle, possibly the greatest battle of all time unfolding before our eyes.

In front of us on the beach, and by now inland we could see evidence of a fierce encounter between what we knew to be the 50th Division and the defending German stronghold on the beach and beyond, up the hill that leads from the shore to the relatively open country, behind the small resort of Courselles.

Every few seconds the huge battleships standing farther out to sea thundered out a  terrifying broadside shaking our ship as if it was a tiny cockleshell, the smaller destroyers darting in and adding their not inconsiderable voice to the proceedings, all manner of other vessels going flat out to ensure that they would not be left out of the party, and yet, in spite of the apparent chaos one felt that it was all going to a well designed plan, and that it was certain to succeed.

Standing on that deck waiting for our orders we might have been forgiven for thinking that this was a massive film set, and that we would find it was not reality, but pure fiction. Suddenly our illusions were rudely shattered. Imperceptibly we had been slowly moving toward the shore and some of the empty landing craft were passing us and moving towards some ships lying farther out to sea. As they passed close to us and we saw the rows and rows of stretchers lying there we suddenly realised that these men had already paid a terrible price for the small piece of land that had been won back in the early stages of the battle. Then, all at once the battle became a very personal fight. We had quickly been loaded into landing craft and we were off towards that very unfriendly shore to make our contribution to the invasion.

On reaching the beach we drove into about six feet of water, sitting on the back of seats, then up the now fairly well trodden track between the white tapes, up the narrow road for a couple of hundred yards, and into a field where I gave up my driving seat to another chap and went to find my own particular section, the Signals Unit. I had been temporarily attached to a gun crew because of the shortage of experienced drivers.

As soon as I caught up with the Sergeant I/C my group he told me to dump my kit in a radio truck and join a party setting out to establish field telephone contact with our forward observation post, some half a mile away. Because the few roads were full of traffic there was no chance of using a vehicle to run out the telephone cable as we would have liked. The radios were almost useless because of the close proximity of so many other units so we had to carry out the task manually, cutting across fields, and using hedges and trees to support the cable, and keep it up out of harms way. After the link had been accomplished I was ordered to take a signals truck along some farm tracks to check that the cables were still in a safe position, and to check that it had not become dislodged or badly damaged by the almost non-stop barrage of mortar shells, heavy machine gun fire and small tracked vehicles that were rushing about in all directions trying to make their way forward without using the main roads.

The cable at one point had been taken around a small clump of trees away from a well used track, and I followed it around checking as I went. I was so intent on making the line safe that I did not notice a destroyed German machine gun post at first, and as I came right up to it I saw that lying partly in the bushes and partly on the track was a German, obviously quite dead, and partially blocking the way forward.

I got out of the vehicle and walked towards him warily in case he was shamming and would suddenly start shooting at me, but I realised quickly that he was not in any way a threat to me, and started to make my way rather gingerly past him as if I might become contaminated in some way. I walked around a small clump of bushes until I was almost out of sight of him, then, remembering my training I went back to see if he had anything on him to identify his unit.

He was lying partly on his side so I decided that I would have to move him to get into his

61

The bombardment. 14" guns of the Battleship USS Nevada paving the way for the landings.

tunic pockets, and I was not very happy at the prospect. I looked around rather desperately to see if I could find any of my mates to give me a hand but there was nobody near enough to help me. When we were coming through the shallow water on to the beach, and all the way up to the Battery position I had seen dozens of bodies, but, everything had seemed so unreal, as if it was happening to someone else, in another time and dimension, and being brought face to face with this situation was something my previous life had in no way prepared me for.

I was very aware at this point of the warnings we had received in training about booby traps, but I did not think that there would have been time for the retreating Germans to have used such devices in this case, especially with one of their own men, although I did hear of many instances of this happening later. Failing to attract the attention of my mates I decided to drag him farther into the bushes, and to try to establish his identity. After a bit of a struggle I succeeded in moving him into a better position and I took his paybook out of his pocket with the intention of handing it in at B.H.Q. when I got back to base.

As I opened his paybook a photograph fell on to the ground. I picked it up and found it was a picture of the dead soldier with a very charming girl, obviously his wife, standing behind two beautiful little children, equally obviously his daughters.

I felt at that moment as if I had intruded into very private family grief, as if I had been personally responsible for that young man's death, and that it was me, and the thousands of Allied troops were the villains in this terrible conflict. I sat down close to this former enemy. I no longer thought of him as being part of a Nation that had enslaved almost the whole of Europe, and by its dreadful example precipitating a Holocaust on a scale that the world had never even dreamed of.

I was brought back to earth, and to reality by a voice calling me from a a signals truck that had managed to find its way through the fields to where I was waiting.

"Everything OK to here mate?". It was one of my pals, the Signals Sergeant. He had realised that I was a long way out and came to bring me back safely. I handed over the paybook I had taken from the dead man to the Sergeant. His only comment was, "That's one less of the bastards to bother us," while the driver, a hard bitten cockney merely walked back to the truck without giving the body a second glance.

I think their reaction might have been influenced by the fact that both had served in the Western Desert with the 8th Army, and all of this was fairly routine to them.

For a short while after this incident I felt some sympathy with the rank and file of the German Army especially during and after the Falaise Gap battle when thousands of their dead lay everywhere, even clogging the tracks of tanks and bren gun carriers. But when stories of the atrocities in the Concentration camps were proved to be even worse than most of us imagined I believe the whole attitude of those people I had contact with changed substantially. Instead of looking on the German soldiers as being just like us, fighting for what they believed was a just cause, by this time all Germans were evil, to be wiped from the face of the earth. Any feelings of revulsion when dealing with dead people soon went at the end of the war.

I was present when two large death camps were liberated, and for some time after the war finished I was part of a Transport Unit engaged on clearing several camps over a wide area.

I have spent many happy hours in Germany on holiday, and I love the country, and respect the local traditions, but I have a terrible feeling that if another Hitler should emerge it could all happen again.

Eric Morgan, 9 Knighton Court,
Caerleon, Newport, Gwent

German sniper lying dead at the base of the Church tower at Denouville. See photo on page 236.

My D-Day was on June 5th. It was a day I will always remember for the rest of my life. Myself and 19 other men under Major George Payne plus 20 other men, all from 22nd Ind. Para. Coy. moved off to Harwell Airfield in Oxfordshire. The time for us to jump was 0020 hours (H-6 hours 55 mins) from four Albermarle aircraft. Us 40 men were among the very first of all Allied assault troops to land in Normandy but half of us were dropped by mistake on D.Z.N. at Ranville, instead of on D.Z.K. at Touffreville four miles east of Caen and eight miles from the coast.

Our tasks were to set up the Eureka radio homing transmitter beacons for D.Z.K. and to prepare the flare path for the six Horsa gliders of the Bn Group on the adjoining L.Z.K. The 8th (Midlands Counties) Battalion was a new Parachute Btn. It consisted of young men who had never heard a shot fired in anger. Commanding the Battalion was L/t. Col. Alastair Pearson D.S.O. and two Bars and the M.C. for bravery and leadership. 8th Para Bn Group was an independent force of 760 men and the Group's tasks were to capture and destroy three bridges over the River Dives in Normandy before 0915 hours (H+2 hours). Two of them were at Bures and the other was at Troarn. After that they had to hold this remotest area of the Airborne Bridgehead to protect the extreme left flank of the Allied beach head against any German counter-attacks.

At Harwell airfield the time had come for us to go. Major Payne came round to say "good luck. I know you will give them hell." At the time the only hell was in my guts. I just felt sick and wanted to get it over with. We had blacked our faces and hands and looked more like chimney sweeps. We all got a mug of "Sgt-Major" to drink before getting on board the Albermarle, a bloody awful aircraft. It carried 10 men and we had to squeeze up tight to the top Gunner, not like the Dakota which was a lot more comfortable.

As we flew over the channel the sky seemed to become lighter, I could see the waves breaking on the shore. As we passed over the coast gun-fire was making little red blobs in front of us but could not hear a thing because of the engines. We were already hooked up just in case we were hit by flak, but so far no worse than flying in a thunder storm. Someone said "five minutes to D.Z." Red on. We all stood up, took up positions ready to jump. This was it. No turning back, no calling it off this time. Someone shouted "good luck boys". Green go. Out I went. Done it lots of times in training. Just like dropping on Salisbury Plains! The ground came up fast. I hit it with a bump and never saw it because as I came in lower the ground got darker and darker. Got out of my chute and looked around. Not a bloody person could I see, and I was too scared to call out in case a German heard me!

What little I could see was not like any of the models we had studied or the maps we had looked at for hours at our Transit Camp. Thought I saw some one move towards me. My sten was already cocked with two mags taped together so I could reload without much trouble. It was a German. He fired as I rolled to my right and missed getting hit. I fired a mag of 32 9mm bullets and got him in the guts and both arms and nearly cut him in half. I didn't feel bad about it, in fact later after seeing the number of lads in the Btn on June 7th that had been killed only wished it had been more at the time. Up came Tommy Green my pal, "got one then Frank?" He'd heard Sten-Gun fire and came over to help out but could see I didn't need it. "Have you seen Taffy Burt?" I said "no, and let's get away from here."

Just then gun fire came from our right. I guessed it must be Caen. Tommy was doing a recce. When he came back I said "I don't think we are in the right place," and then heard planes and down floated some Paras. A Sgt came running over. "7th Btn mate?" "No 8th Btn" I told him. "Bloody hell they've dropped us on the wrong D.Z." "You're O.K. Sgt, us silly buggers have got to get to Bois-De-Bavent. This is Herouvillete. You are not far from Ranville." Just then it

...n of the 12th Battalion, Parachute Regiment, 5th Parachute Brigade. They fought for 3 days before linking up with the ...asion troops.

seemed like daylight. The Germans had fired up Parachute Flares and then opened fire on us with two M.G. 42s and small arms. The Sgt said "what shall we do rush them?" I said "not bloody likely. Let's out flank them from right and left and leave the Bren Gun to draw their fire then when we are 40ft away knock them out with 36s (Mills bombs)." Took ½ hour to get in position. The two groups must have read each others minds! Mills 36s fell down on them like rain. Then we went in to find 18 dead Germans and not a live one in sight.

I then decided to try and reach Touffreville. Tommy said we'd never make it. Too many Germans about in this area. We must have been four miles from D.Z. so on we went. After about a mile we had a bit of luck and met up with a patrol from 8th Btn led by Sgt Fred Baker from our own B coy. Said to Fred "don't mind if we tag along do you?" We heard later only 140 men had reached the R.V. out of 650. A lot had dropped in the River Dives and drowned also many killed and wounded. C.S.M. Jones in a stick from 4 Plt was saved when their Dakota was hit by 88mm and caught fire. At the time he was standing in the door waiting to jump so he did! He was found by the French Resistance and got back to England via Spain!

The rest of the Parachutists were killed. 14 men from 4 Plt B. coy., 5 men from B. coy H.Q. Two of the men were Cpl Smith and Alen Humphries, both mates of mine. Also the Aircrew from 233 Squadron were killed. We do know that they are all buried in a Collective Grave V.B. 1-22 in Ranville War Cemetery Normandy.

We soon reached D.Z. K. Six Horsa-Gliders of Btn Group were supposed to land on the adjoining D.Z. but only 2 did. Then we saw Dakota Aircraft, 37 in number, from 233 and 271 Sqns. Only 130 jumpers landed on or near D.Z. K. because of flak.

Two lads from Btn Signal Platoon were captured by the Germans when helping the Pathfinders to set up Flare Path for Gliders on L.Z. Pte. Arthur Platt and Tom Bilington were executed shortly after capture. On a farm track just outside Touffreville each with a bullet in the back of his head. Their bodies were left face down in the hedgerow at the side of the track, and were discovered next morning by a French woman from Touffreville, Mme Yveline Langevin. On June 10th when the 51st Highland Div. arrived nearby their bodies were taken by the Germans to a field near Demouville about two miles away and buried there to remove any incriminating evidence from the scene of the executions.

Arthur Platt's grave was found when the area was captured in July. His body was exhumed in September 1945 and reburied in Ranville War Cemetery. Tom Billingtons grave was never found as it was probably blown to pieces in the very heavy bombing and shelling which took place in the area at the start of Operation Goodwood on the 18th July. He is commemorated by name on the Bayeux Memorial opposite Bayeux War Cemetery.

Major Tim Roseveare, Commander of 3rd Para Sqn. R.E. had been dropped by mistake on the D.Z. N. at Ranville. He commandeered an ambulance, jeep and trailer, loaded them with explosives, and with eight men on board raced through Troarn and blew a gap of 20 feet in the bridge there at 0530 hrs. On the way from Touffreville to Bures a lance-corporal by the name of Stevenson and four men of the anti-tank platoon, armed with piats were left where the lane crossed the main road from Troarn to the coast.

At 0630 hrs they knocked out the six armoured half-trucks that we had seen. They killed three Panzergrenadiers. The others ran away and reported back that a large British force had ambushed them, so no more enemy attacks were make up the road on D-Day! In reality a small force of Nazi Heavy Panther Tanks could have probably swept along the same road straight through to the bridges over the River Orne at Ranville and over the Canal at Benouville.

They could have wiped out the small Airborne bridge-head as only 17 Anti-tank guns had been flown in intact by 0330 hrs for the whole Divisional area. Fifteen of them were 6-pounders, which were too small to knock out Panthers, leaving only two 17 pounders capable of doing it.

A lot of men who had been dropped in the wrong areas managed to rejoin the battalion group and by the evening our strength was about 350 and were surrounded by the Nazis for five days.

We had done all that was asked of us.

Frank Ockenden, 5 Kings Avenue, Rye, Sussex

oops of 1st Corps moving up to the front near "Jerusalem". Knocked out scout car by woman with cycle.

Landing Craft Tank 645: Commanding Officer: Charles Summers, Lieutenant R.N.V.R.
First Lieutenant: Bryan Wyatt, Sub. Lieutenant R.N.V.R.

I have kept a copy of my Log Book and together with what I remember I have laid out the events as they happened.

L.C.T. 645 was attached to the American Command based at Dartmouth where we loaded up with a contingent of the U.S. Second Army with the following equipment and personnel:

6 Half Track vehicles. 6 Anti-Tank guns towed by the half-tracks. 10 Jeeps one of which towed a trailer with radio equipment. 70 U.S. personnel of varying ranks from a Major downwards.

Monday, June 5th 1944

04.30 hours: Weigh anchor and proceed to sea.
07.00 hours: Form up in convoy in accordance with previous orders.
10.00 hours: Exercise Action Stations.
17.40 hours: Spot and report floating mine on port beam. Progress very slow, about 5 knots. Steaming southward.
18.00 hours: Minesweeper escort on fire on port quarter.
21.00 hours: Close up to Action Stations. All seems quiet and convoy is still steaming slowly. The Channel is brilliantly lit by marker buoys showing up in the gathering dusk.
22.40 hours: Note spasmodic firing to the South.
23.30 hours: More firing ahead. Tracers. Probably on French coast.
24.00 hours: Firing ahead now more concentrated. A myriad of lights dropping from the sky. Reminds me of Guy Fawkes Day!

Tuesday, 6th June 1944

H-Hour. Destination Utah Beach. Gunfire to the South is now continuous but there is little interference with our convoy which is proceeding through swept channels lit by buoys.
04.15 hours: There is now a constant stream of aircraft – bombers, fighters, gliders.
05.45 hours: We arrive at the Transport Area and the coast of France is now visible.
06.30 hours: *H-Hour arrives.* An ear-splitting bombardment from the Capital ships further out to sea begins. Smoke screens are laid. The air cover is continuous and a heavy smoke now covers the coast line.
09.50 hours: We weigh anchor and form up in the 24th wave for Utah Rendezvous Area.
10.30 hours: Leave Rendezvous Area for Line of Departure.
11.30 hours: Leave Line of Departure for the beach. On the way an L.C.I. coming off the beach and about a cable's length on our starboard beam strikes a mine and sinks. There is no time to pick up any possible survivors. The bombardment from the Capital ships is still deafening.

12.00 hours: Utah is now clearly visible and ruined buildings can be seen. A lot of gunfire is in evidence in the adjoining Omaha Beach. There is a two hour delay in unloading on Utah.
14.00 hours: We beach on Utah!

NOTE: As we beach there is now an ebb tide and the U.S. Major in Command is repeatedly warned by me to disembark in 5 minutes otherwise L.C.T. 645 will remain beached. He promises this will be accomplished. Unfortunately this does not happen and I am forced to threaten the Officers with a .45 revolver. Whether they are scared to disembark into three feet of water or frightened at the sight of the burning vehicles on the beach I shall never know. Anyway by the

71

German prisoners being marched off into captivity somewhere in Normandy. Members of the 58 LAA take time off to have a ringside seat whilst the Armour of the Division also provide a grandstand viewing position.

This was followed by the whistle and explosion of the shells, as we were seeing them explode before we heard them. The next two that arrived we heard first as they passed over us, landing between our ship and the next in line.

Eventually our L.S.T. ran into the beach and the ramp was down, and after all that water-proofing, it looked as though we were going to have a reasonably dry landing. The vehicles out of the hold were disappearing up the beach, making for a flag that denoted a gap in the sandhills, while we were waiting on the deck. Gradually the shelling got worse, not only spouts of water going up, but also great spouts of sand as shells landed on the beach, which by now was practically empty, except for vehicles going hell-for-leather towards the exits.

Finally the hold was clear and the first vehicles were on the lift, which never seemed to stop, but just kept going up and down. Then it was my turn, and there in front of me were the open doors and the ramp leading straight onto the sand, and it looked an awful long way to the top of the beach! Also there were those spouts of sand still going up in the air, and the noise and racket, which by now we had taken for granted, as it had become part of our world.

Now, the instructions for landing had been: Get in first gear, four wheel drive, and stay in that gear until you were out of the water and through the sandhills. That was all very well, but with all the racket going on, as soon as I hit the sand I was changing up, and within a few yards I was in top gear, going like a rocket for the red flag in the sandhills! At the same time ripping the waterproofing material from around the carburetor, through the inspection trap door on top of the engine cover. I was told later, that as I raced up the sand, a shell fell right in front of the ramp, but on the sand and did no damage to the ramp, but made it very awkward for the remaining vehicles to get off. Also two shells hit the ship, one making a mess of four jeeps, which had been parked behind where I had been. The other hit the Galley. Bang went the perpetual coffee supply!. Being a U.S. ship, tea was unobtainable.

Our destination, where we were to 'Harbour,' was the village of Cainet, where we finally arrived after taking the wrong road, and almost running into Caen, which was still in enemy hands. I remember it was a warm and sunny day, and everything was covered in dust. The hedgerows and the fields were grey with it, and every now and then you would see a cross with a British or German Tin-Hat on the mound, or sometimes a rifle stuck in the ground, where somebody had 'bought it.' The refuse of war was visible everywhere, burnt out trucks and tanks, and you suddenly realised that this wasn't one of the dozens of schemes we had been on back in England. This was the real thing.

After we had got our vehicles and guns camouflaged, I was instructed to make my way back to the beach-head, to try and round up some of the guns that seemed to have gone astray. This was easier said than done, as I was 'going against the grain'. All movement was inwards, and it was getting dusk, and by the time I had reached the beach-head, the nightly firework display had started. How on earth we found any of our own Troop in that shambles, I will never know, but we did, and after setting some of the guns off along the right road, I was left with one demic tractor that had gear box trouble, and its attendent gun, so I decided to tow them back to where we were harboured. What a picnic! Pitch black lanes, lit only by the light of gunfire. We were sniped at twice going through villages, got into a cul-de-sac and had to turn everything round. It was a case of unhitching the gun and manhandling it

knocked out Mark V German Panther tank in the centre of Lingèvres.

When I sailed out in command of the destroyer "Ulster" in Force G – officially on exercises – we all knew pretty well that it was the real thing: I personally had received a cyphered signal indicating that D-Day would be June 5th. As we steamed down the Firth in a depressing drizzle, I suddenly remembered it was my daughter's sixth birthday. I wondered if I should ever see her again.

As we steamed up Channel on the afternoon of 5th June from every port and inlet on the South Coast there poured out convoy after convoy of craft of every shape and size, sailing in accordance with the minute to minute programme of the vast operation. There were ships visible in all directions for miles and miles, and it seemed impossible that the enemy could not find out that the invasion forces were on their way at last.

About six p.m. we in "Ulster" were passing close inshore along the Dorset coast. The English countryside was clearly visible in its perfect summer setting; among the checkboard panorama of grass land and crops, the farms and cottages showed up white in the evening sunshine. Little wisps of blue smoke rose vertical from their chimneys in the still, warm air. It was England at her best bidding us all farewell on this great adventure.

And just before dusk there happened something else that was typically English — the Admiral made a signal to his ships in Force 'G', the ships who were to do the bombardment next morning. He knew well enough what we were feeling like; he knew if we could batter down the defences before our troops landed, their casualties would be reduced enormously; he knew also that we had no easy task, and that hundreds — if not thousands — of British lives depended on the accuracy of our gunfire. It was a great responsibility for us.

He might have made a long and platitudinous signal, but it so happened that he was a keen cricketer, and his message was short and simple. It read — "Best of luck to you all. Keep a good length and your eye on the middle stump, and we shall soon have the enemy all out." That was just the sort of signal that was wanted; the sort of signal that made every man say to himself, "My God, we will." It made us on board "Ulster" more than ever before determined to put up a good show. Personally, I thought it ranked with Nelson's famous signal before Trafalgar.

The excitement on board was intense; men spoke in whispers as though the enemy might hear them ninety miles away; the words of Henry V ran through my mind all night – "Once more unto the breach, dear friends, once more..." as the minutes ticked by so appallingly slowly. It seemed an age before we reached the little green flashing dan buoys halfway across, where the swept channels through the minefield started. We glided past the first one, with an M.L. sitting patiently there like a policeman on point duty, and altered course five degrees to starboard.

Apart from the navigational problem, the thought of our task on the morrow weighed heavily on my mind. For the hundredth time I studied the orders under the shaded light of the chart table. We had to anchor literally within yards of our appointed spot, and then knock hell out of those forts: the forts whose photo I had gazed at so often in the last few days. Unless our shells dropped on those two pinpoints on the chart, we would fail in our duty.

If only we weren't mined first! For I remembered some words at the final conference. "The destroyers will lead the way, of course. If the minefield hasn't been properly swept, it will be cheaper to lose a destroyer than a cruiser." "Ulster" was leading one section of Force 'G'. Slowly the night dragged on. Suddenly the Sub lowered his binoculars and turned to me.

"Land in sight, sir," he said quietly.

The tension on board was terrific, and as if to encourage us even more, a continual roar of aircraft passed overhead southwards – our own bombers going to play their part. The daylight seemed to come up much quicker now; on either side of us, the faint outlines of hundreds of ships could be made out, steaming placidly along in an orderly array according to plan. It was a magnificent sight, almost unbelievable in its imperturbability; it was Sea Power personified.

As we approached the coast we overtook several convoys of smaller craft, and had a hectic few minutes weaving our way through them; we could not stop as the other ships were close astern of us. Some of these tiny craft were all over the shop, and we whizzed past with only a few yards to spare. I saw a brass-hatted officer stand up and shake his fist at me!

And then seemingly quite suddenly it was broad daylight; houses and forts on the coast ahead of us were plainly visible. A lighthouse, yellow in the light of dawn, stood there like a friendly finger to beckon us in. It was a perfect June morning quiet and still. On either

...e battleships (L to R) USS Nevada, USS Quincy and HMS Glasgow approaching France for the bombardment. Destroyers in ...tween. Taken from HMS Enterprise.

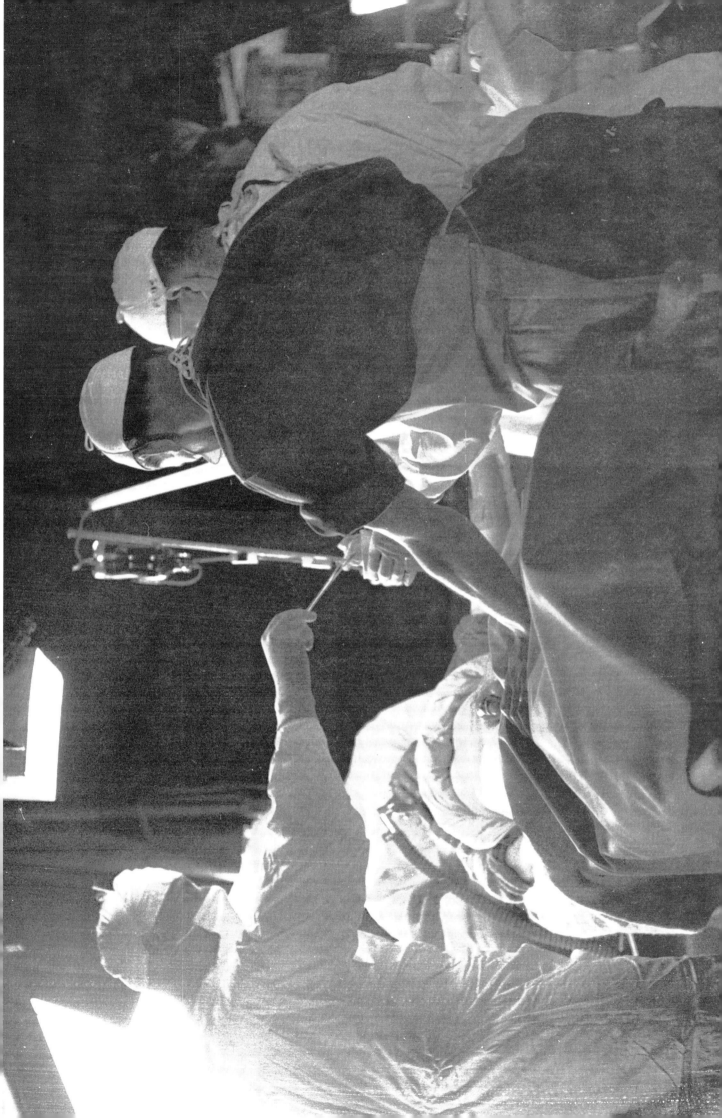

I had been a qualified House Officer at a teaching hospital and within a few weeks of donning uniform I found myself posted to Oxford, to join the R.A.M.C. and a military hospital which was forming up in the Examinations Schools building. However, very soon I was sent with a small unit from the hospital to the Isle of Wight for a couple of weeks to train on amphibious three ton trucks (DUWKs), commonly referred to as "ducks". We learnt how they could be loaded with stretchers bearing "wounded" soldiers and how to unload them efficiently. We were also shown how these vehicles could be driven down a beach into the sea and then "swum" out to mount the bow ramp, let down into the water, of a landing-ship anchored off the shore. It was an ingenious but quite hazardous procedure. If the DUWK when loaded failed to hit the ramp dead centrally and at reasonable speed it was liable to topple over or slither down the ramp depositing its luckless and helpless human cargo into the sea. However, once safely aboard and unloaded, the "casualties" could be simultaneously treated while in the process of being transported to base.

After training at Oxford and Southampton we were yet again moved by the same mysterious organisation which had recently so taken control of our lives. This time we ended up on board an American Landing Ship, Tanks, (LST), (Medical) anchored in Southampton Water. This vessel, a sort of "roll on, roll off" ferry with a lift to the upper deck like an aircraft carrier, was already fully loaded with a miscellaneous collection of vehicles ranging from armoured half tracks and bull dozers to ordinary trucks and staff cars. Deep at the rear of the cavernous vehicle hold was our "theatre" tent, neatly "concertinered" back against the rear wall but containing our main medical and surgical equipment and ready to be pulled out once all vehicles had been unloaded.

The units on the ship were all from the 50th Division, to which we were being temporarily attached as a sort of sea-borne field ambulance. Including the American naval crew there were possibly three hundred men on board waiting in cramped accommodation to hear exactly what was going to happen next. At last we were informed that we were due to start unloading our vehicles by rhino float on to a strip of beach referred to as Jig Gold, next to the village of Le Hamel on the Normandy coast, at H+2 hours the next morning. Our emotional tension was not lessened by a 24 hour delay because of the weather, but real fear was subdued by growing confidence in the mighty organisation we saw assembling all round us. This confidence even grew as we finally set sail, towing the most enormous raft I had ever seen, into a wet, windy, grey channel. Before darkness concealed everything we saw many strange looking vessels including what looked like floating castles, and others like colossal cotton reels. When allowed back on deck in the grey light of next day's dawn we gazed out on a massive collection of ships of war, transports and landing craft of all shapes and sizes. A mile or so away the grimly grey coast line in front of us spewed up a few columns of smoke. Suddely a shattering explosion from behind us, followed by the tearing sound of a shell made me cringe and reminded us of the business in hand. A war ship had loosed off a salvo over our heads at some invisible target well inland. Next time it happened I was better prepared.

Very strangely, at about this point a naval launch approached us, thumping its way through the choppy seas in bursts of spray, and soon a notice was given out over the "tannoy" that a naval chaplain had come aboard and would shortly celebrate Holy Communion on the fore deck. All were invited to attend. In those days I had not heard the saying that there are not many atheists in foxholes and when I surfaced to present myself rather sheepishly on the fore deck I was astounded to find that I had been beaten to it by well over two hundred armed men. The scene could not have been embellished even by Hollywood. The chaplain, in a fluttering white surplice over his uniform, was standing at the bow of the ship with landing craft heading for the shore line behind him as a back drop.

Immediately in front of him there was a small table covered with a white cloth, anchored down by pieces of weaponry, on which there was a small silver cross, chalice, etc. And all around were the men mixed in with the parked vehicles. Tin helmets were reverently removed. Some found space enough to kneel at least on one knee. The words, sometimes blown away by the wind so as to be inaudible, of the hallowed prayers of repentance, forgiveness, humble access, and consecration were recited. Then the elements of bread and wine were shared out, and the men returned to their places of waiting, a little subdued, perhaps, but with a new degree of calmness. I personally knew that I had made my peace with God, at least for that day. I felt nothing now really mattered. What had to be, just had to be and that was that. It was a great feeling of release from the emotional tension.

ı operation at a Casualty Clearing Station at Reviers.

I was born in Dublin in 1922 but I was here on holiday in Knebworth when I met a young man whose name was Lionel Shadbolt who lived in Tower Road, Codicote. That was in 1939 and in 1940 he wrote to me asking if I would write to him which I did. We wrote for four years. He wanted to get engaged until the war ended but I said no, although I gave up dancing and singing on the stage and ballroom dancing etc. to come over to England to be near to him. I gave up everything to come over to Lionel who was in the 6th Air-borne Division. He was a Lance-Corporal and when we met again after four years it was love at first sight really. He had saved as much leave as he could for when I came over and we saw each other as often as we could.

I worked at the Norton Grinding Wheel Factory and what a wonderful factory it was. From the workmen to the bosses one could not have met better. We did shift work of course at Norton's and on the 6th June, 1944 I remember we were on the 6.00 a.m. to 2.00 p.m. shift. As we walked to work down Peartree Lane oh what a noise overhead. I have never heard so many planes and gliders in my life. My two friends who were with me were also from Dublin, Maureen Walsh and Kathleen Nolan and we all stood looking in amazement.

I realised it was the invasion and Lionel was up there too. I thought of him and all the other lads and I went cold and started to cry and I can remember amongst the sobs saying "God bless all our boys up there." The tears were streaming down my face and by this time my friends were crying also. As we walked along the road to the factory people were stood solemn and many of them wiping their eyes. As I looked up I bumped into an old lady and she was crying. I said "Sorry dear", and she said, "God bless and help them all. My son was killed just before last Christmas and now my youngest son is up there."

When we eventually got to the Norton factory usually you would hear everyone singing or chatting over the machines but not this time. It was so quiet it was unbelievable to feel the empti-ness. Then we got to our machines and got stuck in but it was all still so quiet when suddenly one of the girls shouted out "Come on everybody. Are we downhearted?" and it seemed to shake us all up and we all shouted "No" and immediately we felt better about things. Then, as if it knew somehow, the sun came shining through the window and the factory and all of us seemed to come back to life again. But I will never forget the sadness that had swept over that factory as we thought of these young men heading off to France overhead.

Of course Lionel was amongst those young paratroopers but he came back, bless him. He was shot down. The pilot made a belly landing and Lionel damaged his knee in the crash. I don't know what happened to the other lads, neither did Lionel because he came back on a hospital plane, and his picture was in the newspaper. I didn't even know about it – I was still worried stiff if he was safe in all the fighting that was going on.

Then my dear mum came to my billet at 72 Salisbury Road but I wasn't in! That day I was out doing the shopping in the Welwyn Stores so my mum came there to find me. What a shock to see my Lionel in the newspaper but I just thanked God he was safe and home. We married on 6th December, 1944 and we had a wonderful married life together. We had two sons but sadly

Lionel died in 1972. I still miss him so.

So that is my memory of D-Day. We all just lived for today as tomorrow might not come. What a happy and sharing country it was. If only people would act like that today. If life's changed now I don't think it's changed for the better. In mentioning my billet it has brought back to mind all the times we had there and so I must say a big "thank you" to all the landladies and the people of Knebworth for the way they looked after us. They were wonderful and so "Thank you all" and thank you for sharing my memories.

Mrs. Maureen Shadbolt, 2 Gun Road Gardens, Knebworth, Hertfordshire.

Stirling bomber dropping supplies to 6th Airborne Division. Note gliders and "obstacle poles".

THE BEACH

She looks about four. Blonde, piquant and bubbling with merriment as she builds sandpies with her mother. A young father looks on fondly in between working on an elaborate castle. The mother draws the little girl to her and whispers something playful because she suddenly screams with tinkling delight.

Even as I watch this tender scene the little scream is transformed into the unforgettable, unforgotten clatter of metal on stone as tanks in a dozen monstrous shapes silhouetted against the rising sun mount the beach into the tiny resort waved through white tapes by crazily gesturing marshals, each tank with its tense phalanx of sheltering infantry behind. Offshore the big cruisers plumed in smoke vomit shells and rockets above the village. Behind, a cavalcade of scarred landing craft belch vehicles and men, some from flaming infernos, while smaller craft draw away with their inert packages of dead. Overhead the heavens thunder to the screeching solace of protecting planes.

An infantryman becomes a grotesque crimson mound of butchered meat by an avenging roadside mine. Blood spatters our tank's tracks. Rich green Normandy grass and golden buttercups are his shroud. The rest of his section stand up and move forward without a backward glance. That was the moment when the sombre image of death invaded my hitherto cheerful universe and fear became my fellow traveller. Fear. That dry feeling engulfing the mouth, the cold sweat running down the back, those icy fingers creeping up the neck. After that it never left me.

THE ROAD

It runs up the gentle shelving escarpment – straight and true like all good French roads. Fields of green corn and maize and vegetables stretch away endlessly on either side, lush and simmering in the early summer noon sunshine. Silent today except for a tractor lumbering down to the village with a load of hay.

This was the road stalked by selective death as it spat from superbly sited guns someone had forgotten to silence. Like toy ducks in some macabre fairground booth down went the six tanks as they nosed and probed out of the shelter of the grey dusty village. Hissing steam and resonant ringing echoes as each one exploded, armour-piercing shell destroying the men inside and igniting ammunition and petrol. Each one its fiery tomb as a few luckier crewmen escaped to scramble for the ditches under a hail of machine gun fire, stunned and sickened by the first blood of war. Each one now marked only by a large patch of smoke forming shimmering ringlets against the azure blue sky.

But today the tractor is alongside us now, the driver perched nonchalantly atop and whistling something from Abba, a Gitane clenched between his teeth. He wishes us a cheery "ça va" as we pass.

THE ORCHARD

I found it after some searching, found it much as it was on the evening of that day. The same mellow-stoned farmhouse, flat-stoned limestone walls, lofty hedges, apple trees in blossom, lovely copse of elder and ash at one end, fat brown and white Normandy cows, larks high above.

Over that wall the mortars rained on the laagered tanks and resting crews followed by stream upon stream of spandau fire. Three of us were spared because we were foraging for cider in the cellar of the house. Stunned by blast we emerged to find rustic peace transfigured into a holocaust of dead and dying amid an inferno of burning tanks and exploding shells. Later we returned to the scene to claim and bury our dead amid the scattered deitrus of their last moments. Here an abandoned diary, there a last letter home, an opened book of poems, a pair of socks.

89

Hermanville – infantry moving off from Landing Craft and sheltering behind Sherman tank.

April 1939, I joined the Green Howards Regiment Territorials, 6th Battalion. I went to France 1940, evacuated from Dunkirk, April, 1941, went to Middle East, served with the 8th Army until March 1943. I was buried in my slit trench, and after a spell in hospital and in a convalescing depot, I was sent to a transit camp in Tripoli.

From this camp there were about 90 of us from the Green Howards transferred to the Hampshire Regiment, in Sicily and then Italy. After that we sailed back to England.

I believe it was a couple of days before the landing, we embarked on the ship at Southampton. This was the ship to take us over the channel. It carried our landing craft assault (L.C.A.). On the morning we got into our allocated L.C.A. to make our own way to the beach and on approaching we could see the landing craft rocket launchers firing off their rockets. We could hear the Whoosh, Whoosh as they flew over.

"Fritz" on parade with the Hampshire Regiment.

When the landing craft was approaching the beach I had butterflies in my stomach; yes we were afraid (who wasn't). One of my lads in my section broke down in tears; he didn't land with us. On hearsay after, we heard as the L.C.A. was returning to the ship it was hit. If he survived I don't know. I was a Lance Corporal in charge of the Bren Gun section. On approaching the beach things seemed quiet – we secured a good foothold then it happened; Mortar fire, normal arms fire. As we were making our way inland my section Sergeant was killed by a sniper, but I didn't have the nerve to look at his body and we had to get off the beachead. I knew I had to take over, then my bren gunner died. We believe he died of shock, but some said it was because he wasn't wearing his dentures!

On finding him dead I had to get one of the other men to take over the Bren. He didn't want to but I had to give him the order to do so. On proceeding further inland I noticed four Germans going into some kind of dug-out so I threw two bakelite grenades into them. I must have hit them but I didn't stay to see the result. It was previous to this our platoon Commander was killed. He was a good chap.

It was time to regroup and report to the Company Commander, to mention casualties, dead, wounded, etc. After this I was told to take my section on a reccee. We went along the road into this small looking town; we didn't know any of the houses but just in case we threw grenades through the bedroom windows. But we had our resistance. On passing through the town we went around a bend leading towards the beach. Again there in front of me was a German pill-box. No-one fired at us but on approaching it, this tall German officer came out with his hands up. With him was another German but what amazed me was this massive dog, a Pyrennean mountain dog. This dog was coming for me and I raised my Sten gun to fire at it but the German officer called it off.

I escorted them to my Company Head quarters. They were then sent to England with other prisoners. I found out later that the dog was kept as a regimental mascot to the Hampshire Regiment, but I could never find anything out about the officer. A week later my Bren-gunner had his head blown off when we were shelled by our own artillery.

I was 18 years old when I joined up. This year April 1993, I will be 72 but for all I served with the Hampshires, my heart is still with the Green Howards.

Fred Cooper,
57 Rochester Road,
Billingham,
Cleveland.

18th Hussars. Troops crouching low as they wait to move forward off the beach.

I was a Lieutenant RNVR in charge or G2 591 Flotilla on an LCA (HR). Our tiny open-decked boat, with its crew of four, butted into the Channel with sturdy purpose. It was dark, we were soaking wet and we hadn't eaten for 24 hours. There was a heavy swell and rough seas. It was an unpretentious vessel, low in the gunwhales and flat keeled. It was about the length of a living room and half its width but it somehow gave off an aura of naval heroics. In June 1944 the white ensign was flying bravely from many a strange vessel that went on to perform sterling deeds but the Landing Craft Assault Hedgerow was an exceptional craft which in post-war books on D-Day has largely been disregarded.

It was the smallest of its breed. It carried no defence beyond a Lewis gun but it bristled with armaments. It's task, allotted two days earlier at a briefing meeting, was to get up to the enemy-held beach in Normandy. There, irrespective of opposition, we would pull a switch. That one action would launch a barrage of spigot bombs on to the beach. In theory they would explode on the beach defences and detonate any mines. They would clear away entanglements and leave a safe gap through which troops, tanks and guns could be rushed ashore. It was D-Day, 6th June, 1944 and the beach in military parlance was "Gold".

We were cold, wet, sick, miserable and hungry and we also knew that we would be the first to arrive at Gold Beach. We would have to launch our fighting action well in advance of the actual start of the invasion, and we would have to do it successfully. Through that gap would pour later that day troops, guns and artillery and supplies of the famed 50th Division composed of men from the East Yorks, Durham Light Infantry, the Green Howards and others. The battles which led the troops inland from Gold and the adjoining beaches of Sword and Juno would in fact represent the outstanding successes of that first day of the invasion. But we didn't know that at the time!

Our arrival was precisely timed. We were due to attack one minute before the rest of the invasion forces rushed ashore. That at least was the theory, and I still think the entire plan a masterstroke of planning genius, particularly landing at half-tide, but even the best laid plans can go awry, and ours did! By midnight the tiny craft – the smallest in the entire operation – were in bad trouble. The towing arrangements were proving abortive and most had cast off to make way under their own steam as best they could. They had already suffered casualties. One of my flotilla had been "towed under" with the loss of all crew. Another had returned due to a fouled propeller. A companion flotilla fared even worse. Of the nine vessels involved in that flotilla I don't believe one made it to the beach. It was a rough passage with a vengeance.

I remember flak lighting up the night sky and the sight – oddly enough – was viewed with gratitude! It showed the proximity of land, even if it was enemy held. An aircraft was hit and slowly dropped to earth, a blazing ball of fire. Dawn came and my little fleet passed through the ranks of other ships to take up its alloted place at the front. I remember that the crews of cruisers and battleships, busy firing their guns at distant targets, nevertheless lined the rails of their ships to cheer them on. One had to show a brave front even though we were scared. I certainly was not conscious of the fact that we were on the threshold of any great event. We simply had a job to do and we wanted to get it over with so that we could get out of it!

The beaches appeared – the little boats lined up, lifting and dipping on the rough swell whilst the shells of the British bombardment dipped overhead to land on the shore. Some landed in the water nearby – "fall shorts" from our own ships. At "D minus 1" a minute before the official landings

97

LCT approaching the beaches approximately 30 minutes before 'H' hour. Note camouflage has been removed.

were scheduled, I made my run in. I was on time and according to plan although things had gone wrong for so many others. My crew shut themselves in the engine room. I pulled down the cockpit and navigated through slits in the armour plate. The tide was rising. It was just after 7 a.m. and there came a bad moment. My friend, Bruce Ashton, in the adjacent boat, was rammed by a following landing craft and went down. He and the entire crew were drowned.

And then it was time. I pulled a switch. My spigot bombs lifted into the air and fell on the beach ahead, exploding satisfactorily. I immediately pulled aside to make way for the following landing craft bearing tanks. I watched as one tank drove ashore up the cleared lane and moved upwards, its mine-exploding flails whirring. Two mines rapidly exploded. And then something odd. There was complete silence. The bombardment had suddenly lifted and there was no enemy response. It was an almost eerie moment. This, I felt, is what it must have been like in World War 1 in the trenches before an attack went over...

The silence was brief. Suddenly a tank exploded in smoke and flames as it took a direct hit from a German 88mm gun fired from an emplacement. It was all too clear there would be no survivors. A second tank also took a direct hit. Then a third tank moved in and silenced the gun emplacement. Whilst this was happening we were being fired on from a machine gun post just to the east of our land fall. Bullets were splattering the craft but caused no casualties. Another boat with heavier armament got a direct hit on the enemy gunpost and knocked it out. The post, it later transpired, was manned by Poles who had been recruited into the German Army.

Twenty minutes had elapsed since the first of the assault troops of the 5th Battalion of the East Yorks Regiment had landed and rushed – many of them to their death – up the beaches. They were met by machine gun fire and shells and I watched, shocked, as one man fell and then stumbled into cover, never to move again. I was only 150 yards away from the infantry

Just off the beaches. Note beach obstacles and shells impacting.

action and saw how they dashed to a beach wall where German troops suddenly appeared and dropped grenades on them. And then it was time to pull out. It took us around three hours to get to a large landing ship which lay-to about four or five miles offshore. We were winched aboard and for me and my remaining crews D-Day was effectively over. We had been 36 hours without food and were soaked to the skin and bone weary. I fell asleep and was in the Solent when I awoke. I felt we had done our job well, but my thoughts were with the "pongoes" who were now ashore and fighting. That reminds me. When the Green Howards were issued with French Letters as waterproofing for their rifles in the initial assault over the beaches, the general comment was "I thought we were to shoot them not f....... them"!

But there was to be one more D-Day experience for me. It was in the 60's and I was standing on the same beach that I had helped "clear" about 20 years previously. I looked down at the sand and saw a tin helmet with a bullet hole through it. It was queer – it somehow just seemed to rise out of the sand. It was a helmet of the Green Howards who had landed in that sector. It was really quite strange – almost as if it were an act of God!

H. Michael Irwin, 51 The Drive, Gosforth, Newcastle-on-Tyne.

(Note – the 5 photographs in this story have been kindly provided by H. Michael Irwin, and he retains full copyright. He took the photographs, which have never before been published.)

H-Hour plus 20 minutes.
Note the tank on fire on the beach.

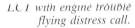

LCI with engine trouble
flying distress call.

PLUTO – Pipe Line under the ocean –
at Southampton.

Where does one start in recounting such a momentous day as D-Day? The 27th Armoured Brigade had been part of the 79th Armoured Division otherwise known as "The Funnies" because of all the unusual tanks and devices which were experimented on and developed and eventually played such a big part in the success of the Invasion. I was in the Brigade workshops which played such a big part in the actual development of these "Funnies" but that of course is a different thing to D-Day and a completely different story. The 27th Armoured was equipped with DD Swimming Tanks which were to be some of the first to land behind the A.V.R.E.'s on Sword Beach near Hermanville. We were to be the first workshops ashore on D-Day in order to keep the tanks in action.

But to start. On 3rd June, 1944 our unit moved to King George Docks on the River Thames, and all our vehicles and equipment were loaded on to an old coal ship which had come down from Newcastle! Talk about being well looked after! We anchored along the

coast near Southend, along with many other ships, which gave us a chance to get used to the type of food we'd have to get used to for the next month – Bully beef and some of the hardest biscuits ever made by man! There were also cans of soup which were heated by lighting a candle set in the middle of the tin. We remained "at anchor" for two more days.

However we eventually set sail on Tuesday in a very large convoy and as we sailed through the Straits of Dover the Germans opened up with their big guns at Calais. Immediately three destroyers sped alongside the convoy putting up a smokescreen but despite this, three of our ships were sunk.

With the dawn, back came our fighter planes and on the shore there were billows of smoke from the fierce fighting and the bombing. As we waited to get ashore there was suddenly a noise like an express train going over our heads and then there was a terrific bang. We learned later that it was one of the battleships further out to sea firing 22" shells at some target near Caen. At high tide our ship went full speed for the beach. We were still in about 10 ft. of water, so we then had to wait for about four hours for the tide to go out. Talk about sitting ducks! I had a three ton Bedford Lorry and, lowered by a crane over the side of the boat into about 4 ft. of water. Very unnerving, especially as you're not quite certain that it is 4 ft. of water you're going into! It took about three hours to get all our vehicles on to the beach and we then formed a convoy and set off to get off the beach as quickly as possible.

After travelling only a few miles we had to all pull on to the verge as the place we had been told to go to was still held by the Germans. One of our convoy just in front of me pulled on to the verge and there was a loud bang as it ran over a mine. The driver was killed instantly and in that same instant the realities of war and what could very well happen to any of us became apparent. We could only bury him at the side of the road and put a wooden cross on his grave so that the Red Cross or someone could arrange for him to be buried properly later. After a short stop we were told to move on and after a few miles we were guided into a field and told to dig a slit trench to sleep in for our own safety. We had only just finished and were getting ready for our can of soup for supper when we were ordered to get back into our vehicles immediately and pull out! This was all getting beyond a joke! Apparently the Germans were only 300 yards away on the other side of a slight rise in the ground.

Driving without lights, dog tired from lack of sleep, our despatch riders guided us back almost to Hermanville, where we had started out from! We pulled into a field which was to be our base for the next two weeks. There we had to start work immediately on repairing tanks and other vehicles. I had a crew of five on my Bedford Truck and early next morning we had to go down to the café on Hermanville beach. One of the Sherman tanks had hit a mine and finished up only 20 yards from the café. We had to get a bogie and track plates off a damaged tank that had been dragged into the vehicle "graveyard" that had already been formed just off the beach! Five hours hard graft and the tank was back in action.

The next few days were busy, repairing damaged tanks and vehicles of all sorts but work slowed down alarmingly for a few days when the whole of our Unit spent most of the time sitting on a long wooden pole over a cesspit! The water we had been drinking was found to be contaminated and we all had acute diarrhoea. One day as I walked past a farmyard with dead cows lying bloated on the ground with their legs in the air, I came to a Bofors gun site. Sitting there in the gun-seat was my younger brother! I hadn't seen him for three years and we had quite a long chat. Suddenly two Messerschmitt fighter planes came roaring in low over us and before I could blink he was firing away like hell at them. I didn't see him again for over two years until we were both demobbed.

As the Germans retreated we set up a new Brigade Workshop. I was given the task of repairing one of our DD Tanks that had run over a mine. I took my crew to it in a field and found that the bottom of the radiator had been badly damaged. I was told to get it repaired as quickly as possible as it was one of only four in the 13th/18th Hussars Regiment that was equipped with a 17 Pounder gun and was desperately needed at the front. We worked like hell until dark getting the engine out under appalling conditions. Apart from anything else we had to get the armour plating off that had been bent in the blast. It was so urgent that we had intended to sleep under the truck but after we'd finished supper the Germans started shelling and hit an ammunition dump in the next field to us. Ammunition was exploding everywhere so we spent a pretty sleepless night in the ditch! The next day, worn out, we had to go back to the tank "graveyard" to remove another engine complete with a good radiator and then get it back to the field. It took another two days of hard work to get the job done.

Back at base I dug myself a slit trench near my vehicle and covered it with the armour plating off the old tank and then soil on top! I was soon very glad that I'd done it! As night began to fall the six of us sat in the back of our truck enjoying our supper of soup and biscuits. Then without warning we heard the sound of a plane diving and bombs falling and with cans of soup and biscuits flying everywhere we dived out of the truck and into our slit trenches. Seconds later the bombs exploded only 20 ft. away and the side of our truck was peppered with shrapnel holes where we had been sitting only seconds before. Three of our Unit were seriously injured.

The very next afternoon we saw an American Boston bomber flying round and round our base in a circle, and then we saw the crew bale out. The plane flew in the same circle for, amazingly, almost 20 minutes and then it started to stall. Then the engines picked it up again and we all stood there watching as it dropped and climbed and dropped and climbed in a fixed circle getting lower and lower all the time. We were all worried sick where it would drop – there was nothing we could do about it. Then it came down in the next field in a ball of flame.

Two days later I was working on a tank with a fellow staff-sergeant when the time came to get back to the cookhouse for dinner. As we walked across the field the Germans started shelling our base and so I dived to the left to my trench and he dived to the right to his place. I'm sorry to say he didn't make it, and he was one of three of our Unit that died that day. I remember thinking: "There but for the Grace of God..." and somehow it didn't seem fair that I should survive and he should be killed. But it was then decided "higher up" that we were too close to the front line for a Base Unit and so we were moved back. We were still only four miles from Caen but at least we were out of shelling range for the first time since we'd landed. Shortly afterwards we had the best meal since we'd landed as well! One of my crew, a lad from Liverpool, found a plot with carrots and potatoes growing and he made us a super dinner, to the envy of the other crews!

A Churchill Tank Crocodile (a flame thrower) was knocked out in the middle of a field not far from Caen and orders came through that the tank and its trailer must not be allowed to fall into German hands at any cost. A battle went on for two weeks with the Germans trying to get to it, and our lads determined they wouldn't. After a 500 bomber raid one night our lads were able to get it back, but first it had to be sprayed with disinfectant as the crew inside had been dead for that time.

At 77 my memories of things perhaps aren't as good as they used to be but my story does show the day-to-day difficulties that everyone encountered and future generations will then perhaps realise what thousands of young lads went through. I'll never forget all my pals.

John Wall, 13 Herrick Road, Loughborough, Leicestershire.

101 Squadron was a special squadron. Flying Lancasters, they carried the most secret wireless equipment and an extra crew member. In F/S Hopes' crew I was that extra man.

Our job was to listen out to German fighter control and interfere with any instructions after identifying the language as German. With the aid of three powerful transmitters we were able to jam three frequencies within thirty seconds. The whole undertaking was known as AIR BORNE CIGAR, or A.B.C. ... that made it easy.

It appeared that whilst training to be a Signaller (Air) at Madley, near Hereford, I had let slip to my Flight Sergeant that, before joining the R.A.F., I had had half a dozen lessons in German. I finished the signallers' course and was awarded my brevet and sergeant stripes in April. Four days later I found myself attached to No. 1 L.F.S. (Lancaster Finishing School) at Hemswell. There I met three other newly promoted air-crew sergeants, all as mystified as I was. The next day the four of us assembled in a hut with a Flight Sergeant instructor. "Through that door," he said, "is something top secret. If you go through you will commit yourself to going on operations. If you wish to withdraw now, you may; and will not be considered LMF." Needless to say, none of us did. So the mysteries of A.B.C. were revealed to us. I was the only one of the four to survive a tour of thirty operations.

There followed about 10 hours flying to familiarise us with Lancasters. On 17th May I arrived at Ludford. On the 18th I was crewed. On 19th and 20th I had completed squadron training. 21st May was my birthday and on 23rd my commission came through. I, at last, got my leave during which I was fitted out with my officers' uniform.

By 30th May I was back at Ludford; and on the night of 1st/2nd June, 1944, at the age of nineteen I went to war.

5th June, 1944 found me a veteran: I had survived two bombing operations. The first was against Berneval-le-Grand and the second was on the night 4th/5th June against a gun emplacement at Sangatte. This was part of the softening up and diversionary tactics prior to the great assault on the European mainland. Returning, we found it impossible to land at base. We landed at another 1 Group airfield ... Faldingworth. This meant that preparations for operations 5th/6th June took place away from our prying eyes.

Rumours flew thick and fast. Eventually, some sort of truth began to emerge. There was to be an abnormally high fuel load. But what of the bomb load? And I was on the battle order. Two nights running ... Ah well!

At briefing, all was revealed. There were to be no bombs. The purpose of the trip was to carry us over enemy occupied territory in order to interfere with radio communications. Twenty four crews from Ludford were to fly over an area Beachy Head to Dungeness, then across Northern France along the line of the Somme, a dog leg towards Paris, then back along the line of the Seine. We flew over this area many times during the night and into the early hours of 6th June. Apart from concentrated jamming, the intention was to give the Germans the impression that this was a gigantic bomber stream. We learned afterwards that the Luftwaffe had put most of its fighters among us, only to find, because of our action, it was impossible to give clear instructions to their crews. All was confusion. The result of this was that the airborne troops, spearheading the main attack on Normandy, were able to get through with casualties far lower than had been expected.

After seven hours in the dim light of our equipment, listening to the chatter and to the wailing note of our jammers, we returned home and crawled into bed, still unaware of the importance of the day.

In the short space of time from 29th April to 6th June I was trained in the use of A.B.C., commissioned, crewed, been on leave and taken part in three operations; one of which was probably the greatest in the history of warfare. I was involved in a highly secret, sensitive operation requiring a knowledge of the enemy's language ... YET NOBODY HAD TESTED MY PROFICIENCY IN GERMAN.

Ron Crafer, 36 Parklands Road, Swindon, Wiltshire.

The Commanders – Back: Lt. Gen. Bradley, Admiral Ramsay, Air Chief Marshal Leigh-Mallory. Front: Air Chief Marshal Tedder, General Eisenhower, Supreme Commander, General Montgomery.

Day after day, night after night, we'd rehearsed our role for D-Day. On moonlit nights when every man, every vehicle, was silhouetted against the backdrop of the silvered sky: on Stygian nights of impenetrable darkness, when a vehicle 3 paces in front suddenly disappeared at 5 paces. Rehearsals were practised under all and every condition, sometimes in silence, when the only sound was the click of a bolt as a live round was rammed home. Yes, absolute realism was essential. Month after month we practised to the state of exhaustion so that every detail, every movement, every tactic could be done automatically, without thinking, in our sleep: in fact many rehearsals were done in our sleep, when exhaustion overwhelmed us. We were all impatient for the word, "Go!" We'd trained to the peak of perfection – we were ready. When we left, as it happened we passed by my

wife's house, en route for embarkation. I kept my eyes front as we passed: I couldn't trust myself to look.

The night was pitch-black; rain slanted down hissing into the turbulent, foam flecked sea. The L.C.T. with our 3 Division badge painted on its funnel wallowed its way through the sea. After several false alarms we were on our way to the Normandy beaches.

There was not a glimmer of light anywhere; it was impossible to see where the lowering sky ended and the sea began. Men whispered together – one wondered why, out here in the middle of the channel? Perhaps because of the secrecy of the whole invasion we were reluctant to disclose our whereabouts by "idle talk!" "No smoking!" was a strict order to be obeyed, but it made a fag all the more desirable.

We were in the last boat but one in our echelon, on the extreme left flank of the convoy, destined for Sword-Queen-Red beach, the furthest spot on the left of the whole invasion force. The skipper's aim was to put us down alongside the Orne canal east of Ouistreham. The boat behind us was the Rescue Launch: in front of us was an L.C.T. loaded with lorries carrying fuel oil and all the other paraphernalia of modern warfare. We were loaded with composite loads of ammunition for direct supply to forward troops of 185 Bde on D-Night. It was comforting to know the Rescue Launch was so close in spite of the explicit order we were given before sailing from Portsmouth Hard; "On no account will any craft stop to pick up survivors."

We ploughed our way on through the night. Suddenly, without warning, all hell was let loose! The sound was as if some giant's hand had torn a large canvas sheet asunder, to be followed by a blinding flash of orange and white light as the L.C.T. in front of us seemed to be lifted out of the water, throwing the vehicles and other equipment like children's toys into the air, before they cascaded down into the water. From a pitchblack night it had suddenly turned into an aurora borealis of light: a rich orange colour with the stark silhouettes of human catherine wheels hurled into the sky against the tremulous motion of the streams of light. The horrendous screams, torn from the shattered bodies, penetrated our eardrums, etching seared scars in our minds to return in the silent nights of future years. I shall never forget. Black evil-smelling diesel oil poured out over the sea – men frantically calling out for help from this turgid mass through which we passed.

Just as our paralysed minds and bodies were recovering from the shock of the explosion, another cataclysmic explosive detonation came from our rear. The Rescue Launch disappeared skywards to rain down as a million disembowelled parts a few seconds later.

Were we next? Against orders our skipper hove-to; a boat was lowered. It rescued as many survivors as possible before the boat was ordered to return. These battered, bemused, shattered men: still covered in the thick clinging oil, which had so polluted the area with its stench that men on our boat were vomiting over the side. The poor devils, snatched from the sea, had swallowed this obscene oily liquid: it was in their lungs, their stomachs. Violent retches wracked their

roops looking towards the coast as an LST approaches France.

Southampton was a city waiting, quietly and with some anxiety for the D-Day announcement. We had lived with troops, tanks and guns on the streets for several months. I was employed as a civil servant by the Royal Navy Armament Depot and we had a small out-unit based on Bugle Street. From here we issued authorisations for the supply of guns and ammunition to the cruisers and small landing craft using Southampton Docks. Before D-Day the docks were crammed with craft. You couldn't put a pin between them.

On D-Day the docks were deserted – all craft had left. The civilian staff of dockyard policemen, maties and civil servants now had to play the waiting game. Aircraft had thundered overhead during the darkness to begin the softening up process. Everyone was on tenterhooks, waiting for news. At last came the announcement that we had landed on French soil. A great big cheer went up for, perhaps now, we could see the end of the war in sight. The news came of heavy fighting and of losses so that we waited eagerly for the first ships to return. As soon as the first sighting came the news spread like wildfire; every one who could be spared made for the Town Quay to await the ships. The WRVS turned up with their refreshment wagon, the ambulances came to collect the wounded stretcher cases and other vehicles to transport the walking wounded. We stood silently, watching for the first craft to dock. From the open doors the first troops returned, battle-weary and dirty, for it had been a rough crossing. In the waiting period I had walked along the High Street and saw on display a hat – a gorgeous hat, black with an emerald green ostrich feather around the crown. It cost £6, an enormous price, but without hesitation I went in and bought it – my "liberation" hat! I stood there, as they landed, wearing my liberation hat and I wept when I saw them. Tears rolled unashamedly down everyone's cheeks as well, even the hardened old maties were affected and as we wept we cheered the lads and touched them and then one soldier on a stretcher said to me 'Don't cry lass, we're home now, out of hell and you look right bonny in your hat!"

The WRVS bustled around with cups of tea and I was aware that several priests had joined the small crowd to help. The ambulance men worked with quiet efficiency and soon the soldiers were on their way to various hospitals around the country.

Another craft docked but this time it did not contain British soldiers but the defeated enemy. German prisoners were being marched towards the wire enclosure at the far end of the dockyard. This was the first time we had come face to face with the enemy but they were met with cool stares and not a lot of pity. For them too, the war was over and they would be transported to camps. Such young grey clad men, but no cheers to speed them on their journey. Then back to the office to await requests for more guns and ammunition, which we readily supplied, provided we had the all-important signature from the Gunnery Officers!

They were exciting days, we all worked well together and formed strong bonds of friendship; and I must add one thing. The American Forces were much in evidence around this area and two weeks after D-Day they gave a big "Thank You" party to all the teams who had assisted them. I was collected from the Office by a beautifully turned out Bomb Disposal Officer and driven to a large country house nearby in a jeep boldly stating its function – BOMB DISPOSAL! We dined well – fresh peaches AND bananas – and it really was a lovely party.

We worked hard keeping up the supply of small arms and ammunition to the Fleet and the names of the Normandy beaches became so familiar to me. Some years after D-Day I visited Bayeaux and was so moved to see how the city gave thanks to their liberators. There were many small monuments to the fallen, still well maintained and all with fresh flowers on them. Not so in Britain – hardly a mention now of D-Day and apparently few memories of what it meant to us all.

Dilys Waldron, 16 Highgrove Avenue,
Beeston, Nottingham.

I was a corporal in 44 Royal Marine Commando and when I was to later wander around the 'war graves' area, my mind pondered the question over the 24hr postponement of the intended D-Day.

"Who now lay dead ... may well have survived ... a quirk of fate that was perhaps to see myself a SURVIVOR?

On the night of June 4th I was told to 'stand by' (I was a Cox'n of L.C.M. 'Landing Craft'). Rumour abounded ... some said "It's cancelled," many were busy writing the 'final letters' home ... some even 'in prayer' with the padre. But all in deep contemplation.

No official word was forthcoming as to the 24hr postponement.

In the twilight of MONDAY JUNE 5th, 1944 ... "we sailed" ... Still no word of our destination. It wasn't till we were well across 'The Channel' we were eventually told "You're going to NORMANDY". Nearing the French coast, and, by now actually manning my landing craft ... two words can only describe the sight AND sound ... "DANTE'S INFERNO"

'My orders'? Keep in line, should you see any survivors in the water, "DON'T STOP" and keep a sharp look out for underwater obstacles. Engines throbbing, and each moment nearing "our targetted beach" ... The gunfire of the huge Battle ships, the bombing, the explosions of little landing craft ... caught in the underwater obstacles ... even cries of "help me" etc. from drowning personnel "ALL HELL LET LOOSE".

Call it luck or was it my steering clear? No doubt credit to the training I received ... for eventually I did "TOUCH DOWN" ... albeit later than expected with a load of precious 'cargo' of supplies. No sooner unloaded than a beachmaster told me to report back to get further supplies. This was to continue for many "runs" to the beaches of COURSELLES-SUR-MER ("JUNO" Beach).

One occasion I chanced to see lying nearby an obviously seriously wounded soldier, clinging to a broken hulk of a blown up landing craft ... I warily went to him. It was now known that snipers were very active in a nearby church spire of the parish Church of Berniere sur Mer ... His ashen face said it all ... blood oozing from a chest wound. I held his hand ... "Speak to me corporal. Am I going to be OK" he said.

"I can't" I said, my own eyes misting over ... Suddenly I said "We've got the ... 'Jerries' running son." He couldn't have been but twenty years old (I was 25). He died minutes after. I ofttimes think of that lad ... and dying like that is not like one sees in a John Wayne film ... nor even a "Rambo" film.

But there were amusing incidents. On June 7th, D-Plus 1 ... still running my little landing craft to and from the "Mulberry" ... I saw, having beached once more, a group of German prisoners being escorted ... One looked at me, and said "F--- Hell THEY'VE GOT ERROL FLYNN with them." He was very fluent in his use of English I must say ... I smiled and gave him our "V" sign.

Another very notable experience was whilst engaged in "supplying the beachhead" I got into difficulties, and found my little craft in danger of drifting into possible minefield area etc. ... and broadside on, thus in danger of overturning, not only with our precious supplies, but, putting myself and my little "crew" of three marines into "Davy Jones' " locker. Imagine my amazement when from nowhere came a small Royal Navy vessel ... and the very willing 'hands' that pulled me inboard WERE TWO OF MY OWN HOMETOWN PALS OF PEACETIME DAYS. Able Seamen Boniface and Stoker Jones, both two very great pals of mine. Can you imagine the odds against that occurring in the huge Armada of shipping involved.

I never saw "Stoker Jones" ever again ... and it was with a sad heart that I attended the funeral of my dear friend A. B. Boniface in November 1991.

Tom Roberts, 57 Juliet Avenue, Bebington, Cheshire.

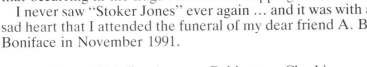

It was a wet morning one day in June 1944 when we drove out of our Barracks in Aldershot. We made our way to what turned out to be Tilbury Docks where our group boarded two American Liberty ships. Artillery Guns, A.E.C. Truck, 3 Ton Lorries, 15 cwt. Wireless Cars, Bren Carriers, Jeeps, Half-Tracks – they all went up the ramps! The vehicles and equipment went in first – reversed up. Then the men to find spaces below deck! I was a sergeant in the Royal Artillery and allowed on deck.

When our time came to land the Captain ran the ship into shallow water and lowered the ramp. Now I realised why the vehicles had been reversed into the ships hold. They were now ready to drive off head first. The first vehicle down the ramp was a Bedford 3 Tonner which

promptly vanished in deep water! Apparently the ramp had been lowered on the edge of a bomb or mine crater. So the Captain resited the ramp and ordered the next vehicle off. Sad to say no one was in a hurry to follow the fate of the Bedford! There were no John Wayne's amongst us – we were butchers, carpenters, painters and rent collectors. Reluctant heroes you might say! "I'll shoot the next bastard who refuses my orders" the Captain bellowed as he drew his revolver and fired into the sky. So with mixed feelings and prayers on our lips we drove down that awful ramp and onto the beach of Normandy. Our training was now about to be put to the test.

"Dig yourselves in" we were told and my four Cable Laying Signallers and myself dug a trench about 12 ft. long and 2ft deep. Should be adequate. The German shells came over and we promptly went down a few more feet! More shells – more digging. By the following morning we had steps to get in and out! A plane circled our position. "One of ours" I said. There was a burst of machine gunfire as the pilot mistook us for the enemy and we all dived for cover! We were learning fast. But many didn't get the chance.

I shall forever remember those simple wooden crosses at the beaches. There were no names – only numbers. One NCO and 12 men of the K.S.L.I. Four men of the Lancs Fusiliers. Two NCO's and six men of the Royal Marines. There were so many buried where they had fallen. Left behind of necessity by their advancing comrades. A sight that brought a particular lump to my throat was of an American Glider which had evidently lost its bearings as it shouldn't have been in our Sector. It had got caught in overhead wires and nose-dived with terrific force into a grassy bank. All the crew were still inside including one man still sitting in a jeep, his hands on the steering wheel ready to drive off should the landing have been successful. The force of the impact had shot the jeep to the front of the glider, causing it to double up and trapping the driver between the steering wheel and the folded back of the vehicle. The sad part of it was that on the side of the glider in big white letters was the message "Home – via Berlin" and "Don't worry Mom – we'll be back". I read those words over and over again and looked at the lifeless bodies inside – young men who had died without firing a shot.

In another location in what remained of a small cottage and orchard was the scattered remains of a fighter plane. The pilot's torso was in what was left of an apple tree and on the ground amongst the debris was a flying boot with part of a leg still inside. Everywhere I went there was carnage. A Sherman Tank with a hole a little bigger than a cricket ball in the turret – evidence of where an armour piercing shell fired from a German 88m gun on a Tiger tank had found its mark, killing the crew. I still picture our Battery Commander, a Major only 23 years of age, shot through his steel helmet by a sniper whilst standing in the turret of his tank directing fire into enemy positions. A small wooden cross at the roadside with his helmet and khaki scarf wrapped round it marking just how far he had advanced into Normandy before he made the supreme sacrifice.

The battle had in fact only just begun. We still had a long way to go, and throughout there was a constant prayer on our lips.

Harry (Bombardier 'H') Hartill, 45 Elm Street, Rhydyfelin, Pontypridd, Wales.

113

It was a wet morning one day in June 1944 when we drove out of our Barracks in Aldershot. We made our way to what turned out to be Tilbury Docks where our group boarded two American Liberty ships. Artillery Guns, A.E.C. Truck, 3 Ton Lorries, 15 cwt. Wireless Cars, Bren Carriers, Jeeps, Half-Tracks – they all went up the ramps! The vehicles and equipment went in first – reversed up. Then the men to find spaces below deck! I was a sergeant in the Royal Artillery and allowed on deck.

When our time came to land the Captain ran the ship into shallow water and lowered the ramp. Now I realised why the vehicles had been reversed into the ships hold. They were now ready to drive off head first. The first vehicle down the ramp was a Bedford 3 Tonner which

promptly vanished in deep water! Apparently the ramp had been lowered on the edge of a bomb or mine crater. So the Captain resited the ramp and ordered the next vehicle off. Sad to say no one was in a hurry to follow the fate of the Bedford! There were no John Wayne's amongst us – we were butchers, carpenters, painters and rent collectors. Reluctant heroes you might say! "I'll shoot the next bastard who refuses my orders" the Captain bellowed as he drew his revolver and fired into the sky. So with mixed feelings and prayers on our lips we drove down that awful ramp and onto the beach of Normandy. Our training was now about to be put to the test.

"Dig yourselves in" we were told and my four Cable Laying Signallers and myself dug a trench about 12 ft. long and 2ft deep. Should be adequate. The German shells came over and we promptly went down a few more feet! More shells – more digging. By the following morning we had steps to get in and out! A plane circled our position. "One of ours" I said. There was a burst of machine gunfire as the pilot mistook us for the enemy and we all dived for cover! We were learning fast. But many didn't get the chance.

I shall forever remember those simple wooden crosses at the beaches. There were no names – only numbers. One NCO and 12 men of the K.S.L.I. Four men of the Lancs Fusiliers. Two NCO's and six men of the Royal Marines. There were so many buried where they had fallen. Left behind of necessity by their advancing comrades. A sight that brought a particular lump to my throat was of an American Glider which had evidently lost its bearings as it shouldn't have been in our Sector. It had got caught in overhead wires and nose-dived with terrific force into a grassy bank. All the crew were still inside including one man still sitting in a jeep, his hands on the steering wheel ready to drive off should the landing have been successful. The force of the impact had shot the jeep to the front of the glider, causing it to double up and trapping the driver between the steering wheel and the folded back of the vehicle. The sad part of it was that on the side of the glider in big white letters was the message "Home – via Berlin" and "Don't worry Mom – we'll be back". I read those words over and over again and looked at the lifeless bodies inside – young men who had died without firing a shot.

In another location in what remained of a small cottage and orchard was the scattered remains of a fighter plane. The pilot's torso was in what was left of an apple tree and on the ground amongst the debris was a flying boot with part of a leg still inside. Everywhere I went there was carnage. A Sherman Tank with a hole a little bigger than a cricket ball in the turret – evidence of where an armour piercing shell fired from a German 88m gun on a Tiger tank had found its mark, killing the crew. I still picture our Battery Commander, a Major only 23 years of age, shot through his steel helmet by a sniper whilst standing in the turret of his tank directing fire into enemy positions. A small wooden cross at the roadside with his helmet and khaki scarf wrapped round it marking just how far he had advanced into Normandy before he made the supreme sacrifice.

The battle had in fact only just begun. We still had a long way to go, and throughout there was a constant prayer on our lips.

Harry (Bombardier 'H') Hartill, 45 Elm Street, Rhydyfelin, Pontypridd, Wales.

aye-sur-Mer. Rough crosses marking temporary graves. (Kindly supplied by Robin Nott of Kings Lynn who served on LCT 319).

When I joined the A.T.S. in January 1940 I was not yet 18 and totally fluent in German. I was assured then that full use would be made of my qualifications and skills (which included a Teaching Diploma) but it was not so. It took a long time to realise that a male "closed shop" operated. We learned about gun-laying radar and then we were posted to Greenford, Middlesex where the first dozen or so girls to qualify were trained in actually repairing radar equipment. The standards and responsibility required were tremendously high.

Despite all this there was still considerable male chauvinism. Despite my qualifications and practical experience when I was posted to Swansea to the Royal Electrical and Mechanical Engineers I was greeted by the Major with the friendly words "They'll be sending us monkeys next". What a thing to say! Then another Officer actually made us remove our trade and profession badges with the words "You couldn't have actually earned them". But we showed in our work and exam results that we were as well trained and qualified as the men, and soon, I am happy to say, our badges were restored. But it may be interesting for people to know some of the attitudes that were adopted.

To be fair that wasn't always the case – we girls mixed with men from all sorts of backgrounds including deprived homes and prisons and they were great to us. They never used bad language in front of us and from them we experienced chivalry and companionship of an order which would be quite impossible today. Anyway, back on to D-Day!

By May 1944 I was helping to perfect the servicing of the radar that would be used in the later stages of the battles in Normandy and I had recently been posted to Gopsall Hall near Twycross in Leicestershire. That would be about two weeks before D-Day. We had briefings on the new Westinghouse generators which were worlds in advance of our diesel generators. Our old diesels were huge, required priming, and often needed six people on a rope round the starting handle in cold weather! Not much fun! But our main job was modifying the old Army WT17 backpack radio sets by adding Rhomboid aerials in order to extend their range to about 250 miles.

After days of concentrated briefings and training we started the first complete practical tests, by coincidence on 6th June. Suddenly as we carried out the tests we heard clearly and distinctly the voices of British soldiers as if they were in the middle of a furious battle. We were hearing a lot of the background communications and appraisal from street fighting in the vicinity of Caen. But the full realisation only came when someone remarked that they were speaking en-clair with confidence and sureness. Significant parts of the British Forces battle communications in Normandy were there in our ears in Leicestershire and we were all transfixed with disbelief. The urgency and reality of the battle situation rang out so clearly it was as if we were there with the troops, and I have never forgotten those magical moments that were so unexpected and unique.

So much was encapsulated in mere words, and sounds that spoke of the horrors of battle. We continued to listen and although we tried to work the atmosphere became more and more subdued as we all silently came to terms with the reality of how those words and sounds would be translated into deaths and wounded. In an effort to "lift" things some of us wandered around and talked about "after the war" because we were all sure it would be over soon now. But three of our girls in the A.T.S. had husbands who were prisoners-of-war and cried with a mixture of relief and fear of what could yet happen. Personally I remember I could not even begin to visualise the return of my husband and three brothers so I understood how they felt. By lights out on D-Day there was total silence but the seeds had been sown for most of us looking forward to being human beings again.

Mrs. Mary Drake, 73 Newmarket Road, Norwich, Norfolk.

mmando troops passing through La Déliverande towards Caen.

I was with a small Royal Engineers Works Section attached to the Third Infantry Division. We were timed to land at Sword beach at 8.00 a.m., and as the light grew stronger we became aware of the immense scale of the operation – there were landing craft as far as the eye could see, and several naval support vessels, around frigate size were buzzing around.

Around 6 a.m. we were about two miles offshore and the game was obviously in progress. Just out of view to the east was the large port of Le Havre, but a number of German gun batteries were visibly blasting away at us from this direction. The first landings which had been preceeded by the paratroops, were in progress on SWORD and JUNO beaches, but vicious small arms and artillery fire was coming from many of the bungalows and buildings above the beaches. The Navy were heavily involved and their smaller craft went quite close in and blasted the buildings involved – one could see tracer shells going clean through some of the buildings. A large battle cruiser, rumoured to be the Ramillies, stood further out firing 15″ shells over our heads, and her attention was then concentrated on to the enemy batteries near Le Havre with telling effect.

The German Airforce then reminded us that they were still in business as a squadron of bombers flew parallel to the beaches, at low level and unloaded bombs. These were the first enemy planes we had seen but were not to be the last. But the R.A.F. usually appeared to have monopoly in the air, and we had seen many of our fighters.

As the shelling from Le Havre reduced we prepared to land. Our landing craft grounded on a rather steep section of beach and the ramp was lowered. I had my engine running and drove off the ramp and thud! We had landed but in about two feet of water, and stumbled on for a few yards before the engine spluttered to a halt. We jumped out to inspect the problem but an R.A.S.C. Beach Officer bawled out, "Leave it, we'll tow you off, get out of the landing area," and I then saw that a number of vehicles were in the same plight. Drowned, as we called it and awaiting tow, so we then contacted our Officers near the sea wall and they had better luck with their vehicle a four wheel drive jeep. The remainder of our unit had waded ashore and we were a complete technical unit of around 15 officers, N.C.O.s and Sappers.

The truck has been towed clear, with a tracked vehicle, and I stripped off the waterproofing materials and dried off plugs, leads etc. It appeared the ramp had not properly beached due perhaps to catching one of the many obstructions kindly left by the enemy, and my truck had dropped almost 12″ off the ramp and displaced the seals. I was thankful when it started and we followed our Officers off the beach, and I saw a street sign marked Le Breche D'Hermanville. As we moved cautiously through the village, my attention was drawn to a lady waving near a cottage gate and I stopped. She did not understand my poor French but clearly wanted me to go inside. I had no time for niceties, but her face was grave and inside I found a dead officer, shot through the head. He had headed the initial assault earlier that morning and had crawled into the cottage to die. She wanted me to arrange the brave man's burial, and as we had a Pioneer Corps section attached to our Group I therefore informed Captain Josey and this was done together with that of several other brave lads who had given all.

We were then encouraged to see a few groups of German prisoners being marched off under the supervision of British soldiers to compounds prepared for them. Apart from these and our own units now moving through the village in large numbers, as heavier transport and armoured vehicles were landed, we saw nobody. Civilians were 'keeping their heads down' and I saw no welcome committees, as we moved into a small farmyard to regroup and receive instructions. We were warned that a German counter attack was likely, as our forward troops had not taken Caen, and were in fact about two miles away. On our West flank near the village of

on-sur-Mer. Crashed Thunderbolt on beach.

Douvres la Delivrande, a well equipped German fortress guarded by a massive concrete wall, and armed with a full range of artillery and ammunition held out against all our attacks. They were to dominate the road to Caen for a few days, until a monitor which I understand was the Warspite, standing just offshore, bombarded them continuously for almost two days with their maximum firepower of 15″ shells. We were instructed to dig slit trenches for cover, and prepare to stay overnight, and we dug ourselves trenches in a mole ridden paddock. In the adjoining field was our attached Field Co. R.E. about 250 strong, also digging themselves in. Around 2 p.m. we opened our ration packs, and I vaguely remember chocolate, beans and soup.

During the day we had seen several groups of British fighter planes, but few German planes since the morning raid, but we had a sharp reminder that they were still in business. Around 4 p.m. a squadron of twin engined bombers zoomed low across the fields, and as they unloaded and the string of explosions came nearer I screwed up in my trench, face down with helmet on the back of my head. The last bomb had exploded just through the hedge and I knew there would be casualties in the next field, but we were not permitted to get involved and were warned not to discuss casualties with anyone. One of our jobs would be to supervise road repairs near the Pegasus Bridge approaches, and this was a continuous job due to bomb, shell, and persistent mortar fire from German positions just beyond the tiny bridgehead. We were also to be involved with repair and improvement to The Third Lateral which was a posh name for the narrow coast road linking Hermanville with Lion sur Mer. I was to be involved with a check on water supplies of which large concrete water towers were a feature, but most of them had the legs blown off or large shell holes through the reservoirs. Our discussions were sharply disturbed by the rhythmic explosions of mortar bombs as they exploded nearby. These became more intensive and nerve racking, and continued for more than one hour, so we took to our dugouts.

The mortaring continued intermittently after dusk and seemed concentrated just south of our position and we prayed they were perhaps just out of range as we lay on our blankets unable to sleep.

So ended D-Day for 205 Works Section R.E. – a long nerve racking day which had started after midnight, and we thanked God we had no casualties and looked forward to doing useful work on D-plus 1.

Eric Saywell, Three Gables, Station Road, Fiskerton, Nottinghamshire.

In June 1940 I was Signal Platoon Sergeant in the 4th Battalion The Border Regiment and on the 10th we were all encircled by the German Armour at Fécamp. Half the Battalion got away to Le Havre, and half were taken prisoner, except me. I was walking down the N138 towards Saintes when I was taken in by Monsieur Huby's father and mother. They sent me to their son's place in Verneusses "for a few days." I stayed until I was repatriated in October 1944!

The village of Verneusses where I found shelter with the Huby family is to be found just south of the main N138 road between Bernay and Gáce. It has between 200 and 300 inhabitants. In 1944 there were five of us – the mother, Marie-Louise aged 45, Pierre the father aged 39, Yvette the daughter aged 13, Jean the son aged 2 years and myself. Monsieur Huby had a well equipped workshop and was variously the village carpenter, joiner, undertaker, wheelwright, cartwright and sometime blacksmith. Usually there were three or four of us in the workshop.

In 1942 there was a faint glimmer of hope that an invasion would take place, to be reinforced during the spring and summer of 1943. But by 1944 the French were convinced that it was inevitable to happen at any time now. The Allied preparations for such could not be totally camouflaged, either in the aerial attacks on the Atlantic Wall, the marshalling yards, communications or the heavy bombardment of German cities.

The situation throughout the village was worrying, even thought I had been there four years. Several people knew my nationality, some were suspicious and apparently all the kids at school knew I was an Englishman! German troops had frequently occupied the village, and indeed in previous years had even used the workshop. But in 1944 they were hardly ever away and during July several were actually billeted in Monsieur Huby's house. There was, to say the least, a mounting tension and increasing nervousness!

On the night of 5th June 1944 I went to bed in a neighbour's house but later than usual.

119

The old lady would be asleep. It would be about 11 p.m. when I quietly climbed the stairs and stretched out in the soft feather bed. I propped my head up on an extra pillow in order to listen more clearly to a bombardment taking place. I guessed about 30 miles away towards the coast. They always seemed to last about 20 minutes. Then there would be the usual inky black silence broken occasionally by the barking of a dog, and then I would sink down into the bed and sleep. This night however was different.

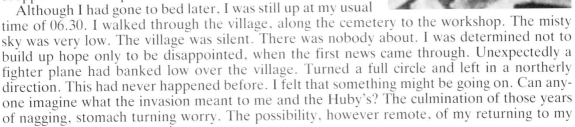

The house shook slightly, the windows rattled, and even the panes of glass vibrated. It must be heavy stuff I thought. It might even be naval broadsides. Whatever it was, it was music in my ears! Long gone were the depressing days of September 1940 when I had counted 750 German bombers passing overhead on their way to London. Recently I had seen happier sights – 1,500 Fortresses in broad daylight flying eastwards! Waves of 1,000 had become almost a common sight. I gradually realised that the "usual" 20 minutes were up, and it was still going on. I became excited. Twelve o'clock midnight struck and still the windows rattled! It was well after 1.00 a.m. when things quietened down and I dropped off to sleep.

Although I had gone to bed later, I was still up at my usual time of 06.30. I walked through the village, along the cemetery to the workshop. The misty sky was very low. The village was silent. There was nobody about. I was determined not to build up hope only to be disappointed, when the first news came through. Unexpectedly a fighter plane had banked low over the village. Turned a full circle and left in a northerly direction. This had never happened before. I felt that something might be going on. Can anyone imagine what the invasion meant to me and the Huby's? The culmination of those years of nagging, stomach turning worry. The possibility, however remote, of my returning to my family in Carlisle once again.

"What a night" exclaimed Monsieur Huby, "Do you think it could be the landing?"

Not wishing to build up too much hope I simply said "Something special is going on" and I told him about the plane I had just seen but had been unable to recognise. After breakfast I went to work with the others. It was now 7.00 a.m. Monsieur Huby turned on the radio. Nothing. It was too early for the BBC news.

At the workshop René Beautier, the young hand, related that the Germans from the Tremblay Château, usually so quiet, were assembled already for leaving. From the village came the news that the Germans in Villers-en-Ouche, with tears in their eyes, had left quickly in the direction of the coast. It was now quite obvious that something WAS happening, but what? Every half hour the by now over excited men left the workshop to get the latest news. Still no mention of anything special. I tried to remain as calm as possible and got on with my job.

I was using the planing machine with deliberate slowness, alone in the workshop, trying to keep my mind on the job when it finally happened. The others had just gone once again to listen to the BBC. It was 11.00 a.m. plus a few seconds. Abruptly, a voice in the courtyard. It was Madame Huby.

"Jean ... quickly ... they have come ... they have landed..!"

She was all excited. Who wouldn't be! What a precious moment. The culmination of four years of anxiety and waiting. Marie-Louise served us real coffee and as an extra celebration we drank the mature Calvados! We all shook hands and embraced. What a delectable moment.

"No more work today" decreed Monsieur Huby! That about said it all!

John D. Vallely, 18 Etterby Lea Crescent, Carlisle, Cumbria.

P.S. Incidentally Pierre Huby and I were awarded the Medal of Freedom by the Americans for saving 14 aircrew who had been shot down, 5 of whom returned to duty via Spain and Gibralter.

121

general view of Caen after its capture.

During the War I was a radio officer (hostilities only) in the Merchant Navy. I was homeward bound on the North Atlantic and on watch in the M.V. Westmoor when the announcement of the invasion was made. I hold the original of the attached message transmitted "en claire" to all merchant ships and recorded by me for our ship's company.

John "Sparks" Bradshaw,
10 Astral Avenue, Hipperholme, Halifax, Yorkshire.

M/V. Westmoor

MARCONIGRAM

SHIP TO SHIP / SHORE TO SHIP

Prefix	Handed in at	NEWS — TUES — JUNE 6TH, 1944	Date Received	
Number	No. of Words	Date handed in 6-6-44	Time handed in 0600 gmt	Service Instructions	Time Received	By

To GT. BRITAIN — OFFICIAL — "This morning the Navy with strong air score began landing the Allied Expeditionary Forces on the N. coast of France under supreme command of General Eisenhower". No details from Allies but Germans say Le Havre heavily bombarded. This follows yesterday's attacks by over 2,500 bombers & fighters on rail centres & strong points in France & Belgium: 750 Bombers (incl. above figure) dropped 3200 tons bombs on area between Boulogne & Calais — 6 heavy bombers & 2 fighters lost.

ITALY — Since fall of Rome 2 days ago U.S. & British troops have advanced northwards after retreating German troops. Rome almost undamaged. Pope held thanksgiving service for city having been spared devastation of war — German evacuation at first was orderly but as allied trap closed it became absolutely disordered — 500 U.S. heavies bombed targets between Venice & Rimini (main German supply route to front) king...

BRITISH WIRELESS MARINE SERVICE
Joint Service Department of :—
The Marconi International Marine Communication Co. Ltd., Radio Communication Co. Ltd., and Marconi Sounding Device Co. Ltd.
MARCONI HOUSE, CHELMSFORD.
Registered Office : Marconi Offices, Electra House,
Victoria Embankment, London, W.C.2.

Form 53. Printed in England

Many stories have been told of D-Day and many more photos published of the event. All portray strapping six foot Commando types rushing up beaches armed to the teeth, determined to dislodge an Enemy deeply entrenched and equally determined to defend their position at all costs.

But was it really like that?

What about the many ordinary blokes, who make up the majority in all crowd scenes? After all there was a crowd! Hundreds of ordinary blokes all carrying out their 'orders' to the best of their abilities. This is the story of one of them. A Driver in "231 Brigade, 50th Northumbrian Division" who after four long years of very active service, had risen to the dizzy rank of Corporal.

First on our barge was a Bofors gun, carriage, and crew, then a Brengun carrier and crew, two Sherman tanks and crews; finally our two Jeeps side by side nicely positioned to be first

...mmando's and Sherman "DD" tanks passing through a badly damaged village. Note collapsed "skirts" of tanks.

off as soon as the ramp went down. Our Zero hour was H+ 11, which meant we were due to hit the beach eleven minutes after the first assault wave went in.

It must have been about the 31st May; when we were loaded on, we were towed out into Southampton Sound tied into large raft-like formations and covered with camouflage nets, then lay there, slapping, sliding, pitching and rolling waiting for the 'off'. Barges don't have keels like any self respecting boat should, and I felt sure the sound of all this slapping around would have been heard for miles, right across the Channel in fact and that 'Jerry' would be well aware of our coming!

I'm a poor Sailor at the best of times, but this period of waiting was made completely miserable not only by the movement but also the stench of diesel which pervaded everything. I remember very little about that week's wait; most of the time I spent curled up over an anchor chain which I had found in a little cubby hole alongside the ramp, filling thoughtfully supplied vomit bags! I suspect it was all part of a grand overall plan. I was quite sure that if I lived to reach the other side, even had 'Jerry' been as thick on the beach as Blackpool on a Bank-holiday, nothing, just nothing, would have stopped me getting ashore.

We were all so well equipped; the order of the day was 'Battle Order', which meant we carried our small-pack on our shoulders attached to our webbing equipment with sten-gun ammo pouches on either breast. On my right hip my water-bottle; gasmask on my chest and gas-cape on the back of my neck. Steel helmet and sten-gun at the ready, all as laid down in the Army Hand Book. But as I had the mine detecting apparatus on my back, my small-kit had to be carried on my left hip, and because I was serving a Field Ambulance Unit I couldn't carry my Sten-gun! This had to be packed with my other gear which would follow later.

The Army realised we may well get our feet wet, so they issued us with 'waders'. These were two tubes of gas-cape material sealed together at one end to make trousers and on the end of each leg had been sealed a plate shaped piece of hard board, to make feet, not unlike snow shoes. They had tapes at the waist to hold them up. In my case these waders came right up over all my equipment, and tied up over my shoulders!! It was thought 'Jerry' would use gas, or even chemicals, so we were issued with a second gas mask, which also had to fit around the waist; to detect these attacks quickly, we were issued with shoulder detectors which needed fitting under the shoulder straps. By the time I had all this on I looked like a pregnant turtle stood on its tail with helmet tipped over my eyes caused by the gas-cape on the nape of my neck! The Army hadn't finished yet! As I waddled to my position at the foot of the ramp, a long rubber tube was thrust into my hands. "Blow that up and tie it across your chest" I was ordered!! "It's a Mae West you may need it."

As I was doing this there was an almighty explosion and the barge shuddered to a halt. It had impaled itself on an under-water obstacle and detonated a mine. Still the Army hadn't finished with its surprises even now! As the ramp went down the Order rang out "All those wading ashore grab that rope and take it with you." This rope apparently would unroll an enormous roll of coconut matting intended to make the undersea surface better for the following vehicles. I grabbed the rope and leapt in. We were further out than planned and I leapt into at least eight foot of water. Down I went – fortunately the Mae West brought me to the surface again just in time to see my helmet float gently away out to sea; down I went again, this time the waders filled with water, the straps broke and they started to fall down my legs, making it impossible to use them. I surfaced again and started to struggle for the shore. Looking around, I realised, I would never make the shore unless I freed my legs. Just ahead, to my left, I could see the core of the coconut matting roll floating like a giant cotton reel.

I felt I could just about make it. I said to 'Charlie' a Medic struggling alongside; "Charlie I'm not going to make it. I shall have to let go, and make for that." "I should" he said "You're the only bloody fool pulling it!! I'm coming with you." I let go and looked over my shoulder and there was the matting billowing out up in the air like a darn'nd great sail. No wonder I was making so little progress! I struggled to the reel and hung on for grim life. Soon Charlie joined me and I struggled to free my legs. Taking a moments rest I looked up just in time to see that as we rose up with the big rollers coming in, on the same rise a floating mine was coming up with us, fortunately falling away again as the roller passed, leaving a gap of about 3′ between us. I yelled to Charlie "look at that, lets get to hell out of here."

Fortunately just beyond us, another barge had just started discharging lorries. "I'm making for that" I shouted "and hope it'll tow me ashore." "Good idea" said Charlie "I'm coming with you." As we got nearer to the lorry it slowly started to sink, and by the time we had reached it, it had sunk! The Driver had to scramble first onto the cab and then onto the canvas back covering his load. First he pulled Charlie on board and then between them they dragged me over the side, looking more like a stranded porpoise than an Invader.

Meanwhile the barge off which we had leapt was still firmly fixed onto the underwater spiked girder and had been swept by the strong tide parallel with the beach so that the back end of it was now only about 20′ or so from where we were stranded. A Sailor stood there. I yelled to him to get a rope to pull us back on board, and this he did. I walked to the front of the barge to see what was going on. "Oh! hello Tubby" was the greeting "We thought you'd been swept out to sea. Nice to see you – we got the first jeep off, and the sea promptly turned it over. You've lost your mine sweeper!!" "What a pity, what a pity" I said. "But we'll have to get this other Jeep off, we're stopping the others from going." Just then the Commander of the first Tank came up and said "There's an urgent call for armour, we shall have to get by." "Right," I said, "if your lads will help, we could push the jeep to one side and you might to able to squeeze through, and then, if you do would you let us fix our tow rope to the back of your tank and tow it ashore for us?" "Right" he said, and no sooner the word and the action. Anderson, the Jeep's driver, said "Look Tubby you're already soaked through, why don't you take the Jeep. I'll scramble on the back of the Tank, and perhaps share some dry clothes with you later." It seemed a sensible idea, so I agreed.

The Tank squeezed by, up the ramp, and then down the other side at full throttle – the tow rope tightened – the Jeep took off, the wheels hit the ramp once, up it bounced – flew to the top, the wheels just caught the top of the ramp, and there I was sailing through the air, hanging on for life once again! It hit the water with an almighty splash, and off I rushed through the water like a champion surfer. All went well until the Tank hit the beach, when on pulling clear of the water it churned something up from just below the sand which stood up above the surface, caught the two front wheels of the Jeep stopping it dead in its tracks. The Tank went on up the beach trailing my front bumper-bar and radiator grill in tow, leaving me still sitting in about 2′ of water!!

The only thing to do in these circumstances is to keep the engine running to keep the water out of the system. You can't engage gear or water will get into the clutch; and wait for help. The Beach Master saw the problem and sent an armour-plated Bulldozer which had just come ashore to push me the last few feet to dry land. I was then able to engage gear and drive to where Anderson was waiting to take over again.

I then gathered myself together and looked around for the path along which we were being directed. I was wet through and thoroughly dishevelled. I joined the Infantry making my way inland. Just then a voice bawled "Down, get down." I just did what everyone did and threw myself flat, Automatic fire from a nearby pillbox was raking the 'crown' of the beach. I gently peeped up over to see what to do next, just in time to see the same bulldozer which had pushed me ashore, slowly cover the pillbox over with sand, completely covering the slit out of which the automatic fire was coming.

We were all then able to make our way foward to our various rendevous. By now not only was I soaked through, thoroughly dishevelled, but also covered with sand sticking all over my drenched uniform and equipment. I am quite sure that had 'Jerry' seen me coming ashore looking the sight I did, he would have died laughing, and lost the War anyway!

So, when in future you see pictures of these fine specimens of Manhood rushing around causing havoc to our enemies: – spare a thought for the many, many supporting Bods, who were also there doing their bit to the best of their ability – very very few of them are born Heroes.

Len (Tubby) Lane, 187 Canterbury Road, Margate, Kent.

On 6th June 1944 I was 14, living with my Mother (my Father was at sea) close by the River Medway, in the vicinity of the Naval Dockyard. I was wakened before first light by a deafening roar of aircraft, as wave after wave of bombers thundered overhead. Sleep was impossible. It seemed to go on for hours, shaking the house, the bed and me with it. I could never remember such a prolonged bombardment of sound, even during the worst nights of the Blitz. It was obvious that something important was afoot, but all that I knew was that they were 'Ours' – going 'Over There.'

Suddenly I heard the unmistakeable whine of a machine plunging earthwards and sat up in bed to see, unbelievably, the huge wing tip of a plane skim past my bedroom window, followed immediately by a roaring crash. My mother and I ran downstairs, opened the front door and stepped out into a swirling cloud of smoke and dust. Somewhere people were shouting, bricks and glass were falling but for a while we could see nothing. When the dust did begin to clear we saw the Special Constable over the way shrugging himself into his trousers before dashing off down the road, presumably to the telephone. The road and pavement outside our house was covered in rubble and the upper floors of the two houses opposite were gone. The enormity of this struck me at once and I began to cry. Where was my friend, Pat – her father, mother and brother?

Joan Taylor, killed in the crash on 6th June 1944.

We gingerly stepped over the rubble in our bare feet and then to our horror saw, 6 houses up the road, on the same side as ours, an aircraft laying across the roofs and hanging out over the road. It had crashed through into the bedrooms and was blazing. The shouting continued, together with cracks and bangs from the burning plane as of ammunition exploding, but for a while we could see no sign of life anywhere until neighbours emerged from next to the burning buildings and my mother brought them indoors. Of course she made tea – the remedy for all catastrophe – but no one drank it. A Policeman came to say we should all leave immediately as the plane would have been carrying a full complement of bombs and the whole street would go sky high at any moment. No one was given time to pack a thing.

My Mother told me to go to school and thereafter to meet her at my grandmother's, so I snatched my satchel and went exactly as I was – hurriedly dressed, tousle-headed and unwashed. Of course, I arrived far too early and was discovered by a member of staff, wandering around in a daze. Then comes a really bittersweet memory of that day. Bacon and egg, toast, marmalade and tea from a tray in the Head Teacher's study. A treat indeed!

I was overjoyed to find that Pat had been dug out alive and that her mother and brother had also been rescued. Sadly, her father was killed – and her mother also died later that year. Where the plane came to rest another friend of mine, Joan Taylor, lost her life together with her aunt, and a man who lodged next door. Ironically Joan's uncle was on firewatch duty on top of the gasometer and watched the plane fall on his house. What a dreadful thing that must have been.

And of course the poor young American airmen all lost their lives in the fire. Two Marauder B-26 bombers, each with a crew of 6 had collided, the one I saw crashing in Corporation Road, Gillingham, Kent.

Mavis Syred, 3 School Lane, Mewington, Sittingbourne, Kent.

Note: Amazingly we've heard from Eddie Harrison who was on guard duty and witnessed the crash, and Byron Jones of the "Buddies of the 9th Association" who has a vast amount of information.

127

...e crash site. This was Joan Taylor's house. (Courtesy of Kent Messenger).

It was soon evident when we embarked a number of civilian "boffins" together with a variety of packing cases on HMS Inman that this was not to be one of our usual convoy escort duties. Soon after we sailed from the U.K. the Captain announced over the Tannoy that we were to be stationed in mid-Atlantic as part of a force of three ships each acting independently, to measure and record prevailing weather conditions and data from the upper atmosphere to be radioed to the U.K. every six hours. Our initial amusement at watching the meteorologists coping with the sea conditions of the North Atlantic as they filled their observation balloons and operated their assortment of equipment soon wore off. Most sea trips are rather boring but usually have periods of excitement especially on convoy duties when we

at least had the satisfaction of protecting the convoy from enemy attack. But the endless steaming around in circles whilst the meteorologists carried out their functions was particularly tedious. It was only enlivened by the occasional sighting of an aircraft or ship, or the detection of a "U" Boat which caused us to be closed up at "Action Stations."

We were not however particularly happy at the necessity to break radio silence every six hours to transmit meteorological data to the U.K. as this could readily be interrupted by enemy listening posts on ship or shore and our position plotted by them with consequent enemy action against us. We were most apprehensive throughout our stay on station but were lucky enough not to have any unwelcome visitors. I have however often wondered what the enemy thought we were doing sailing around way out in the Atlantic for such a long time, ignoring the most basic rules of radio silence!

Eventually after some weeks of the same routine, the Skipper announced that the invasion of Europe by Allied Forces had commenced and that the weather information we had been radioing had been of inestimable value to the meteorologists at SHAEF back in the United Kingdom in forecasting the expected weather over the invasion beaches in the English Channel and had been instrumental in the final decision of whether or not the invasion fleet was to sail. We were of course delighted to know that we had taken part in such a vital operation and all our disgruntled thoughts of the past weeks at sea were immediately changed for the better! Unfortunately I do not recollect the ships crew receiving the ultimate accolade of "splicing the main-brace" which, in view of the dangers we'd faced for some weeks, was most disheartening!

By the very nature of their good sea keeping qualities ex-Royal Navy Flower Class Corvettes were used by the British as civilian weather ships following active service. Initially HMS Marguerite, HMS Thyme and HMS Genista were so employed, followed by ex-Castle Class Frigates, HMS Oakham Castle, HMS Amberley Castle, HMS Pevensey Castle and HMS Rushen Castle. I am sure that the crews of these fine ships that gave such good account of themselves with the escorting of North Atlantic convoys during World War 2 will be pleased to know of their ships extended lives which prevented their being consigned to the scrapheap immediately following the cessation of hostilities.

Finally may I say that our work wasn't John Wayne stuff, but it was hard work and very dangerous. I have read a few accounts of D-Day but no mention has ever been made of that assignment we undertook which was so vital to the ultimate decision. I don't want any laurels for me or my shipmates but it is disappointing to read sometimes of the involvement of so many on D-Day and for there to be no recognition at all for those lads who acted as "Sitting Ducks" to get essential information to England. Perhaps everyone should remember something else. Whilst General Eisenhower had to make the final decision — "Lets go!" — about the invasions, it was the "Weatherman" Group Captain Stagg who put his reputation on the line by forecasting better weather was on the way. That DID take courage, and it was based on our reports.

Eric W. Airey, 2 Cambria Close, Sidcup, Kent.

HMS Inman".

Whilst in the WAAF, because of my art college training, I was assigned to the team who made models used in the planning of assault landings, commando raids, for the briefing of air crews and for the use of resistance organisations. For 'Operation Overlord' there were 97 panels, each 5ft. x 3ft in size.

The work was carried out by three teams of American and British model makers each working eight hour shifts for twenty four hours a day and with approximately 20 members to each team. A rigid wood and hardwood covered base was made and onto this, boards of suitable thickness cut to the shape of selected contours traced from maps were mounted. The resulting terraced assembly was waterproofed and provided the control for the modelling of a basic landform with a mixture of paper pulp, Plaster of Paris and size, affectionately known as 'Jollop'. 'Jollop' hardened very quickly, so whilst one lot was being used another was being 'bashed' by throwing it as hard as possible against the sides of the sinks until it reached the right consistancy. It was a great release from any build up of tension caused by the precise nature of the work! Photographs were carefully studied through a stereoscope and more detailed modelling of embankments, excavations, spoil tips, rivers and lakes and changes of levels not shown on the map were completed and the basic colouring applied, taking care to register the position of fields and other surface detail of a two dimensional nature.

Meanwhile, another group of model makers would be busy constructing houses, churches, factories, engineering works and other three dimensional installations and on average, an ordinary three bedroomed dwelling house would be about one eighth of an inch square, but roof detail was an all important feature for recognition purposes from the air. Heights were established by measuring the shadows shown on the photograph, taking into consideration the time of year and the time of day at which they were taken and using what was called a 'shadow factor', to work out what the exact height was.

Small buildings were usually made out of linoleum and cut into shape with a sharp razor blade whilst holding the minute pieces with a pair of eyebrow tweezers – a slip of the tweezers could often result in one of these tiny buildings being flicked into oblivion in the dust and debris of the workshop and was usually accompanied by a frustrated bellow – or something even stronger – as twenty minutes or so of painstakingly detailed work was lost for ever.

The painting of roads, rivers, tracks, railways, airfield runways and other relevant information was added and the buildings then transferred and stuck to the model. Hedges were applied with something like a fine cake icer filled with a coloured mix of alabastine and paint and coloured sawdust of varying degrees of fineness were used for scrublands, woodlands and forest etc. and finally, any military or other required annotations or symbols were added. Throughout, the model was known only by a number and any names on maps that came into the section had them obliterated first to preserve the utmost secrecy.

The Model Making section was concerned with virtually every major operation in World War 2, and a fitting tribute to the Section's skills and ingenuity was included in the book

'The Eye of Intelligence' by Ursula Powys-Lybbe, when she referred to the 'realism and beauty' they portrayed and it is sad that none of the original models can now be traced.

Secrecy was such that for some considerable time we had no idea what these particular models were for but on the morning of June 6th, 1944 as I sat with several colleagues at breakfast, the announcement was made over our crackly old radio set that the invasion of Normandy had begun.

Suddenly there was complete silence in the Mess as we looked at one another, not only in disbelief but in comprehension.

'So that's what it's all been about,' said the quiet voice of reason, breaking the silence but I wasn't the only one to shed the odd tear over breakfast that morning.

Mary Harrison, 4 Parr Court, Main Road, Radcliffe-on-Trent, Nottinghamshire.

n LCT(R) Rocket Ship converted from an LCT (Landing Craft Tank) to fire rockets in an assault.

I was a navigator of a Stirling four-engined bomber on Squadron 149 engaged on "special duties" – mainly dropping supplies to the Maquis, which required flying low-level, at about 500 feet, above enemy occupied territory at night.

We learned fairly early during the morning of 5th June, 1944 that "Ops" were planned for that night. Then stories came from the armourers that the "bomb" load we were to carry was extraordinarily light in weight and that they had been told that if any canister failed to release, they would be court-martialled! As the day wore on, we learned that the interior of our aircraft was being filled with two tons of "Window" – metalised strips of paper of varying lengths in bundles, each of which looked like an aircraft on the enemy's radar screens – and that we were to take with us two extra volunteer aircrew, who would help us throw it out!

At the navigators' pre-briefing that afternoon, we learned that the dropping point for our canisters was beside Caen in Normandy, and that two other crews were detailed for the same dropping point. This was a great relief, as our usual trips entailed long flights into France and occasionally, Belgium. However, our route was to fly from Portland Bill, then to the west of the Channel Isles, turning east once we had passed south of Jersey.

At main briefing, we were told nothing about the purpose of the trip – nor did we guess, even though it was common knowledge that an invasion was planned! It seemed an unnecessarily long way to get to Caen, since Caen was only a dozen miles from the coast, but it was not ours to question why. From Portland Bill, our bomb-aimer was required to throw out of the front hatch two bundles of "Window" every 20 seconds and our flight-engineer to throw one bundle of a different size down the flare chute every 10 seconds. The two volunteers were required to carry supplies to them. We were to cross the Channel at 1000 feet and keep our height 500 feet above the hills of Normandy, then gently dive when we came to the plain surrounding Caen so that we would drop the load from 500 feet at an airspeed of 130 knots. This would necessitate the use of flaps to slow us down. Unusually, I was required to drop the load on specified co-ordinates of my navigational radar. We always asked whether other aircraft were expected in the area, because they attract enemy fighters, and we were astonished to be told in a matter-of-fact voice "about 1000". But we still did not guess the purpose of the trip! Maybe our minds were on more practical matters.

When we arrived at the aircraft at 9 p.m. in the gathering gloom, we were glad that we were all slim young men, because the interior was filled on both sides with boxes of 'Window" to the roof, leaving a corridor about a foot wide. I had difficulty dragging my bag of navigation equipment through. The hour before take-off was always the most worrying part of an "Op" if all the instruments etc. were performing properly, because there was nothing to keep one's mind away from the trip ahead – but this night we had to appear nonchalant to our volunteer aircrew. We took off at 10.10 p.m. and had no difficulty in keeping to track. Fortunately, over France there was intermittent cloud cover, because in the clearings we saw many flashes of small arms fire shooting at us. The load was dropped according to plan and there was some light flak as we turned starboard returning on the same track, arriving back at Methwold, Norfolk at 3.30 a.m.

After returning, we learned that we had been simulating a parachute drop, in order to draw German troops away from the shore just before the Army was to land on the beaches. The "Window" was intended to make our three aircraft appear on German radar to be an armada, and the "bomb-load" were fireworks, which appeared and sounded like small arms and parachutists. To our surprise, the other two aircraft did not return. We learned later that one pilot had miraculously managed to make a wheels-up landing and the whole crew had escaped uninjured, and were smuggled back across the front line a couple of weeks later.

Derek C. Biggs, DFC, 16 Crown Drive, Inverness.

German "Ace" Joseph Priller in Normandy. His face shows his frustration.

I was corporal crew commander of a Sherman tank in the 10th Canadian Armoured Regiment (Fort Garry Horse). We were attached to 3rd Canadian Division and landed on Nan Red Beach.

The secret of our tanks, known as DD (duplex drive) was that they could be converted into an amphibious vehicles by a canvas screen providing buoyancy enough to support a 28 ton Sherman, fully armed with one 75mm cannon and two 300 Browning machine guns, one in the turret and one in the hull. The crew of five consisted of a driver and co-driver in the forward hull, gunner, loader/operator and crew commander in the turret.

The collapsible screen of heavy rubberized canvas was raised by inflating rubber air pillars by compressed air from a single cylinder, (barely enough air for two inflations). When fully raised, struts were locked into position by kicking each one with foot or hand by the crew commander.

When the screen was inflated and the tank was afloat guns could only be seen from the air. About fifteen inches of screen was above the water, making it look like a shallow boat and thus hiding its true identity. No one would believe that such a flimsy looking craft could possibly be an armoured vehicle. D.D. meant that the tank not only had tracks but had two propellors which could be lowered to engage in sprockets coupled to the rear track bogies to become a boat capable of about 8 knots. When not required the propellors could be disengaged by the driver as the tracks made contact with the beach.

The D.D. tank was one of the best kept secrets of the war. We spent months training with these vehicles usually under cover of darkness and with Valentine tanks instead of Shermans. We were on the south coast of England near Calshot across the water from Portsmouth and used to swim the tanks to the Isle of Wight one night, hide them in the grounds of Osborne House and then swim them back the next night. The longest swim I had done was from a L.C.T. (Landing Craft Tank) about seven miles from shore.

On the 4th June, my troop embarked on L.C.T. 1406, manned by the R.N. and under their orders while onboard. I was the first of five tanks to embark which meant that I would be the last tank to disembark. We spent the night of 4/5 June and all day 5th June on board in the harbour waiting for weather conditions to improve. We set sail during the night of 5/6 June and at daybreak were nearing the French coast.

Myself and crew were among the very few who slept or made a breakfast. Most of the crews were seasick but those who had eaten were in better shape than those who had not. I'm sure many thought it would be a blessed relief to be killed!

After having breakfast we checked over our tanks, released our chocks and inflated our screens ready for the instructions from the R.N. to disembark. The four crews in front of me all got into their respective tanks ready for disembarking. With screens up crew commanders were unable to see while in their tanks and with radio silence imposed were completely unaware of what was happening.

I ordered my driver and co-driver to get into their seats and to make ready. My gunner, loader and myself remained out of our tank, standing on the hull so that we could observe what was happening. From our position we had a clear view over our screen and over the front and sides of our L.C.T.

As we approached the coast of France we could see and hear the naval guns firing over us, rockets from rocket launchers mounted on some L.C.T.s, fighter aircraft and heavy bombers overhead, going in to soften up the coastal defences and disrupt the support areas. I have never seen anything like it since and will remember it forever.

We were still several thousand yards off France when our L.C.T. naval No. 1 climbed onboard each tank in turn to tell us that due to the rough seas they would take us as close to shore as possible, and hopefully right in to make a dry landing.

On receiving this information the front two tanks

remained ready for either situation keeping their screens raised, but tanks 3 and 4 immediately dropped theirs, the crews remaining in their tanks awaiting instructions. As I was still out of my tank I could see that it was unlikely that we would make a dry landing so I too kept my screen raised. Our guns could not be used whilst on board the L.C.T. even with the screens down.

By this time we were under fire from the enemy shore defences and our L.C.T. had been hit. The No. 1 then ordered the tanks to disembark and the ramp was lowered. I could see we were about seven hundred to nine hundred yards from the shore. He (No. 1) ordered the tanks to disembark under his direction. The first tank went down the ramp, engaged propellors and swam clear followed closely by the second tank. The third tank with screen down was ordered to the ramp and then into the water where it immediately sank from sight. The crew commander, who was also the Troop commander, swam clear of his tank followed by his gunner and the loader operator. They inflated their escape devices and became buoyant. The driver and co driver drowned in their seats.

In the meantime the commander of the fourth tank had realised a dry landing was out of the question so opened the valve on his partly emptied air cylinder and started to raise his screen. The low air pressure and volume was just enough to finish raising the screen as the tank went off the ramp into the water. He was able to engage propellors and move clear. He came under fire from shore defences, his screen was holed and his tank sunk in shallow water. His crew evacuated, inflated their escape devices and survived by holding onto their tank's aerial. When the fourth tank was clear of the ramp it was my turn to disembark. As I proceeded down the ramp and into the water, the L.C.T. received another hit, or struck a mine, and the crew abandoned ship from the stern.

We managed to swim our tank to the beach and though under shell and machine gun fire we remained afloat until our tracks engaged and pulled us out of the sea. We were able to drop our screen and use our guns to defend ourselves and to support the infantry regiment with covering fire as we fought our way off the beaches and into St. Aubin Sur Mer. We supported the infantry and some engineers by shooting up possible observation posts, machine gun nests and any enemy troops who appeared.

The beach became strewn with various vehicles that had struck mines or had been hit by cannon or mortar fire. There were also a number of dead and wounded soldiers lying where they had fallen. We got through the town by about mid day although some snipers and other pockets of resistance were not cleared up for a couple of days.

I knew my immediate objective was the village of Tailleville so I proceeded in that general direction. I saw my squadron O.C. and informed him that I was the only tank from my troop still in action. He allocated me to another troop and we proceeded to Tailleville, a walled hamlet held by German soldiers. My own troop was reformed a few days later from reinforcements and I was promoted to troop sergeant. After more casualties to tanks, crews and infantry, we eventually routed the enemy from Tailleville and headed in the general direction of Caen but that was only taken after many days of hard fighting.

We carried on during D-Day until darkness when we formed a laager and waited for supplies. We had food, sleep, and when I removed my helmet I found that it had been gouged by a bullet. It could have happened at any time during the morning but with all the excitement I had not been aware of the near miss!

When we replenished our supplies during the night 6/7 June I had only seven shells left for my 75mm cannon and the barrels of both machine guns had been so hot that they could no longer be removed and so both guns had to be replaced. The rifling in them had become so worn that I could see the tracer bullets leave the barrel in an ever increasing spiral with absolutely no hope of hitting a target. Both guns were replaced D+1.

Thus D-Day had ended, we were exhausted and had an hour or two of sleep before being available for action again by daybreak. It was days before we realised what we had been through! D-Day was probably the most exciting day of my life although not the most frightening. I was too inexperienced at that time to know what to fear. From the moment we embarked on our L.C.T. on 4th June I became oblivious to everything else. I had a carbuncle start to swell on my right elbow that day but was able to ignore it until D+1 when it became extremely painful. Every time we made tea my crew would make a poultice with the hot tea leaves. It came to a head and burst late on D+3 and my gunner pulled out the core with a pair of pliers before applying first aid. I still have the scar!

Harvey (Willie) Williamson, 174 Standhills Road, Kingswinford, West Midlands.

At 9.15 p.m. on the 5th June the 8th Parachute Battalion was all packed up and raring to go. The load each one of us was carrying was horrific. What with different types of grenades, mortar bombs, rifle ammunition, rations and spare clothing, a pick or shovel or trenching tool etc. etc. we could barely walk with the load let alone jump from an aeroplane! But we all fell in on parade and marched across the road to the airstrip on which was lined row upon row of Dakota aircraft.

I remember the Officer in charge of our group of 18 noted that one of the lads was carrying a canvas bucket of 6 Bren Gun magazines in his hand and on being challenged admitted that he intended to jump with them in this manner! The Officer snatched them from him with some rude remark and then he took the magazines out of the bucket and distributed them around the section, handing one to me. I objected, stating that I just had nowhere to carry it, but I wasn't allowed to get away with an excuse like that and I was told to "find somewhere"! There's logic for you! In the outside breast pocket of my parachute smock I had a phosphorus smoke grenade and a tobacco tin full of cigarettes but I found the inside pocket was empty so I put the magazine in there which, as you will read later, proved to be rather fortunate. And so we enplaned and took off, safe in the assurance from our Commanding Officer that a lot of us were making a trip from which there was to be no return. Not a comforting thought! I remember the flight over very well; I was No. 16 to jump. I can remember looking along the plane and wondering what the other chaps were thinking. There was a dim red light along the plane that apparently would not affect our eyesight when we jumped out into the darkness. A few of the lads were relaxing as though trying to sleep. Some were chatting. A couple I remember were reading war comics! Despite the situation there did not appear to be any stress in that plane at all and there certainly should have been! On the contrary it was rather relaxed.

That is until we went over the French coast and then it was hell let loose. Everything seemed to be coming up at us. The sky seemed to be full of anti-aircraft shells exploding and tracer bullets coming up very slowly and then speeding upwards. The plane was being thrown all over the place. It was the nearest thing to "hell" I ever want to be, and there was only one way out of it and that was down into it! Eventually the green light came on over the door and the time had come to carry out the job for which we had been training for so long. Out we went into the darkness at 00.50 hrs. on D-Day 6th June 1944.

The plan was for all of us to land in a dropping zone close to a village called Touffreville. We were then to move to a rendevous point on the edge of the village by following red and blue Very Lights being fired into the air by some of our lads who had dropped about an hour before us. We were then to form up and carry out our first task which was to move through a small town call Troarn and with the Engineers to blow up bridges on the River Dives to prevent German tanks crossing the river into our area.

After all the planning and briefing it was soon realised on landing that most of our Battalion had been dropped over a very wide area, and out of 670 men only 110 arrived at the rendevous point to carry out the first tasks. I had been dropped eight miles from where I should have been! On leaving the plane I can only say I felt very lonely except that the sky was full of bullets coming upwards. Fortunately it wasn't long before my feet hit the ground with a thud. Almost as soon as my feet touched the ground I was to find that I had landed directly in front of the muzzle of a German Machine Gun and I received a burst of fire straight at me. I can remember being hit and spinning round with a sudden yell of shock and finishing up flat on my back. The gun continued firing bursts over me for quite a while and I was getting the "flash" from the gun all the while as I was only a few yards in front of it. I

136

lay there rather dazed for a while, expecting to be hit again at any moment. It was difficult but I was able to keep control although not really aware of how many wounds I had received. The only defence I had was three Grenades in my waist belt but that was under my jump smock. That meant pulling a long zip down at the front to even start getting at one. My rifle was in a bag at the end of a rope about 25 yards away.

After a while the gun stopped firing and I was close enough to hear the Germans talking. I couldn't understand what they were saying, but they appeared to be very excited. When the firing resumed I realised I was not getting the "flash" from the gun and they were now firing in another direction. I then decided to get hold of a grenade expecting to be shot at at any time. I managed to get the grenade out and pull the pin and then I threw it at the gun. It seemed a very long four seconds before it exploded! Then I was aware that I had hit the target — the gun had stopped firing and there was no reaction from the gun position.

I got to my feet and retrieved my rifle. That made me feel better! But I now felt lonely and isolated, still dazed and in pitch darkness and with still a lot of anti-aircraft guns and machine guns firing around me. I was aware that my left arm was now useless, but unable to check the extent of the damage. Whilst unpacking my rifle and collecting myself I became aware of a figure advancing towards me along the hedgerow and to my relief found it was another Parachutist of the Royal Engineers. We moved along from this spot to the corner of the field we were in and after finding a wound in my upper arm where a bullet had passed right through my muscle my new pal applied a shell dressing to the wound. He then told me we were on the outskirts of the village of Ranville which was about eight miles from where I should have been and that his rendevous spot was too far away as well! It was then decided that as he had a Sten-gun and I had a rifle that it would be better if we changed weapons. I could handle the Sten-gun better with one arm. We also agreed that even though we were both miles from our Rendevous Points we should part company and try to find them. So he left and disappeared into the darkness and I moved away in the opposite direction, towards Ranville to try to find my way towards Troarn.

After moving a short distance I picked out the outline of a church in Ranville and became aware of German soldiers rushing about in a state of panic and my arm was now getting very painful. So I made my way by a circuitous route to the churchyard, narrowly avoiding the Germans in the process. The tower of the church is a separate building, and at the bottom of the tower are three doors. One is a toilet, the middle one leads by steps to the top of the tower, and the other is a coal hovel. I chose the toilet in which to take refuge, so I went in and sat on an old box type seat! This proved to be a fortunate choice as I found out next morning that the next door leading up to the top of the tower was a German machine gun position manned by a number of German soldiers.

I hadn't been sat too long when I heard someone trying the door of the toilet and I was soon aware from the noises the person was making that he was in a lot of pain. So I opened the door and found a German soldier on the ground who had lost most of his right foot. So I dragged him in with me as best I could. By this time two things happened. It was beginning to get light, and there was quite a battle going on around us. There was not a lot that I could do for my companion but I decided we could have a cigarette and so I undid my top left hand pocket and took out my tobacco tin full of Woodbines. When I did so I found that a bullet had hit me just below the button, gone straight through my tin of Woodbines and into the Bren Gun magazine in my inside pocket and stopped there. Otherwise it would have gone straight through my heart. All my Woodbines were unsmokable but thankfully the German had cigarettes which he produced and we smoked them instead!

Before long we found ourselves in the middle of a battle for Ranville. The top of the tower was blown off to destroy the machine gun position, and before long the Para's had taken the village and I was soon on my way to a Field Dressing Station and two days later on my way back to Blighty to hospital. I guess I was one of the lucky ones thanks to that Bren Gun magazine that I had grumbled about. I was back in Normandy within five weeks and fought right across Germany to the Baltic Sea.

Every day since then has been a bonus to me and I am and have always been so proud to have been a member of the Parachute Regiment. As a matter of interest I still have the breast pocket cut out of the battle smock that I was wearing on D-Day, plus the tobacco tin with the hole through it! And I often wonder what happened to the German who shared his cigarettes with me because I hadn't any to share with him! I wonder what happened to him and where he is now?

John Hunter, 79 Carron Drive, Werrington, Peterborough, Northants.

I was a member of the Royal Observer Corps, and after volunteering for operations was put on a training course at Bournemouth. Life here was one mad rush. Lectures on discipline, first aid, survival etc. and above all Aircraft Recognition. We were expected to pass 99.5% in that. British planes were known thoroughly from Albacore to Whitleys and German planes from Arado AR 230 to Messerschmitt 410's.

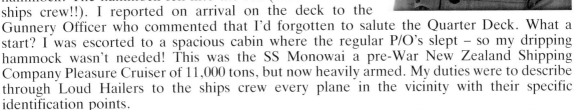

On passing the tests we had Seaborne flashes to add to our R.A.F. Observer Uniforms and R.N. brassards as Petty Officers. Quite a mixture. We were then secretly moved in RAF vans early one morning to Cowes Isle of Wight to board our respective ships.

Have you ever tried climbing up a rope ladder up the side of a heaving ship – I tried – carrying my kitbag and my hammock. The hammock fell into the sea (cheers from the ships crew!!). I reported on arrival on the deck to the Gunnery Officer who commented that I'd forgotten to salute the Quarter Deck. What a start? I was escorted to a spacious cabin where the regular P/O's slept – so my dripping hammock wasn't needed! This was the SS Monowai a pre-War New Zealand Shipping Company Pleasure Cruiser of 11,000 tons, but now heavily armed. My duties were to describe through Loud Hailers to the ships crew every plane in the vicinity with their specific identification points.

On the Sunday we steamed out – only to return – operation cancelled because of inclement weather. The real thing was then on – we left Monday evening for France. We could hear overhead a constant stream of our planes as they flew to bomb their targets. The route was marked clearly by a series of buoys of various colours as we zig-zagged towards our destination. I was on the bridge – binoculars ready – next to the Gunnery Officer. Though we'd had strict orders not to look at the sea but constantly search the skies for any intruder, very early that morning, I THOUGHT I saw a submarine on the starboard bow and pointed same out to the Gunnery Officer who said "excellent". "All guns range so and so prepare to fire." The ships Captain asked: "What is it Guns?", on being told he said: "Good show Taff" then looked carefully with his binoculars and shouted "Guns, Taff, haven't you seen a so and so (strong words these) paravane before?" (Drawn by minesweepers to clear mines). That was a good start.

On the dawn of 'D' Day the French Canadian Commandos on board embarked on their landing craft which bobbed up and down in the very rough sea and many were sea-sick. I waved to one very young Sergeant from Regiment de la Chaudiere (who had many a chat with me previously and had asked me to say a Prayer for him on his departure). Between watching carefully for any sneak raiders, I watched the landing craft approaching Courseulles sur Mer and saw my little Sergeant and his Company land safely only to be wiped out by the German machine gun from the sand dunes. What of my prayer?

Scarcely any planes to identify – though the black and white stripes made our planes easier to spot. I saw two of our Spitfires shot down by our own rocket gun ships as they swooped down from the low clouds. The shelling from the battleships behind us was terrific – Cherbourg to our right being a special target. The activity was intense – while we bobbed up and down at anchor – landing craft on both sides emptied men on beach-head JUNO.

Sirens sounded on some ships and suddenly from the coast flying very low towards the ships came Spitfires. I shouted "Spitfires." The Gunnery Officer disagreed. "They're Messer-

schmitts. All guns prepare to fire."

I shouted: "You are not to fire Sir."

"Pity help you Taff if you've made a mistake." They roared overhead – with perspiration running down my face I smiled at him and he winked back. "Good show Taff." They were Spitfires.

For 28 hours I stayed on the bridge – not moving – watching – and being proud to be part of the spearhead of the invasion that liberated Europe. I like to think I deserved the Gunnery Officers remark: "You were worth your weight in 4 inch shells."

The Canadian troops come ashore at Bernières.

Let us with pride remember those very gallant men who 50 years ago gave their lives that we might live. "Greater love hath no man than this, that a man lay down his life for his friends."

René Jones, Penrhiwfawr Isaf, Felindre, Llandysul, Dyfed. (Sadly we record that René Jones passed away on 24th March, 1993, after a short illness. His wife Mary has agreed to allow his story to be published as a tribute to him and to all of his colleagues).

I was in a Company of Engineers formed specially for the invasion at Blackwater in Essex. There were only 4 of these type of Company in the Army and we were called Inland Water Transportation Squadron. I was in 940 IWT, Royal Engineers. Our job was to deal with the landing of special tanks on the initial assault and in our Company we had Lightermen from Liverpool and London especially – men who understood and were used to working on small craft. I was 18 at the time. In the Company we had a wide range of boats and equipment. There were PBR's (Power Barge Ramp), Rhino Ferries, large U.S.A. Raft with 2 large engines with propellors that could be winched up when going in to beach in shallow water, and other items as well.

The U.S.D. Rafts were used to support L.S.T. ships 3 miles off shore in the early stages of the assault. We went back and forward through the smoke screens unloading "Funny Tanks", field guns etc., and to help us we had various tug boats to clear away damaged Landing Craft and other obstructions as quickly and as best they could. I was once the "Ramp Sapper" on a Rhino Ferry which was loaded completely with "Jerry Cans" of petrol – dozens and dozens of them. As we came in we were hit and the petrol cans blew up. There was a hell of a roar and fire and explosion and we had to just grab our issue life belts and jump into the sea and manage as best we could to get away.

There was the added danger of landing-craft ploughing back and forth through the smoke screens which gave a dense smoke cover, but I managed to float inshore safely where I eventually got on to the beach. It had been my first or second trip and when I landed it was still only about 7.00 a.m. on D-Day and daylight was still breaking! There was very little smoke on the beach at that stage, but as it got lighter the beaches became covered in black smelly oil. The smell was always there for many weeks afterwards: the smell held in the texturing of your uniform. The only gear we had was what we stood up in – "Battle Order" was the name and it was very appropriate. When we had time for a break on the beach later we were told to dig into the ground – 2 to a hole. I remember on D-Day night that snipers left behind gave us trouble from houses on the beachfront and an Infantry Regiment with flamethrowers mounted on Bren Carriers was called up to clear them out. That included the cellars and some tunnels that connected some of the houses which had been dug by the Germans.

I remember seeing the German signs "Actung – Minen", and also, which perhaps many people don't know about, our own signs "Dust Means Death". That was an important one. Lorries travelling at speed could easily make dust clouds, and I remember one lorry doing exactly that being subject very quickly to German .808 shell fire. I also remember having very sore gums with having to eat hard tack biscuits for too many weeks! It was ages before we got any bread and some men when going out to ships at anchor would gladly swap a German Steel Helmet for a nice slice of decent bread!

I still have many more thoughts and memories even after all these years and I often sit and think of various comrades. When you are a member of such a Unit, formed and trained for a special job such as the invasion, your comrades meant such a lot to you. I was the Units youngest sapper when it all happened and I still have a few mementoes of what was undoubtedly the most historical part of my life.

Richard Fisher, 35 Lake Road, Keswick, Cumbria.

141

German tanks attached to 3rd Infantry Division loaded on to an LCT.

I was living in Andover in 1944. The R.A.F.'s airfield just outside the town had been taken over by the U.S.A.A.F. in 1942, and military convoys were a common sight. Some road routes were closed to facilitate aircraft movements, and to enable vehicles to be hidden in copses alongside the verges. Harewood Forest was used for storing bombs and the Headquarters of the R.A.F.'s maintenance organisation was housed in one of the western villages. Southwards, the area banned for travel by civilians without special passes extended to within five miles of the town. Men and women of the Allied Services, including many G.I.'s spent off-duty time in Andover, often being invited into people's homes.

"We've opened the Second Front: we've landed in France," my father called up the stairs.

I dashed down the stairs, still clad in pyjamas, eager to hear the rest of the news issuing forth from our old Cossor battery powered wireless set. My mother sent me back to get dressed, saying that there would be many more bulletins during the day!

I was three weeks short of my fourteenth birthday. I attended the Andover Senior Girls' School, and had been head prefect since the beginning of the summer term. There was an air of excitement and optimism amongst the girls and boys that day, as they streamed up the hill to their respective school buildings situated on the outskirts of the town. My first duty on arriving at school in the mornings was to report to the Headmistress in case she had any particular tasks she wished me to undertake. She told me that she intended to hold an Assembly to pray for our forces, and asked me to ensure that all the Form Mistresses were advised accordingly. When I returned to tell her that everyone was assembled in the hall, she said: "Bring the flag."

I picked up the Union Jack, which stood in a corner of the vestibule at the main entrance. She directed me to bear the flag into the hall and to position myself just below the stage. I was not, and have never been, of standard-bearing physique, being only 5ft tall. However, I was a good soldier and obeyed orders. I lifted the flag aloft and proceeded into the hall. Meanwhile, the Headmistress had gone on to the stage, and as soon as I was in my allotted place she began the service. I continued holding the flag up, because I didn't know what else to do! I was concentrating hard on trying to keep it steady, but I must have wobbled it during the address, because the mistress who played the piano accompaniments for the singing crept across the stage and whispered to me: "Lower it." I was very grateful to her! She gave me the nod to raise it again as she struck the first note of the National Anthem.

As a leisure activity I used to attend the local School of Art on one or two evenings a week. At about half past six, someone called out: "Look what's coming over!" We all ran to the windows. The sky was filled with light aircraft (Dakotas, I think) all towing Horsa gliders. There were hundreds of them, and they kept coming for the next two hours.

"These must be the reinforcements," we all said. "The landings on the beaches have been successful, and we're pushing inland." We cheered and waved frantically, hoping that some of the soldiers on board could see us.

On the way home, everybody seemed to be craning their necks skywards, to see this great armada of the air. Some people were in the streets, but many others, like my mother and our neighbours, had spent the time in their gardens waving and cheering.

The war was by no means over. Tomorrow we should hear about the casualties, there would be hard fighting in France, and within a few weeks southern England itself would be back in the front line – the target of Hitler's V1s and 2s. But, for a brief spell that fine evening the horrors and privations of war seemed to be forgotten in euphoria which treated "tomorrow" as "another day."

Miss June Harris, 14 Humberstone Road, Andover, Hampshire

My bomber Squadron was the 552nd B26 Marauder Medium Bomber Unit of the U.S. 9th Air Force in the U.K. I was aged 22, and we flew to England from Homestead Air Base in South Florida, our departure point from the U.S.A.

It was to be a remarkable journey, especially for an inexperienced crew, with a real "round-about" route with England the final destination. The route was designed to fit the range limitations of the B26 and involved an engine failure, a forced landing, horrific storms over the Caribbean, skimming across the Amazon delta, searching for Ascension Island in the wide open spaces of the South Atlantic and then 2 nights in primitive Africa. Finally up through a cloudy pass in the Atlas Mountains and to marvellous Marrakesh in Morocco where to my delight I fixed up a date with a charming French girl! Then on up the Atlantic, on the lookout for German fighters from France, and finally a very nervous night-time landing at Lands End.

After two combat missions as co-pilot in another B26 I was told I was now ready to fly my own plane in combat. And so to bed on June 5th. At 03.30 the next morning (which turned out to be D-Day) I was woken and told that I was to fly on that morning's mission. So, full of high excitement I reported to the Briefing Room where our Colonel told us that General Omar Bradley had selected our Group, because of its fine record, to be the last to strike the Germans just before our troops landed on the beach. What's more, as best I can recall, we were to bomb an artillery position somewhat behind the beach fortifications and then dive down for a low level attack on shore line gun turrets just before the allied landings were to begin. So that was to be my FIRST Mission as Pilot with my own crew!

All this was enough to shake my confidence even before take-off. But to add to the problem I was then told I was to fly in the "Tail End Charlie" position. That meant that in all the "groups" of planes that were flying on that Mission I was not only in the LAST Group, but I was in fact the LAST plane in the LAST Group – in short there was no-one behind me to cover me! Well, tremendous excitement is an emotion that is hard to explain. Our mission was important. Our lives were very much at risk. Who could foresee the outcome? I knew that for me it would be the hardest job I had ever undertaken – and it was! I decided that the only solution was absolute dedication to the controls of my aircaft. I remember mostly the sweat and the muscle aches which came from that concentration and trying to keep in position. It was probably that supreme concentration that temporarily put aside my fears. At first we flew through German fighters but these were soon driven away by our fighter escort. Then came the flak and the machine gun fire which downed several B26's but I came through unscathed. Just getting to the target that was an unforgettable experience. Below us were thousands of Allied ships in the Channel. We looked down on them in utter amazement. Their deadly ordeal was ahead.

Then the bombing attack itself. Lou Hengst our Navigator/Bombardier had his moment of glory when he let our bombs go right on time and on target. Then somehow we survived the low level attack after which we pulled up and headed back to our base at Great Dunmow in Essex with enormous relief. We chortled in our joy!

On the ground I have to admit that I walked with perhaps a touch of macho pride to the "debriefing" tent where I poured out my story of the raid! I was then offered my "Mission Whisky" – a small shot of liquor for the nerves! It was by now about 9.00 a.m. and, knees shaking a bit with nerves and excitement, I walked back to my hut for a rest. But we couldn't – we talked and talked and talked with other crews about the events of that momentous morning. Later that afternoon we took off on a second D-Day raid – but it was such an anticlimax after what we had been through early that historic morning.

Colonel John Cutler, U.S. Air Force (Retired),
235 San Juan Drive, Ponte Vedra, Florida, U.S.A.
and 74 Burton Court, Franklin's Row, London SW3.

I was a member of a 15″ gun crew on the battleship H.M.S. Warspite. When the Captain told us over the tannoy there was a complete stillness throughout the ship. The only thing to be heard was the continued thud of the ship's engines and the wash of the sea over the bows as we ploughed our way to the place of operations.

D-Day arrives and at approximately 0500 hours the first allied shells begin falling on the French coast. I didn't know a great deal of what was going on since my action station was between decks, but I did know that our 15″ shells were being fired at an alarming rate.

We had been closed up at action stations for almost 24 hours and had very little to eat, in fact all we had eaten was a couple of sandwiches and our action ration which consisted of two barley sweets, two packets of chewing gum and six malted milk tablets. Needless to say, hunger was very prominent, so when the order to 'stand down' came through at approximately 1700 hours our thoughts travelled as indeed did our bodies, to the

mess deck for a good meal. Not all of the guns crews were able to relax and those manning A.A. guns had to remain closed up ready for emergency. We had our first view of the enemy coast and never before had such a conglomeration of ships from Battleships down to small assault craft been seen in any one operation. By this time of course the infantry had established a beach head but even so the coming and going of tank and troop landing craft was still on a large scale. We didn't have much idea as to the extent of casualties suffered by the assault troops but we had picked up several chaps whose craft had been literally blown out of the water. We did see one or two dead bodies and these poor devils had paid the full price of war.

Now came the most awe-inspiring sight I have ever seen or for that matter am ever likely to see. This spectacle must have been a definite boost to the morale of our lads on the beaches – not that their morale was low, far from it I would say. No doubt the enemy felt otherwise!! The approach of the Airborne Forces was the cause of all this excitement. The sky was literally black with aircraft – it reminded me of a flock of starlings, the only difference was that the 'planes were continuous whereas the birds are only momentary. We never saw the actual dropping of the paratroops because the dropping zone was further inland. Of all the thousands of aircraft taking part in this operation we saw only one shot down and this particular plane was a Halifax and I think the pilot deserves a word of special mention. The glider he was towing had just been released and no sooner was this done the Halifax received a direct hit from flak and it was obvious that he would crash. It appeared as if nothing in this world could prevent him from crashing on the assault troops but whether it was by a miracle or sheer gallantry on the part of the pilot, he somehow managed to keep the plane in the air until he was well away from the landing forces. So it was then that yet more men paid the full price of war.

That night we only saw one enemy plane and this came swooping in very low along our port side and all our A.A. guns opened up and for a moment all hell was let loose. I think our gunners were too excited because they never as much as touched him! No further incident occurred and I was intent on watching the coast. I have seen some very good firework displays but never anything to equal this. The sky was ablaze with light and purely artificial – with tracer cross fire forming a steel curtain around our troops.

Next day we were called upon by the Americans at their beach head along the Cherbourg Peninsula to dislodge a formation of enemy tanks. We proceeded with all haste to help the tanks and received this message from the American Commander: "Good shooting," so it was evident that the enemy tanks no longer existed.

D-Day plus two. We go back to Portsmouth to re-ammo ship. We get shore leave for one night and we are asked how things went "over the other side". The daily newspapers carried headlines of the Warspite's exploits – what do you know, we were in the news!

Arthur Hopcraft, 137 Banbury Road, Brackley, Northants.

The battleship Ramillies bombarding enemy positions.

The training was over – no more manoeuvres sending the Skipper white haired with anxiety. This was the real thing. We loaded up with five tanks of the Green Howards at the Hards at Portsmouth. As is pretty well known D-Day was cancelled for 24 hours due to inclement weather, so we had some pretty miserable squaddies on board I can tell you! They were feeling a bit sick even at anchor. We eventually sailed with our craft L.C.T. 1079, twelve little Tank Landing Craft in our group, setting off for who knows what.

That night there was a strong feeling aboard that we were going to do this damned invasion all on our own for all that we could see! But as the dawn broke gradually came the most incredible sight. Everywhere you looked there were Landing Craft and ships of all descriptions including just astern of us H.M.S. Warspite which made me feel a hell of a lot braver than I had been until then!

Gradually the French coast came into view and about 6.30 a.m. the Skipper told me to hoist the Battle Ensign and pipe all hands to battle stations. This I did, feeling quite a bit proud of myself as I did it I can tell you. I still have the pipe and a remnant of the Ensign to this day.

With the Ensign flying we headed on towards our objective, Gold Beach, and as we passed under a posh cruiser, the Belfast no less, she let go a broadside which scared the hell out of every one of us! I don't think anyone had to dash for clean underpants but it must have been a close run thing!

As we came in nearer we could now see and hear the Rocket and Gun Landing Craft letting fly. Things were really hotting up now. Then we saw our planned landing point on the beach and if anyone had looked on the bridge all they would have seen were two steel pimples – the Skipper's and my steel helmets! We were not afraid of course – just being very careful! But as a matter of course nothing ever goes to plan, and this was no exception. As we headed for our planned arrival point we realised that there was nowhere to land –amazing but true! We just had to manoeuvre and change course until we did find a space which fortunately for us was still in roughly the right area. That fact in itself perhaps will give people today some idea of the number of craft and men that were there – all heading pell mell for the same beaches.

Suddenly we hit the beach with a crash, there was an almighty explosion on the port bow and two winchmen shot out of their little cubby holes with eyes popping and mouths wide open and looking up at the bridge as if to say "What the bloody hell did you do that for!" The Skipper who sported a natty ginger beard suddenly changed from being "Wavy Navy" to "Royal Navy" and told them both to get back into the winch house "There's good chaps." Or words to that effect!

We dropped the ramp and the first tank managed to get ashore although submerged to a depth of about four or five feet, and amazingly, bearing in mind the noise, shells and God knows what else, we managed to get all the troops, tanks and equipment ashore in pretty good order. Whilst all this was going on remember that other Landing Craft were also charging in and generally having a rough time of it. Two on our starboard bow blew up in short order before they hit the beach, bodies being thrown in all directions.

Just after the two Landing Craft were hit a report came in that our engine room was flooding. I went belting down and found the stoker with his feet on the control panel with about 2½ feet of water sloshing around him. I also saw a chunk of iron rail sticking up through the deck! One of Rommel's little gadgets had worked only too well on our craft! However, the stoker assured me he was confident he could keep the engines going so I returned to the bridge to report.

Having done so I looked about and could see army men in the water and on the beaches, all heavily loaded and wearing battle green. Some of those in the water were struggling and some of their mates on shore were trying to throw heaving lines to them but to be honest they hadn't a clue. So we joined in and managed to pull five or six chaps out of the surf which was very heavy at the time, but there were others we weren't able to help in time and it was heartbreaking to see some of them drowning in front of your eyes. I think that more than anything else upset me and my shipmates.

Eventually the tide went out leaving us high and dry, and we were able to get ashore and assess the damage. The port bow had a hole in it about seven feet by three feet, and was turned back like a sardine can. As mentioned before, the engine room had a tetrahydron up through the deck and we were lying on a hump on the beach which had buckled the craft amidships.

Some distance away I could see a body lying just out of the surf. Walking over I saw it was a young Marine Commando aged about twenty. I looked down at him and I remember thinking, I wonder what your mother will say and feel when she gets that telegram in a couple of days time.

A few of us explored the gun emplacements which our ships had been plastering; we found that they had not done all that much damage but the Commandos had gone up to the embrasures with flame throwers and the ammunition inside the gun emplacements had exploded.

All we could find were three or four charred boots. The walls were lined with steel plate and it looked like a collander where the shrapnel had pierced it. But the emplacement itself was completely intact. These guns were not taken without loss as the five British bodies outside testified. By this time German prisoners were arriving on the beach and it seemed about one in four were Russians which seemed very odd to us at the time. The R.N. Beach Parties were also there and were busy welding up the holes we had sustained while making the landing.

We were ordered to anchor for the night and to proceed to Portland at first light. None of us had had much sleep for 48 hours, and me less than most being the only one that could read the signals. So guess who had the midnight watch. Yes, muggins was on watch for four long hours. Whilst on watch and listening to the rumble of gunfire off the beaches, I was staring at three tanks burning just on the shoreline and should mention that I was stood on the iron ladder leading down to the messdeck with my arms leaning over the hatchway. The next thing I knew was Jimmy shouting Bunts Wake Up, Get up on deck Immediately!! Well, my brain registered this but my legs were as dead as doornails, I could not, repeat, could not move. What with him hollering at me and an almighty effort on my part I somehow got up on deck.

Of course this meant I was in a lot of trouble. Asleep on watch, off the enemy coast. I was put in front of the C.O. next morning and I gave him the blarney about having no sleep for two days which he knew was the truth because he hadn't had much sleep either. Anyway, I got a fortnight's No. 11 which didn't matter much because we were on duty non-stop anyway.

Now the Skipper had a nice little Wren back in Portland and when we finally set sail, instead of going through the swept channel, he went diagonally across the channel to Portland. Quicker you see, but bloody dangerous, but we made it. I had managed to get my head down for a couple of hours when there was the dreaded cry "Bunts. On the bridge at the double."

When I got up there, there was a big red lamp about two feet across, flashing away like mad. It read S T O P O R I F I R E upon which I made the fastest recognition signal in the annals of the British Navy! The ship flashing was the harbour guard ship and although it was only a big trawler she had a four-inch gun trained smack on us.

Well, that is more or less the tale of D-Day as I remember it. We were sent on leave for two days while repairs were carried out and, while visiting an old aunt who lived in King's Road, a woman stopped me in the street and asked me what I was doing walking around Banbury while her son was across the channel fighting Germans. Well, to say I was stuck for words and non-plussed was putting it mildly. It was not a pleasant feeling, being handed the verbal white feather. I think I managed to convince her I had done my little bit, but as they say folk is funny.

Ray ("Lofty") G. Fletcher,
58 Beargarden Road, Banbury, Oxon.

I was in the Kings Regiment No. 5 Beach Group. Everything in our training was geared up to the landing on the Normandy beaches and although talk of the invasion was a daily occurrence in training, it was almost unknown outside the beach groups. The long and indeed arduous days of training came to an end when we moved south to Havant, near Portsmouth. It was like a tented city as troops moved in from all over the countryside for the final briefing and kitting out. Each man was given two 24-hour food packs, two bandoliers of ammunition, hand-grenades, a complete change of clothing, a jerkin and lifebelt and a blanket wrapped in a groundsheet. We also received 200 "Liberation Money" French Francs, a can of self-heating cocoa, and a can of self-heating soup, both of which turned out to be excellent and satisfying.

We were all keyed up and ready to go on June 4th but the weather changed and the whole show was delayed for 24 hours which was a real anti-climax after such a massive mental build-up. Next day we returned to the Landing Craft at Newhaven and moved out into the Channel into the assembly area. As we started the journey it was a fantastic sight – everywhere you looked you could see ships of every shape and size, an Armada that had to be seen to be believed. It was very comforting I can tell you to realise that we had such magnificent support, but that didn't help with the weather! It was still rough and most of the troops on board were sea-sick. In fact if truth be known, some of them were in a hell of a state.

When we got within shelling distance of the French coast it seemed as if all hell had broken loose. Landing Craft on either side of ours had been hit and were on fire or already sinking. Our ramps were dropped when we came close to the beach and we charged out through the water as best we could. The waves were very rough and the water was still shoulder high. There was one consolation – as we hit the water our minds were so concentrated on getting ashore safely that the sea sickness disappeared!

Actually, as we stepped on to the beach, despite all our fears, was a marvellous feeling. As we made our way forward there seemed to be mines and mined obstructions everywhere, and many landing craft and tanks on fire. There were dead and wounded everywhere on the beach both on the sand itself and in the water and at the waters edge. It was painful but we had to press on – the medics would see to those that could be helped. Indeed as the Germans were pushed back from the beach the Beach Group Organisation took over and the whole system amazingly started to work exactly as had been planned in our training. All that in spite of continued heavy shelling and gun fire.

At about 5.30 p.m. our Company managed to reach the first road from the beach after heavy fighting. I was operating a controlled-radio set but was unable to make any contact with one of our platoons. As the Company Commander was worried about the missing platoon the Sergeant Major took over the radio and sent me off to try to locate them. Making my way along the road I heard a salvo of shells over my head and then an enormous explosion. The next thing was the excruciating pain of shrapnel in my back and right forearm. The worst part was that the missing platoon turned out to be all right and in position. The only problem was that their radio had gone on the blink!

I was badly wounded in my back and forearms and destined to spend all night lying on a stretcher in a dugout in the sand. That in itself was quite traumatic as I was on my own and could only use one hand to try and keep away the sand which covered me each time the guns fired. Lying on my back, unable to sleep, I had at least the privilege of seeing the second wave of paratroops coming in that night. The parachutes mixed in with the searchlights and all interlaced with tracer bullets created a fantastic sight, never to be forgotten.

At about 7.00 a.m. next morning all the stretchers were lifted on to a DUKW and we were taken along the beach and then out to the ships lying offshore and finally back to blighty. They called D-Day the "longest day". It was certainly the longest day of my life!

James McCall, 2 Douglas Road,
Standish, Wigan, Lancashire.

yoops of 4th S.S. Brigade taking cover from snipers at St. Aubin-sur-Mer. Note tank obstacles.

"One spring morning, perhaps for the first time in his life, the little boy got up before his parents awoke. He opened the kitchen door and saw the sun shining in, and the things prepared for this new day. Like his Creator, he looked on his world, and saw that it was good." Sometime in infancy we acquire the ability to produce our first memory that can be retrieved at will. That is mine – precious, in spite of its utter triviality.

Rather like a jigsaw puzzle, other memories accumulated around this one. I realised that my home had a long back garden, with a magical place at the bottom, a small stream. Beyond that was the railway, up on an embankment. Over the road was a wood, which concealed a cluster of Nissen huts – empty, though newly built. At the top of the road were a few shops, and the bus stop leading to the unimaginable world beyond.

The village, now part of Crawley, in Sussex was quieter, with very little traffic – and far fewer men in evidence. There was only one minor nuisance – an "old aeroplane" which produced a wailing noise, rising and falling in pitch, sometimes followed by distant bangs. I never actually saw it, but if it was heard while we were out for a walk, we had to hide behind trees or bushes. My mother, told us that, being old, it was unreliable, so that it was better to be out of its way. With this little story, she kept my illusion of paradise intact. The word "war", heard from time to time, gave me not the slightest understanding of the dreadful experiences being undergone, at that very time.

Children could play alone in woodland in those days without fear of molestation; and the Nissen huts were an obvious attraction. As I had no inkling that anything in my world would ever change, I was quite surprised to approach them one day, and hear strange, stirring music coming from inside. I looked through an open doorway. Men in uniform were sitting side by side, their backs to the walls, while a bagpiper walked slowly up and down. I remember that they seemed to be waiting, quietly – not much was being said. Someone asked me inside; I was taken on knees, and made a fuss of, while I listened, entranced by the pipes. When I had to go, the men seemed sorry, and a week later they were gone. But other novelties succeeded them – the sidings full of carriages, marked with the red cross on their roofs and sides; and a relentless succession of planes and gliders, floating serenely across the sky, all in one particular direction.

In later years, I understood my privilege, in seeing a tiny part of the greatest drama in history. The struggle between Good and Evil is as old as mankind – but this time, modern science had multiplied the scale a thousand fold. But the enormity of the evil was only to be seen in full when victory revealed the nightmare of the concentration camps.

What I wonder, did my little visit mean to those men, quietly waiting to face the battlefield where they would see their friends burnt or shot to death; might suffer that fate themselves; or might be spared, but as cripples in body or mind, needing care for the rest of their lives? Was I to them, for a few minutes, their own child that they might never see again? Or a symbol of the children of Europe, whose freedom they were ready to buy with their lives? Quite a sobering thought for me, when I wonder whether I would be man enough to do the job that they carried through.

The huts are gone, and the wood has been "developed". The roar of a motorway pollutes the peace of the little Saxon church where I was christened. In a crowded island, one's own freedom often has to be sacrificed, in fairness to others. But the vital freedom remains – that of publicly demanding (if need be) that Authority mend its ways. Take this keystone out, and everything else crumbles around it.

This was the prize our Heroes bought for us. This is why I buy my poppy with humility – the money only a token — of a debt I can't repay.

But I wear it with pride.

Chris D. Bristow, 28 Bridge Way, Shawbury, Shrewsbury.

...rman tanks of a British Armoured Regiment waiting to set off. Note they're already on the "Continental" side of the road!

The assault landing craft bobbed up and down on the choppy sea; on board were men of the Ox and Bucks Light Infantry, part of the 3rd Division.

The beach head was now in view. Smoke and flame could be seen all along the wide front. Shells continued to pound the positions ahead, the screaming noise as they passed over our heads was horrific as I am sure they were only passing a few feet above us. I understand that it was guns from our battleships out at sea. I remember seeing the "RAMILLIES" when we passed through on our way in.

We were getting close now. I still recall the intense noise, the cold sweat on my skin. I was not aware of any fear, perhaps a tinge of excitement, a strange feeling that I was not there! Everything was in a confused mixture. I do remember checking my kit for no reason at all for I had done it a dozen times before. I tried the magazine on my Bren gun to make sure it was secure in position and that the safety catch was on.

There was a sudden lurch of the craft as it struck the sandy beach. The ramp was down, and the lads in front of me were taking to the water. I heard the commands, move, move. I walked off the edge of the ramp into the water. I could smell the sea water as it ebbed around my waist. I held the Bren gun above my head and slowly moved forward.

Not far away, to my left, I saw a body, face down in the water. His still inflated Mae West was keeping him afloat. The air was filled with a pungent smell of burning oil tinged with what I assumed to be cordite.

Through the heavy smoke I ran, oblivious of the load I carried and heard the sound of heavy machine gun fire. I scrambled up the slippery dune, saw an abandoned tank perched on the top, its engine still running. To my right was a large house, and through a hole in the roof an enemy machine gun was spraying the beach behind me. I slipped over the top of the dune as more machine guns began to open up. In front of us I saw a couple of our lads fall. I then went to ground, took up a firing position, and opened up covering as wide an area as was possible. My number two came alongside changing the magazines. We must have fired six before I realised the barrel was now getting quite hot. It was a great relief to see tanks passing through at great pace. I think they were the Polish Brigade. Things got a little easier as we pushed inland. I suppose we must have penetrated a couple of miles when the order came to dig in. Our point of position was a hedgerow somewhere near the Caen road.

The platoon officer came round, said all was going well, but be prepared for possible counter attacks. He collected the little brown cards that were issued back in England. They were a simple card that were already printed out saying, you were O.K. and you would write soon. All one had to do was address it home, put your name and army number in the space provided, and sign it. The officer promised it would be on its way home that night. I remember feeling good about that.

I did return on the 6th June, 1985, as did so many others. During my visit I met up with a Canadian, a tall figure, aged now, with the need of a walking stick. It inspired this poem, dedicated to all who took part in the greatest invasion of all time.

He stands beside the waters edge,
Stooped with age yet alert,
Deep in thought he sees once more,
The race across the hostile shore.

Dawn awakes with thundering sounds,
Of firing guns, and all around,
The cries of beings duty done,
Fall to the ground, one by one.

Friend and foe on blooded sand,
Find peace at last, on foreign land,
Stillness shrouds their final quest,
No more in battle, they lie at rest.

Now the thinker in faultering gate,
Moves once more over the sands of hate,
Looks for comrades, who perished there,
They did not falter, they did not dare.

The lonely beach is empty now,
Save for the figure on the dune,
Standing in silhouette against a ghostly moon,
His tear washed eyes mournfully,
Scan the horizon to eternity.

Have I in ignorance, made intrusion,
Upon this sacred past illusion,
Or can it be that I was led,
To see a ghostly spirit, of the 'D' day dead.

Arthur Saunders, 8 Oakland Crescent, Riddings, Alfreton, Derbyshire.

164

Mrs. Sheddon, then Rhea Lang, with her class in Germany, 1944.

Like the other eighteen young women teachers I was in my very early twenties and in charge of a small village school, the men having all been called up. Although born and bred in Cologne and having chosen quite a different part of Germany for my first post, bureaucracy, classically, had sent me totally elsewhere from my desired domain, and I, therefore, found myself working in a part of my country I barely had heard of.

The authorities took good care of us budding paedagogues. We assembled regularly in one village or another in this fine, fertile region near the Dutch border, to observe a forenoon's teaching. In Germany children still go to school only a.m.

During this day's dinner-break we women walked through the woods near Wyler, "Wunderbar, ... truly wunderbar." This was later to become the well-known Reichswald battlefield where thousands perished. The birds were singing, the light filtered lovely through the glades; we were at peace. Then someone, who had heard the one o'clock news on the radio, mentioned the Normandy landings.

My uncle and co-guardian, an elderly E.N.T. man cum-plastic surgeon had been a medical officer in the 1914-18 war. He thus knew history first-hand and had often in domestic discussions Cassandra-like predicted Germany's fate would frightfully repeat itself. I, in my youthful idealism and ignorance of life itself, never mind politics or demagoguery, thought the Fatherland had as good a chance as any. On hearing of the breaching of Fortress Atlantic I was not so sure any more; neither were many of my colleagues.

I remember we had a lengthy, loud, angry exchange, with those fanatics one finds anywhere in the world, who swear blind "we'll win," regardless of reality. Total war indoctrination tended to make them blinkered badly.

Nevertheless it was only too easy for all of us to dismiss disturbing thoughts from our young minds and return through the lovely landscape to the small village school that afternoon to carry on with our in-service training course.

The real irony was, that in the time it would have taken to create a new human life, from June 6, 1944, to the late Spring 1945, this whole once bonny, blooming, fine, fertile German land in the county of Cleves was to be transformed into a vast void; a desolate desert, with towns, villages and farms totally destroyed. The carcasses of cattle stinking to high heaven for months, its people refugees and good serving soldiers, on both sides, slaughtered by the score and score and score.

Incidentally, whether Welsh, Scottish, Irish, Canadian, German or American, wounded and/or dying they all cried for their mothers.

The very forest, where I walked and talked on that D-Day, did not exist at all any more. Its tall trees swollen stumps like some survivors limbs, the earth scorched.

Since then I have been totally anti-war ever, anywhere.

Mrs. Rhea Sheddon, Ph.D., 8 Castle Crescent,
Kennoway-Leven, Fife, Scotland.

14404865 Signalman Flint KW 2nd War Office Signals

Our medium range wireless telegraphy section left Dover in May '44 to go to Portsmouth. I had mixed feelings, having had a fairly near-miss from a shell but not wanting to part from my girlfriend in Dover. We went in convoy, passing through my home town of Lewes en route. I kept a sharp lookout for anyone I knew but saw nobody, yet a few days later my mother wrote to say that Mrs. So-and-So had glimpsed me at the open rear door of our Bedford QL radio truck and I was eating a sandwich! I remember the haversack rations the army cooks used to provide us with for journeys – doorsteps, and the rind was never cut from the cheese (and it was invariably cheese or jam so one had a fifty-fifty chance of a reasonable sandwich).

We were housed at Pompey in one of the three forts at Portsdown Hill, Fort Widley. The main Combined Services Operations and Signals HQ was underneath Fort Southwick.

Apart from the odd spell on fatigues and occasional guard duty we were left to our own devices for a couple of weeks. The food was nothing to write home about and one evening I skipped the tea meal entirely because the blokes coming back from the early-serving said it was worse than usual!

So I went out for a long walk instead, out in the countryside. There seemed to be quite a deal of fighter or light bomber aircraft about and all with double white stripes on their wings – a marking I had never seen before. Then several formations of planes came over towing gliders. I at once assumed that quite a big raid on the Germans was afoot. Probably some sort of preliminary operation to do with the projected Second Front, an event which as a born pessimist I thought would perhaps take place in 1945.

Towards dusk I made my way back to the fort only to get an almighty blasting from the regimental policeman and the orderly sergeant at the gate. Where had I been? Didn't I know the entire unit had been confined to barracks? Did I know I was for the high jump? Did I realise I could be put on a 'fizzer' (charged) for the offence of missing a meal? Here were the Allied Armies about to go ashore on one of the most momentous and hazardous undertakings in military history and here was this NCO worrying about the niceties of military law. In the end commonsense won and I went back to our hut where I was assured that 'it' was definitely on.

Our section sergeant produced a duty roster and I found I was due on shift at Southwick after breakfast. So I thought I would get a bite to eat in the Naafi, a meat pie or something and a cup of tea, and then get an early night.

The Naafi was crowded. Certainly it had better business that evening than perhaps at Christmas. The queue at the beer bar was too daunting, there were soldiers I had never seen before (perhaps they were 'skivers' who with the security clamp-down could not 'dodge the column' for once), the air was blue with tobacco smoke and the canteen piano was beating out boogie woogie. I managed to get a 'char and a wad' but not consume them in comfort, and it was no better back in our hut because nobody could settle and speculation was rife – a cliché but true on this occasion. The following morning as we went down the wide steep stairs to the underground headquarters at Southwick there was a sort of different mood evident. More chatting, more laughing, people buttonholing others – I can only describe it as like the atmosphere outside a football stadium when a big match is on.

Normally when we went on shift a corporal would allocate us to a particular radio circuit and we would liaise quickly with the operator coming off watch (frequency, callsigns, radio conditions, ability of the distant radio operators and so on) and then take over. This time there was a Senior NCO placing operators in certain positions and I was miffed to find that I was to be just a 'check'. This was Royal Signals jargon for the man who merely carries messages to and fro.

For the whole of that shift I burned with a mixture of shame and indignation. I had volunteered for the army and to be a Royal Signals radio operator. In fact I had cut short leave earlier that year in order to sit and pass a trade test that put my rating up to Operator/Wireless and Line B2 – something that in peacetime would have been almost unthinkable at my age. Yet I was being treated as a military errand-boy.

Paradoxically, when I was out in the corridor letting off steam to an ATS girl, along came a staff officer – very grand in his WW1 medal/ribbons and red gorget patches. We stiffened to attention and expected he would sail majestically past as was to be expected from such grand personages. But no; he stopped and enquired would we like to be given the latest 'griff' (we scorned the RAF slang 'gen' for information and always used the army slang). Of course we would.

So we were taken to a quiet part of the ops/sigs complex and given a very brief outline of the extent of the landings and what was currently known about their success. We were also given sight of the elaborate communications diagram. Coloured lines radiating out from circles (the radio control stations at Southwick) to groups of other circles (the HQs of the Brigades and Divisions carrying out the assault). Radiating out from these formations were lines to other small circles – the battalions

Ken Flint in centre.

engaged in the fighting. Overlaying those were radio circuits for air support communications, various special voice circuits (using the, for us, new VHF) and other ramifications in the communications in the command network. Men of the distant stations were marked as being on 'HQ ships' and I wondered briefly whether the personnel on these were under fire and whether they would get ashore in due course or be brought back if the landings were not consolidated.

Eventually I got my own personal message through to the powers-that-be and I was taken off errand-boy's duty and put on the control station of the air-support 'net' – handling 'operational immediate' messages calling for air strikes and so on. Much of the lower priority 'traffic' on the air dealt with the results of our own air reconnaissance. It seemed strange that in the middle of such a large-scale campaign that we would bother to tell such-and-such headquarters that a lone enemy despatch rider had been seen going southerly on a minor road at such-and-such a time. But of course this was all grist to the mill of Unit Intelligence Officers on the ground and might well have given pointers to the location of German headquarters.

The one thing that impeded the smooth flow of our work was the recurring problems of being unable to get 'bomblines' from units. Daily at first and last night all battalions should have given map references of their forward defended localities so that a line could be drawn on the map forward of which our planes were at liberty to strafe or bomb at will. We used to fret and curse, sometimes bitterly, the operators who were not providing this vital 'griff' but of course it was easy for us, comfortably ensconced at a bench with paperwork neatly laid out in front of us, a couple of pencils nicely sharpened (at both ends because if the point snapped when reading a morse symbol we could reverse the pencil in one quick movement and carry on writing), ashtray and cigarettes handy, occasional tea breaks (very occasional though) and equipment that was solidly installed. For the operator in the field (and perhaps as often as not it was actually a field his truck was in) things were never ideal. He might be under fire, he could certainly not have had a decent sleep in a proper bunk, his rations would have been the ingeniously worked-out 24-hour or the 'compo' ration, his morse key might be strapped to his thigh like a Wild Western gunslinger's or else resting on a bench cluttered with weapons and other impedimenta. Nevertheless we would continue to criticise and take the mickey out of the distant operators on the net.

But of course what was nagging many of us, certainly myself, was that **they** were out doing what we had all been trained to do and we were sulking underground in safety – while the chance of more active service and of participating in the making of history appeared to be denied us. As soldiers will, we moaned and wished we were over there. I rather think that at one stage we had a pep-talk from someone in authority who reminded us that "we all have a job to do", with the suggestion that we get on with it.

However, before too long the section was kitted up and went across the water as well.

If the day ever comes when my grandchildren ask "What did YOU do in the war, grandad?" I shall mention my discovery that message forms are not only useful for writing messages. On our first night in Normandy we 'liberated' some farm cider which gave everyone in the section who had drunk it the most dreadful runs. In the morning the corner of the field where we had bivouacked was a mass of crumpled message forms!

Ken ("Errol") Flint, 77 Lydia Road, Walmer, Kent.
(Ken is secretary of White Cliffs Veterans of Hellfire Corner and details of membership can be obtained from him).

It was approaching midnight on the 5th June, 1944 and the engines of my Dakota were droning away, awaiting take-off. For days we had been confined to camp, together with the Airborne Battalion, spending hour after hour at briefing, studying large models of the French coastline and the countryside beyond. We had memorised every house, road, telegraph pole, tree. Even the cows in the fields!! My task was to drop a number of paratroopers alongside a gun emplacement which needed putting out of action. Their faces were blackened and they presented a frightening sight.

We took off in Vic's of three, and both to my Port and Starboard sides were Dakotas only a few yards away. All lights and intercommunications were extinguished very soon after take-off and everything had to be carried out visually. Suddenly, we entered cloud and completely lost sight of the formating aircraft. After what seemed an eternity, we were out of cloud and there in perfect formation were the two other aircraft to Port and Starboard. In the darkness around could now be identified many other aircraft heading slowly towards the Channel and the Allied Fleet could be seen in the haze below; a sight never to be forgotten. Ships of all shapes and sizes, many with barrage balloons at the end of steel cables stretching up towards us from the Channel below. I put the Dakota in a controlled descent, pulling the throttle back gently. At the dropping height, the signal to jump was given. When the last of the paras had left the aircraft, I pushed the throttle fully forward, climbing all the while, and turned for home. Just as we crossed the French coast "all hell broke loose". Gun fire came from all directions, tracer bullets, anti-aircraft fire resulting in puffs of smoke and flashes from what seemed like the whole of the British and American Fleets. It seemed that we were being used for target practice! To my starboard side I saw another Dakota diving in order to avoid the fire and he was dangerously low, risking entanglement in the barrage balloon cables. A burst of smoke, close to my port wing, caused a cascade of glass to fall in the cockpit, through a smashed side window. Even the repeated firing of our Very Pistols Recognition Signal made no difference and I therefore made a tight turn of 180° heading back to the comparative safety of mainland France. After climbing to over 6000ft, I once again tried to cross the coast, heading north, but had to return once again! The barrage from the fleet was extremely formidable.

Continuing my climb in the now freezing cockpit, I headed east along the French Coast and soon Le Havre loomed up underneath unlit, but still recognisable in the distance. There was only spasmodic fire from the ground and no sign of any night fighters. Any puffs of smoke were well off target. Crossing the coast was now easy, not a ship or aircraft in sight. It was still early morning of D-Day and, soon after debriefing, we were fast asleep. D-Day must have been one of the shortest days of my life!

During the next two weeks we engaged in numerous missions to France, including flying SAS personnel to deserted airfields in France close to the German lines. Their missions were completely secret as far as we were concerned. All we ever saw of them was during the off-loading in France. Even then, their faces were covered with scarves. This was to ensure that, if we were ever taken prisoner, recognition was impossible. They were presumably engaged in all kinds of 'devious' activities.

One day I landed at a strip in a cornfield near Bayeux. The farmer was a very agreeable fellow and took me along to his farmhouse to meet the family and drink wine. He presented me with a large box of Camembert cheese which I then transported back to the U.K. and gave it to a doctor friend in Oxford. He immediately designated it to the dustbin saying that "it is too smelly, and therefore absolutely unfit for human consumption; typical of the food eaten by the French". Now I realise that the cheese was in its prime and the gift should have been appreciated and enjoyed!

J. Courtney P. Thomas, Kingsbury House,
6 Stratton Terrace, Falmouth, Cornwall.

nding supplies at Omaha Beach.

I knew all week that something was wrong. I knew that my husband or my brother, who was a paratrooper, had been killed during the invasion — I didn't receive any official communication, I just knew it in my heart. On the Saturday night of 10th June, sitting alone, I broke down in tears. On the following morning, Sunday, at 9.00 a.m. there was a knock at my door and I went and answered it knowing somehow what it would be.

When I opened the envelope and saw the dreaded words that my husband Alex of No. 4 Marine Commando had been killed in action, I closed the door and asked Almighty God to spare me for the sake of my children because I was also three months pregnant. Alex had only seen his little baby girl for 21 days and he never did see the little baby girl who was born six months and one day later. My other child, a son, was only six years old at the time. I remember clutching my son to me and then handing the baby to him. "Hold on to her carefully" I said, "I'm going to Granny to tell her about Daddy." I didn't tell him what had happened because I didn't want to leave him crying, and although my world had been blown apart I couldn't cry myself. I put my coat on over the nightdress I was still wearing and ran to Granny to tell her. After that I can't remember anything — my mind went numb and even today I don't know what happened the rest of that day after I told Granny.

My husband Alex was a big handsome man, 6ft. 1in. tall and so well built. He had a lovely nature and was always true to me. On going away from his last leave I remember he asked me "If I don't come back do you think you would marry again?" I said "What's making you talk like that" and his reply was simple.

"If you got a lazy man I know you would work so hard for him, and he might be bad to the children."

He was like that — always thinking of us. So I said "If you don't come back to me the only man that will ever come to my door will be the undertaker, to take me away."

I took a vow that night I'd never take another man. And I kept that vow. I wanted to give Alex peace of mind even though the thought of losing him broke my heart. Before I took that vow that night I saw him off on the bus and that was the last time I was to see him. I'll never forget the look on his face as he left. He was honest and true. God bless him.

I've often said I'd like to write a book on what I came through. I got so little for me and the three children that I worked till I dropped. Many's the time I was desperate to make ends meet. I know what my children have gone through. I too never knew my father. He was killed at the age of 29 years of age, in the First World War. I've been to his grave but I paid for it myself by saving what I could. He's buried at Arras in France. Whilst there I also went to Paschendale — masses of graves. Brave men, may they rest in peace.

I often sit alone now and wonder why we were born? Sometimes it seems nothing but suffering and hard work. My children now live in Aberdeen, Surrey and Canada. So I am all alone with my memories, but all I want is those memories of what might have been, and the peace to consider them. There will never be anyone else for me. When Alex died a large part of me died with him, even though I worked on for the children. He was everything to me, and sometimes I think it's harder to live than to die.

Mrs. Ruby Porter, 16 Whitehill Court,
Hillhead, Kirkintilloch.

171

British tanks of 8th Armoured Brigade firing at enemy troops using gliders as cover in an attempt to seize the Caen bridges.

Soon came the order to move forward. This was mainly to make room for more units to come off the beaches. By midday we found ourselves almost halfway between Arromanches and Bayeux. On the way up we had passed quite a number of dead German troops and a few khaki clad figures huddled by the roadsides. The occasional trickle of prisoners with their hands clasped on their heads came slogging back towards the beach, bound for P.O.W. cages in England.

A continuous rumble of tracked vehicles, mainly tanks was kept up as more and more units were unloaded from landing craft. The amount of room in the bridgehead was limited and until the periphery could be pushed out, living was going to be pretty crowded. The armour of 8th Armoured Brigade, our parent unit, was almost the first ashore and had been in the thick of the advance all day. The Dual Drive Sherman tanks of 13/18 Hussars were designed to "swim" in from a couple of miles out, but since the sea had been rough, they had been brought right up to the beach by the landing craft pretty well at the same time as the assault infantry. This could have been why our trip up the beach had been so easy compared to other landings. Later we were to learn that the Americans at Omaha beach had launched their D.D. tanks three miles out and had lost over 75% of them. The Americans had also spurned the use of other British "Funnies" of General Hobart. Among the "Funnies" was the Flail. This was a Churchill tank with a boom out in front upon which was a spindle furnished with lengths of very heavy chain. The spindle was driven from the tank engine and revolved at fairly high speed so that the chains thrashed the ground ahead of the tank, thereby exploding any mines in its path. The Brigadier had led us up the beach in the path left by a flail. No doubt many lives were saved by the use of this marvellous device.

Another of General Hobart's brainchildren was called a "Facine". Here an enormous bundle of logs was carried on a couple of arms above the front of the Churchill. On encountering an anti-tank ditch, the bundle of logs was dropped into the ditch and the tank proceeded on its way across the ditch followed by as many more A.F.V's as necessary. Also there was the A.V.R.E. This was a Churchill with an enormous mortar, about the size of a household dustbin, mounted forward of the turret. This was able to throw a huge charge against a pillbox or strongpoint, which usually disappeared in a cloud of dust. Another diabolical (for the enemy) device was the "Crocodile". This was a flamethrower capable of projecting a terrible jet of flame over a hundred yards. The chemicals were carried in a trailer which was towed behind the tank and pumped to the nozzle mounted on the turret.

Such were the devices offered to the Americans. The only one that they chose was the least effective. The Dual Drive tank. The result was the bloody slaughter on Omaha beach. The troops were unable to move off the beach until almost dark and then at terrible cost.

When the R.H.Q. moved forward we bypassed Bayeux and occupied a position south of a junction which we came to know as Jerusalem Crossroads. As we drove past, we could see scout cars that had been knocked out in the immediate vicinity of the crossroads. Also a couple of Sherman tanks had been brewed up close by. There had quite obviously been a terrific scrap for the area. It was fairly open country and the siting of anti tank guns was easy. Further south the roads plunged into "bocage" type countryside which proved to be a tankman's nightmare.

Since we were pretty well up with the leaders of the advance, the O.C. considered it worthwhile laying lines out to the batteries. Shortly after our arrival the line parties from 8th Armoured Brigade and 50 Division brought in lines from their respective H.Q. It was a pretty hazardous business to lay lines along the main roads since the number of tracked vehicles travelling south was enormous and since the weather had become rather more warm the dust was increasing and reducing visibility to a few yards. The wireless links were kept open for fire orders and where possible the lines were used for administrative traffic.

Several times lines went "dis" and the line parties were pretty stretched to keep them working. Jack Halford asked me to go out with him to clear a fault on the line to 50 Div. starting at our end, the Divisional line party starting from the other end. As we suspected a break was located near Jerusalem Crossroads. I held on to the end of the cable from our H.Q. whilst Jack searched around for the other side of the break. It is possible for a vehicle to pull the end of a cable for many yards and it took Jack a few minutes to locate our cable. I bared the end of the cable and connected it to the DV, (Don 5 field telephone), shoved in the earthpin and called the exchange at our H.Q. Straight away the exchange operator answered and I told him the position. At the same instant a battery of medium guns about fifty yards to my rear fired in unison. The fright I received left me shivering with terror and when Jack Halford returned with the other end of the line was unable to speak for several minutes. As soon as Jack had spliced the line together the exchanges at both ends answered our call. Before we returned to R.H.Q. we looked at a tank silhouetted against the sky. As we walked around to the front we could see by the light of Jack's hand-lamp two figures seated in the driver and gunner's seats through the open hatch doors. When we looked closer we could see that the figures were burnt corpses. No features or clothes, just an awful shape. Jack reached through the hatch and pushed one of them gently with his crook stick. It oscillated back and forth in a nodding fashion as though it was made of rubber. The mediums went off again and gave us another dreadful fright. I was very glad to get on the back of Jack's B.S.A. and return to R.H.Q.

We finally settled in the inevitable orchard at a place we knew as Point 103. We were on the top of an almost imperceptible hill and had extended the slit trenches left by the infantry as we were likely to be resident for a couple of days. The cooks had brewed up and a hot meal of some sort was being served. Visiting us from one of the batteries was their B.S.M. (Battery Sergeant Major) whom the R.S.M. had invited to have some food before he returned to his Battery. Most of us were sitting in our slit trenches eating as the B.S.M. walked across the orchard to join the R.S.M. at the latter's jeep. We all ducked when we heard incoming "moaning minnies" approaching. After the explosions we looked up and saw that the B.S.M. had gone. The blast had stripped all the foliage from one of the apple trees and had replaced it with shreds of khaki cloth. The B.S.M. had literally been blown to pieces and later we had the doubtful pleasure of disentangling intestines from the branches of the tree. The rest of the bits were shovelled into a sack and buried. I wonder what the War Graves Commission made of it when they disinterred the remains.

Later we were told that an armoured counter attack was coming in opposite our position. The gun positions were told to have A.P. (armour piercing) ammunition ready for use as well as H.E. We were all well below ground level. All that is except the on duty people who were mostly in light armour and fairly safe from shrapnel. One of the off duty operators, namely R.D. "Bob" Bruce got out of his slit trench and stood relieving himself against the rear wheel of a three ton truck. When a mortar bomb burst on the other side of the truck, a piece of shrapnel pierced the water jerrican on the near side storage rack, crossed the back of the vehicle, pierced the oil container on the off side and entered Bruce's buttock. We took him to the R.A.P. (regimental aid post) and handed him over to Bombardier Spurling, the M.O.'s orderly. Bruce returned to the section nine months later with the piece of shrapnel on his watch chain. They had not removed it straight away by surgery, but had let it work its way to a point near the alimentary canal and at the opportune time had fished it out via his rectum!

The Naval F.O.B. had gone forward to see whether he could see any concentration worthy of his big guns. He was in our full view when he got out of his halftrack and stood looking forward with his binoculars. We saw the bomb explode very close to him and when the dust cleared we could see that he had been hit. I shouted Cpl. Halford to come with me and together we ran out to bring him in. As we approached we could see him on his knees grubbing about on the grass. He stood up when he saw us coming. Jack wrapped a length of spunyarn around the stump of his left arm and used his pliers to wind up the improvised tourniquet, blood flying everywhere. When we finally got the F.O.B. over to the doctor, who had barely finished attending to Bruce, the incredibly brave chap said to Jack Halford. "Corporal will you take my watch off the hand you will find in my trousers pocket?" Jack Halford died several years ago.

Douglas ("Pete") C. Morris, 48 Pen-y-Cefn Road, Caerwys, Clwyd.

LONDON
BRIDGE

I served in the Royal Engineers. We were briefed to get inland as fast as possible, and get a Bailey Bridge over a waterway. No locations or names were given. The Officer Commanding asked "Any questions?" No response. My mind went back to four years earlier when we, as conscript recruits issued with 1914 equipment and old Springfield rifles and five rounds of ammunition, sat as we did that day listening to the Training Battalion Intelligence Officer lecturing on the German Army. He spoke at length of its superior weapons, the use of dive-bombing as artillery, and the famed Blitzkreig attack. A flutter of apprehension ran through the assembly. To end the address came the invitation "Any questions on the German Army?" A lone voice from the back. "Yes sir. How do you join it?"!

After the initial postponement for 24 hours, we were taken by road transport to Newhaven on 5th June, and at 18.00 hours boarded an L.C.I. (Landing Craft Infantry). Thirty minutes later we pulled out, a solitary Wren witnessing our departure from the quay. The L.C.I. is not built with sea-going comfort in mind! It is in fact a flat bottomed pitiless engine of war! Quickly responding to a fairly heavy sea, it began a continuous programme of rearing and plunging which it kept up for the following 14 hours. Below deck were arranged three tier bunks now occupied by stricken personnel, and from which hung discarded assault equipment soiled with cascades of vomit. The fetid atmosphere, a malodorous cocktail of retching and diesel oil, induced a nausea as overpowering as the sea-sickness itself. Presently I fell into a merciful, if fitful, sleep.

An hour or so after first light some of us, now fully equipped, were up on deck to see for the first time the great armada of assault craft and attacking battle-cruisers around us. The French coast now appeared in view, draped in fire and smoke. Had the first assault gone in? How strongly were the beaches defended? These questions thrust themselves into our minds to be resolved as the moment of landing approached. Whatever lay ahead I would not be sorry to see the back of that L.C.I.

The craft rammed the beach at about 08.45 a.m. lowering the port and starboard ramps into about 4½ ft. of water. I went into the sea, chest high, sten-gun and mine detector held above the water. With mortar bombs exploding some 50 yards to the left I made my way up the beach and in that traverse of about 40 feet I was struck by the sight of the corpse of a British soldier lying atop the 8ft. floodbank, face up, with hands across the chest as though in peace on that foreign shore. Enemy artillery was ranging onto the beach as we began the advance inland in deployed order. The advance, halted at times by enemy fire, took us near Colleville. It was here that the flank of the 3rd Division, under whose command we came, was being secured. A number of British infantry lay dead in the locality.

Fifty yards past the Church at Benouville and round a slight bend we came within sight of a building from the roof of which flew the French Tricolour. This proved to be our objective —the Mairie (Town Hall) of Benouville. Two hundred yards to the east of the Mairie the bridge, captured by the Airborne troops in the early hours, crossed the Caen Canal. We now came under small arms fire and being in an exposed position, we doubled forward towards the Mairie. This brought us into close contact with the 6th Airborne Division. I recall one of their number asking what we were doing "up here." Greeting us from a slit trench he was obviously surprised by our early arrival!

We "dug in" at Benouville, and sustained casualties — one man killed, three wounded

Commemorative stone marking the site of the first Bailey Bridge built in France at the Caen Canal – Bob Heath on right.

181

and a fifth man to die from his wounds. The Company had also taken a number of prisoners. They were marched back to the beach under escort — presumably bound for the U.K. By Landing Craft Infantry we hoped!

Very late at night, possibly in the early hours of D+1 an enemy soldier, fully armed, was found hiding in a thicket. He surrendered his weapons and ammunition and appeared to be very scared. Someone gave the poor sod a cigarette — he was surely the last of the Benouville defenders.

So ended D-Day. That night I slept in the courtyard fronting the Mairie and woke at daybreak. A nearby garden boasted a water pump by the side of which lay the body of an Airborne Division soldier. He was lying half sprawled from a stretcher. His right arm was forward as if reaching for water. How long he had lain there, how much he had suffered I shall never know. Now it was too late. We had to go on regardless. So we refreshed ourselves and breakfasted on the "compo" ration that each man carried, and then began the bridging operation over the water-way we had heard about at the briefing — the Caen Canal.

Bob Heath, 96 Lancing Road, Orpington, Kent.

Breakfast that day started like any other. A typical hospital breakfast distributed on trays to those of us still confined to bed, by staff and those other patients in the early stages of recovery. It could have been any conventional hospital ward — except for the cage-enclosed fireplace, the bars at the windows, the bat-wing doors leading to the bathroom and toilet, and the two single-bed padded rooms at one end of the long, narrow room, to mention but a few of the differences. Those and the doctors in their military uniforms, and the walking patients in their blue suits, white shirts and red ties!

For this was Winwick Hospital, Warrington (then in Lancashire, now in Cheshire) — a peace-time mental institution partially requisitioned by the military authorities for the treatment of (principally) orthopaedic casualties of war.

In one of the ward's two end rooms lay a lad scarcely out of his teens but already with whatever future he had cruelly reshaped by severe abdominal wounds sustained when he stepped on an Italian anti-personnel mine in North Africa.

I never came to know the lad's name, or if I did the memory of it is long dead 50 years on. For some odd reason, even though I am sure it was not his name, I remember him as "Paddy." But my mental picture of him in his bed remains clear; that and the memory of his constant moans of pain, even in his drugged state, with a daily crescendo to screams to which we other patients could not close our ears, and which ended for us only when further injections having failed to stem his cries, a nurse closed the padded door of his padded room.

Though we never discussed the moral issues involved, and most of us would not have recognised the word in isolation, we other patients forcefully argued the case for euthanasia as a merciful end for Paddy's unending agony. By witnessing his suffering, ours became so much less important. His pain almost became our panacea.

It was against this background, at breakfast time one day, someone switched on the ward radio. (We called them wirelesses in those days). Suddenly the daily round of ward chatter and clatter was stilled as the radio voice disclosed that at dawn that day, June 6, 1944, allied troops under the leadership of General Dwight D. Eisenhower, had begun landing on the coast of Normandy. The remaining part of the announcement was lost in a riot of cheering.

But when each anniversary of D-Day arrives it is not so much the cheers I recall as the lad I remember as Paddy, for whom not only the war but a meaningful life was already over.

Denis Taylor, 56 Rochester Crescent,
Sydney, Crewe, Cheshire.

183

rah beach. US soldiers moving inland whilst supplies build up behind.

I was a twenty year old parachutist, qualified as a signaller R.A. a member of the 53rd Airlanding Light Regiment R.A. — the 75mm Field Gliderborne Regiment of the Sixth Airborne Division.

Our forward observation section was to consist of twelve parties of three men, one officer and two signallers to each party. One party to each parachute and airlanding regiment, plus a party to each of the three brigades headquarters companies.

I was scheduled to parachute in with the 1st Canadian Para Battalion, Lt. Ted Ayrton being my Commanding Officer and Ken Lamzed who was my fellow signaller. Ken and I had joined the army together and had been together on initial training and courses and shared the same barrack rooms. We were the best of pals. However we were now split up. Gunner Webster became Ken's fellow signaller and I was moved to another group. Frank McGinley was to be my fellow signaller.

We attended a briefing and were told that the invasion would be into Normandy. The Division's task was to capture the Caen Canal and River Orne bridges, capture and hold the ground to the east of the bridges, blowing up all bridges on the River Dives, from Troarn to the coast. We were to go in with Third Parachute Brigade whose tasks were — 9th Para Battalion — to capture and destroy the heavily guarded gun emplacements at Merville. The Eighth Para Battalion's job was to blow up bridges at Troarn and Bure and hold the extreme east perimeter. 1st Canadians Para Battalion's task was to blow bridges at Varaville, and hold the high ground at Le Mesnil. All battalions to be accompanied by sections of 3rd Para Brigade's squadron of Royal Engineers. We in 3rd Para Brigade H.Q. company, were to get to a farm house, a short distance from Le Mesnil crossroads. We would be dropped on the same dropping zone as 8th Parachute Battalion, which was the farthest inland of all the Divisions dropping zones.

We carried a field dressing in our battledress trousers and were issued with a pair of buttons to sew on to our trousers which when removed and one button placed on top of the other, improvised a compass! We were also given a small hacksaw blade to insert in your trouser seam. This was accompanied with a silk map of the area, so one could find a way back to divisional lines if captured or lost!

To carry our equipment from aircraft to ground we used specially designed kitbags. The kitbag was strapped to your right leg, a rope of twenty foot length was tied to the bag, and secured to your webbing. When your parachute opened, you pulled a quick release pin and lowered the bag, so that it landed a split second before yourself. This method had worked well during several practice jumps.

I was to carry the radio transmitter, a No. 62 set. They were heavy and awkward to carry, but had a range of several miles, which would be needed to reach the seaborne regiments, as they got established beyond the beachheads. My fellow signaller Frank McGinley would carry the two accumulators needed to power a 62 set. Each kitbag weighed about 60 lb.

On the morning of June 5th we were given a final briefing, told to pack our parachuting kitbags and small packs. The small packs were to carry all the personal kit we would need. Later on, our big packs would follow on by sea. A small pack carried mess tins, knife, fork and spoon, washing and shaving gear, spare pair of socks and two 24 hour man ration packs. These contained a block of oatmeal (for porridge) meat cubes, bar of chocolate, powdered milk and tea blocks, and toilet paper! We checked our Sten guns, filled our pouches with

ammunition, fitted camouflage netting to our steel helmets, wrote letters home etc. (which would be censored and posted after the invasion had started). We were told to sleep in the afternoon. In my case I was much too excited — or scared — to carry that order out.

We formed up in our "sticks", drew and fitted our parachutes. I think it was about 10 p.m. or so, (double British summertime was in operation during the war), so it was still daylight. We enplaned and took off around 11 p.m. We were packed like sardines, looking like "Michelin Men". Most of us jumping with kitbags, parachute on your back, Sten gun tucked under the harness, airborne smocks bulging with chocolate, sweets etc. Webbing pouches holding

...oops making their way to their positions. Note gliders in background.

ammunition, Mills Bombs etc. Entrenching tool and small pack.

To start with everyone was smiling. We sang all the paratrooper songs we knew, plenty of wisecracking etc. Looking around the dimly lit fuselage, I thought "If this lot were Germans and invading England, I would die of fright"! With faces blackened, camouflage netting on helmets, airborne smocks and scarves, not to mention, rifles, Sten guns etc.

As we neared the French coast, we stood up checked that each others static lines were properly hooked to the overheard strong point, and not caught up under equipment. The aircraft was bucking and swaying, avoiding flak and turbulence. I could see tracer bullets and exploding shells through the open doorway. It was very difficult to stand. The red light came on and we shuffled down the fuselage, green light on, time to get out as soon as possible. Captain Harrington was first to jump followed by Frank McGinley and then me. Captain Harrington got out quite quickly, he carried no kitbag. Frank struggled out with his load then it was my turn. I'm only a little chap and had great difficulty getting through the door, but eventually I made it. Up in the air went my right leg and away went my kitbag, wrenched from my leg and away into space.

I found I was oscillating badly when my chute opened, rigging lines twisted as well. Remembering the drill, I kicked like mad and pulled down hard on my front liftwebs. I think I was reasonably in control, when splash, I'd landed in water! It was pitch black, I was flat on my back, being dragged by my canopy in water a foot or so deep. Struggling to release my parachute harness, and trying to keep my head above water, I lost my Sten gun.

After freeing myself of the parachute I searched in vain for my gun. Getting accustomed to the light I waded to dry land. Lots of trees, so I realised I was nowhere near the dropping zone allocated to 3rd Parachute Brigade H.Q. Company. I had no radio, no gun, no smallpack, soaked to the skin, no idea which way I should go, but, I did have eight Sten gun magazines in my pouches!

After a while I heard someone approaching. What a relief when I heard a whispered "Punch". I quickly replied with "Judy" (That was our code sign). My comrade was an officer, who's still unknown to me. He carried a Sten gun, as well as a side arm which all officers carried. He kindly gave me his gun when I told him of my predicament.

Being a mere gunner, I was more than pleased to let him decide which direction to go. Eventually we met a few paras', some who were heading for my destination of Le Mesnil. I think Lady Luck was on my side that night, not only being given a Sten gun I stumbled into a small pack, which turned out to have belonged to an airborne sapper. Goodness knows how it got there, or what had befallen its rightful owner! When I opened it a few hours later, I was pleased to find it contained the ration packs besides the usual everyday needs.

Dawn was breaking when I reached the farmhouse which was to be 3rd Parachute Brigade H.Q. Only a handful of soldiers had arrived. Brigadier Hill was missing so Colonel Pearson of 8th Para Battalion was standing in for him. The Brigadier was wounded in a bombing raid. He turned up later on D-Day refusing hospital treatment. There was no sign of my two companions. I was appointed No. 2 on a Bren gun and positioned on a vantage point in view of the road into the farmhouse. Chaps were coming in all morning. I thought I was the only survivor of our F.O.O. Section, then much to my relief in walked Captain Harrington and some time later Gunner Frank McGinley arrived, having walked for hours carrying the two heavy accumulators. He wasn't in the best of temper when I told him I had lost the radio!

We dug our slit trenches on ground allotted to us, only a short way away from the farm house. This was to be our home for the next few weeks and as the shelling and mortar bombs increased, we dug deeper and deeper!

On June 7th our F.O.O. party came into its own. Captain Harrington and either Frank or myself went forward to observation posts and relayed targets to the Artillery regiments, as they got established on the beachheads and beyond. I'm not certain, but I think we were the only surviving party in 3rd Parachute Brigade. My friend Ken Lamzed, Gunner Webster and Lt Ayrton were dropped miles off target. Ken was badly wounded and taken prisoner. Lt. Ayrton and Gunner Webster were also P.o.W's.

Captain Harrington M.C. died in the eighties. Have heard nothing of Frank McGinley or Blondie Webster, but am in touch with Ted Ayrton and Ken Lamzed.

David ('Dai') King, 5 Watling Street, Tudor Park, Ross-on-Wye.

oyal Marines of 4th S.S. Brigade 48 Commando taking cover from mortar fire at St. Aubin-sur-Mer.

NOTHING is to be written on this side except the date and signature of the sender. Sentences not required may be erased. If anything else is added the post card will be destroyed.

[Postage must be prepaid on any letter or post card addressed to the sender of this card.]

I am quite well.

I~have~been~admitted~into~hospital

(sick~) and~am~going~on~well.
(wounded) and~hope~to~be~discharged~soon.

I~am~being~sent~down~to~the~base.

I~have~received~your (letter~dated
(telegram ,,
(parcel ,,

Letter follows at first opportunity.

I have received no letter from you

(lately
(for~a~long~time.

Signature only } *[signature]*

Date   15. 6. 44.

Forms/A2042/7.   51-4997.

Standardised postcard to let folks at home know you're alive!

D-Day was the most guarded secret of the War — and yet to Londoners it was the most open secret in the World. Where else could all those military vehicles be going, day and night? For weeks, long convoys of troops, tank carriers and lorries moved along London's arterial roads all heading in one direction — London Docks.

As an army driver in O.F.P. of the 11th Armoured Division, I recall that first week in June 1944 so well. There were flags and bunting all the way with cheering crowds yelling "Good luck, Boys!" and giving us cups of tea to help us along. Yes, even then we had plenty of sugar! Once at the Docks we were sealed off from the outside world. No letters, no phoning, for we had now been officially told our destination was France. Work consisted of waterproofing vehicles and checking equipment. Once aboard we rendezvoused with a Naval Escort and put our vomiting bags to good use!

Luckily our landing was dry. I clearly remember driving across the beach between white ribbons — the sign that it had been cleared of land mines. The few houses were just ruins. British bombers had gone in before us. The Germans had retreated and the fighting was going way ahead of us. But British troops and vehicles were everywhere. We headed a few miles inland to a deserted farm house. Our first task was to unload the camouflage nets and remove sticky waterproofing from our hot engines, and then to dig in. That first night we were ordered to sleep under our lorries but I found a stretcher and had a comfortable night's sleep in the back of mine, the sound of gunfire in the distance. The most memorable thing about that first day in France was the smell: the stench of death. Not human flesh, but cattle. Scores of them all lying on their sides — pot bellied and dead. The sun didn't help much.

It wasn't until we reached Bayeaux that we actually saw any French people. As far as the fighting went, on our front reaching out towards Caen, there was stalemate for some weeks while the Americans battled for Cherbourg. We made up for it later when we covered 400 miles in six days in September to be the first troops in Antwerp.

The organsation and planning of the D-Day operation was brilliant — absolutely nothing was forgotten. Aboard ship every man received a printed message from the Supreme Commander, General Eisenhower wishing "Good Luck on the Great Crusade". On landing each man was given a preprinted Field Postcard on which to write home. It consisted of sentences such as "I am well" or "I have been wounded" which could be struck out. We all had tin rations plus a portable "Tommy Cooker" with tiny solid fuel tablets. I can still recall the delicious steak and kidney puddings. It was several weeks, though, before we had bread and so biscuits were the order of the day supplemented by the compulsory daily vitamin pill.

Special praise too for the Army Laundry Ablution Units. Dirty shirts and underwear were just exchanged for clean ones and if they fitted you were lucky!

Every day was an uncertain one, but the comradeship and spirit has never been equalled. We were the British Liberation Army and we *knew* we were going to win.

John Frost, 8 Monks Avenue, New Barnet, Hertfordshire.

Troop money for use in France.

…ws, once grazing quietly in a field, now lie stinking and bloated in a Normandy field.

The morning was bright and sunny and the time, I think, was about 9.15 a.m. I was a 21-year-old clerk, conscript wartime clippie returning from Liverpool via St. Helens to my Wigan depot. The change had not been easy for me but I can remember I was fussed over and well protected by staff and drivers who, along with tough Liverpool dockers and coal miners, always referred to me as the "10 to 7 Pin Up Girl." Oh happy days!

Leaving the East Lancs Road through Carr Mill we went to the then village area of Moss Bank where we would pick up a regular passenger. She was a thirtyish something staid woman who always wore her dark uniform with the AFS flash — Auxillary Fire Service. Every day we got a brusque "Good Morning". But not today.

As the bus approached the stop I could not believe what I was seeing! Had this poor women suddenly gone mad or beserk with the strain of war? Had there been an accident and had to get to hospital a mile away? I was scared! There she was, clearly visible from the bus as we came in, doing a little jig, arms upstretched and clapping! As we stopped she actually banged on the side of the bus and started shouting something up at the driver who simply sat there and pushed his hat back. Then she ran down the entire length of the bus, still banging as she went, leapt on and cupped my face in her hands and embraced me at the same time! What was happening?

"We're back, we're there" she shouted "We landed this morning" and she ran down the length of the bus again, this time on the inside, and stood with her back to the bemused driver and facing the by now equally bemused passengers!

"We're back, back" she cried with arm outstretched and then clapping. "We're in France, France, France!" and then sang "Rule Brittania" in a voice choked with emotion.

Then she sat down, exhausted from the excitement and exhilaration of hearing the first radio news flash about 10 minutes earlier. It was like a still scene from a film. No one moved. No one spoke. The driver sat there patiently waiting for the signal to move off which I forgot to give! Then suddenly a young woman gasped, and then blessed herself before putting her hands to her face as if in prayer. Pandemonium broke out!

Women wept and cheered alternatively or at the same time! Men talked excitedly. The top deck passengers came down to see what was going on! I was kissed and hugged a hundred times when of course it should have been the purveyor of that historic announcement. But she was now sat weeping quietly in the corner seat.

I lowered my face to the Cross of Lorraine brooch in my lapel, emblem of Free France and a token of my deep love for the French sailor I had met as a 17-yer-old in 1940. Then, as far as I knew, in Portsmouth.

We're in France" the bearer of the news had said. "When we return to France" my French sailor had said to me many times, "You will be 'wiz' me for the new life."

Today, I told myself, is the beginning of my new life. And yet I have no recollection of the rest of that journey!

Off duty at about 2.00 p.m. I went home tired and excited to sleep, to dream of walking with him down the Champs Elysees, by the Seine and to Montmartre. Together, he had said, we would listen to Tino Rossi singing "J'Attendrai". We would visit his friends, Henri in St. Brieux and Joseph in Manosque, Provence. He would buy me "ze beeg dog" to protect me when he was out. He would buy me gallons of my loved "Evening in Paris" perfume, and I would be Madame Guybet. I slept so peacefully that day, unaware that destiny had other plans.

Fifty years later I am as deeply in love with him as I was then. I have never got over him. I am still dazzled by him. His letters and his photographs are always close to me but especially to my heart. I have lived a full, busy, active and satisfying life, but I still play Tino Rossi's "J'Attendrai" and remember what might have been.

Miss Helen T. Murphy, Wigan, Lancashire.

e actual moment of landing. British troops come ashore. Sherman tanks in background. Picture by the British Army Film
it.

I began writing down my wartime experiences shortly after being released from the Royal Marines in March 1946 and some of these eventually appeared in "MARINE COMMANDO, Sicily and Salerno, 1943 with 41 Royal Marines Commando" published by Robert Hale. I am "Unit Historian" of the Veterans of 41 Royal Marines Commando 1942-46 and have written a history of 41 which I hope will be published by the Royal Marines Historical Society.

On D-Day, 6th June, 1944, I was CC/X 100977 Marine Raymond Mitchell, a despatch rider with 41 Royal Marines Commando and landed with them on Sword Beach, the unit's first objective being the capture of two enemy positions at Lion-sur-Mer, codenamed 'The Château' and 'The Strongpoint.'

Prior to the landing we had been kept incommunicado in a 'concentration camp' on Southampton Common, which we knew affectionately as 'Stalag C 19', and to which we had been returned from a boarding point on the River Hamble on 4th June with the news that the invasion had been postponed. We awoke on the 5th to learn that it was 'ON!' After lunch were taken by TCVs (Troop Carrying Vehicles) to Warsash, on the Hamble, to board five LCI(S)s (Landing Craft Infantry, Small) which pulled out into the Solent to anchor while the rest of the armada destined to sail from that part of the coast assembled. At 2115 hours, in the gathering dusk, the LCIs moved into their allotted position as the untold number of vessels moved off, destination France.

The crossing was uneventful and it was in semi-darkness that we were called out of the three small 'holds' of the vessels to breakfast and prepare for the landing. At that time the sea was extremely choppy and many of our number were soon suffering the miseries of sea sickness. As the early morning was rather chilly I decided to eat my tin of self-heating soup, I recall that it was tomato, but the meal stayed down no longer than the time it had taken to prepare and eat! Flashes of gunfire could now be seen coming from the dark shapes of ships at sea and from the indistinct smudge that was France. Disappointingly for us, we were soon dragged away from this enthralling spectacle by being ordered below to 'get rigged.'

And there we stayed for the next half hour or more, as conditions 'outside' became more and more noisy and disturbed. The thunder of widespread gunfire and the scream of incoming shells came down to us clearly, but we could only guess what was happening. The inshore waters, we could feel, were basically calmer, but they were becoming more and more disturbed as our craft rocked and bucked in response to nearby explosions.

After what seemed an eternity, the voice of authority came down to us, "Right lads, we're almost in! — On deck!! — Quick!!" We tumbled out into a medley of sights, sounds and smells, of a beach strewn with burning tanks and other vehicles, exploding shells and bodies on the sand and floating in the sea. There was time only for a fleeting glimpse before getting on with the next (unnecessary) order of, "Move it, lads! Get ashore."

For me, as DR, this meant grabbing my 75lb. Parascooter and starting to push it along the narrow port side deck and, as I did so, the vessel was rocked by the explosion of a shell striking, or narrowly missing, the starboard side. On reaching the bows we found that the port ramp led uselessly down into deep water, pointing in the general direction of England, so we had to queue up to use the starboard one. This, lying askew to both our craft and the beach, was swaying, bucking and bouncing under the combined effects of explosions and our craft wallowing in the tidal swell. To have attempted the standard 'drill' of humping the motorbike onto my shoulder and doubling down the ramp could have had no other results than one very wet Marine and a useless piece of machinery. By the time my turn came to make it ashore, I had decided what to do. Cradling the bike in my arms, I sat down at the top of the ramp and, using the infant's technique of descending a staircase with a Teddy Bear in its arms, progressed by legs and bottom until I could drop off into shallower water and carry my charge safely ashore.

Then it was a case of 'follow my leader' as the Troop doubled forward to take temporary shelter from exploding missiles and small arms fire in a huge bomb or shell crater a score of metres from the water's edge. I dropped my bike and rolled in. As I lay catching my breath, a Churchill tank trundled to a halt only a few yards away, between us and where we had caught momentary glimpses of field grey uniforms. The hatch opened and a crew member, limp and bleeding, was pulled out of the turret and laid gently on the sand.

With the Troop collected together, the officer led us, at the double, along the beach to the right. Burdened with the parascooter, I soon dropped behind, and in only a few minutes my muscles just couldn't bear the weight any more. I dropped the bike to the sand and tried

…mmandos moving off a Landing Craft. Note the amount of equipment being carried.

to push it, but the small wheels sank down to the hubs in the soft sand and I was simply gouging a furrow. After some time desperately alternating between carrying and trying to push the bike, I was lathered in sweat and had come to the realisation that, if I stayed with the bike I would lose the Troop. I was then on the seaward side of a Churchill tank, probably knocked out as two or three of the crew were crouching beside it. "Here, mate!" I gasped, "Want a motorbike?" and, without waiting for any reply, abandoned the thing and ran towards a gap in the hedge at the back of the beach through which the rest of the Troop had disappeared some minutes earlier.

Relieved of the burden of the parascooter, I was able to take in a little more of the chaos all about me. The landing had been planned to enable the landing craft to avoid as many beach obstacles as possible and the narrow strip of dry sand was crowded and littered with burning tanks and other vehicles, with bodies scattered here and there. The air was filled with the smells of smoke and of cordite, explosions and the shriek of incoming shells. One salvo was clearly going to land very close to me so I dived for the only cover close to hand — the body of a dead soldier — I'm sure he would have understood. The water's edge was a similar picture of burning vessels and amongst the wreckage bobbing about in the waves were more bodies, still being kept afloat by their lifejackets.

I reached the gap in the hedge and was amazed to pass some 'Army types' actually digging slit trenches in the sand. The first tenet of any landing (and D-Day was my third the others being Sicily and Salerno) was 'Get off the beach', so I did just that, and moved into a completely different world. The hustle and bustle on the beach had given way to a quiet roadway, draped with the wires from shattered telegraph poles, fronting a row of tall, half-timbered houses. I soon came upon a solitary wounded soldier sitting at the roadside with his back against a wall and asked if I could do anything for him. "Just give us a fag, mate" he said "Then catch up with your pals."

I came upon two other stragglers of our Troop and we caught up with the tail end of the others on the outskirts of Lion-sur-Mer, then doubled along a pavement of the small town, making little sound in our rubber-soled boots, while the white faces of inhabitants peered at us from their windows. With the Fighting Troops of the Commando going about their business some distance ahead, we of HQ were halted somewhere in the town and flopped on to the pavement to catch our breath. My little group had come to rest on the forecourt of a small newspaper shop, and the door was open for business! One of our number, having had his matches soaked in the landing, and knowing that I spoke a little French, persuaded me to go in and buy some for him — which I did, and probably spent the very first 'Invasion Money' of the whole Allied landings!

We waited there for quite some time. Commando Headquarters was operating nearby, with the noises of exploding mortar bombs not so very far away, and some civilians began moving about in the streets. On two occasions I was called forward to translate for agitated French ladies, and found that they were reporting the presence of wounded soldiers in their homes. I went, accompanied by a Sick Berth Attendant with the first lady and found the man fully clothed on her bed, oozing blood from a pretty bad shoulder wound on to her white sheets. The SBA put a field dressing on the wound, and we left him where he was, with some of our rations, as his main concern was that he had lost the small pack containing his food.

Mortar fire was now being directed on to our part of town and the open streets were no place to be in such circumstances, so the CO moved his headquarters into the grounds of a nearby church and we all set about digging slit trenches. As despatch rider, I had to be near the Signals Officer's radio set, and the fact that I had no transport was overcome by someone finding a push bike for me. For the rest of the morning, I delivered a few signals in between flurries of bombs and digging.

202

Early in the afternoon I was sent off on the push bike back to the beach where we had landed, to find the first batch of the unit's transport, about six jeeps, which were due to come ashore from a Tank Landing Craft. For about a mile my ride was quiet, apart from desultory explosions, then I came upon a military policeman, resplendent in white belt, anklets and gauntlet gloves, directing traffic at a road junction and found that the whole beach area had been completely transformed.

The hedge I had slipped through that morning had been bulldozed out of existence and what had been a secluded and empty coastal road was now completely open to the beach and thronged by an unending stream of vehicles all (except me) going in one direction — towards the MP. The beach too had changed out of all recognition. There was still some desultory shelling but, apart from sunken wrecks, the Infantry Landing Craft had gone and the shoreline was lined with Tank Landing Craft, nosed into the beach, disgorging vehicles of all descriptions, or pulling off to return to Britain for more. Royal Engineers were at work with bulldozers, clearing the beach and constructing more roadways of Somerfeld tracking across the soft sand.

I had been given the number of the LCT to look out for, but didn't need it. Hardly had I made my way to a vantage point to watch what was going on, than I saw the ramp of one of the craft which has just beached splash down and jeeps appeared carrying our 41 Commando number '93'! The waterproofed vehicles splashed through the shallows. I collected them on the track, and had soon unloaded a 'real' motorcycle from one of them — one of the small 'Famous James' 125cc two-stroke machines which were to take over from the R.C.-parascooters of the initial landing. The engine burst into life at the first kick, but my triumphant first squeeze of its pathetic bulb horn produced no more than a squirt of water! Leading my little convoy along the track, I had to persuade the MP that this little lot was the exception. All the rest of the unending stream of military traffic was being directed inland, towards Caen, but 41's vehicles were destined for Lion-sur-Mer, further along the coast. In the Normandy landings the role of Commandos was different from 'usual' as such lightly armed units would have been of little use against the strong 'Atlantic Wall'. The plan therefore was for the tanks and guns of Infantry Divisions to 'punch holes' in the German coast defences, then concentrate everything on pushing inland, leaving the Commandos to deal with all enemy resistance left behind.

On regaining the church, it was to find that Commando HQ was getting ready to move, so the jeeps' arrival was fortuitous. All day long the Commando had been without any artillery support because all attached Army and Navy signals personnel in the initial landing had either become casualties or had had their sets destroyed. Therefore, when a strong German counterattack, with artillery support, developed on one of our advanced Troops, the CO decided to regroup in a stronger position. HQ moved to an orchard area about half a mile from Lion and the digging of slit trenches was resumed. Fortunately, one of the jeeps I had brought up from the beach was a radio link with the Navy, so a destroyer 'shoot' on the German positions was called for and our sector eventually quietened down.

It was dusk when the noise of many aero engines came to us and, across a sky made golden by the setting sun, we saw streams of aircraft crossing between us and the Channel, each one towing a glider. The 6th Air Landing Brigade was on its way to reinforce the 6th Airborne Division and No. 1 Special Service Brigade who were holding the bridgehead on the other side of the River Orne only a few miles away. We heard the crackle of German anti-aircraft fire greeting their arrival. As the tug aircraft re-passed us, heading home after having done their job, some nearby wag commented, "Just think, those bloody pilots will be sinking a pint in their local in about half an hour's time." Shortly after the RAF's departure, German night bombers started putting in attacks on the supply ships of the invasion force lying off shore, but we were able to spend a relatively quiet night in our holes in the soil of France.

The Commando, which landed with a unit strength of 27 Officers and 410 Other Ranks, suffered about 30% casualties (123) on D-Day — 4 Officers and 22 Other Ranks killed, 31 Other Ranks missing, believed wounded, and 4 Officers and 72 Other Ranks wounded.

My own saddest memory of that day is that my friend 'Geordie' Swindale was killed. A photograph of him, taken in Sicily appears in *Marine Commando*, and I have dedicated *Marine Commando Despatch Rider* my account of my time with 41 Commando in N.W. Europe, to his memory; he is buried in Bayeux British Military Cemetery.

Raymond ('Mitch') Mitchell, 6 Anscomb Gardens, Newcastle-upon-Tyne.

I was a Naval Wireman on a Landing Craft (Tank) or L.C.T. At last the signal to sail was received and it was off we go to join the biggest fleet the world has ever seen. The organisation of the convoys was a masterpiece of planning. Try to imagine, if you can, 5000 cars equipped with only one miserable candle for lighting, approaching the spaghetti junction outside of Birmingham, on a dark and rainy night with no street lighting at all, and all them then heading off down the M5 in the general direction of Bristol with the road heaving up and down in five to six foot waves with the steering of each car slightly defective. Maybe that isn't the most vivid description of the scene on the night of D-Day but it may give you an idea of conditions. We owed much to the fleet of trawlers etc. which buoyed the course and our escorts who acted as sheep dogs, carefully shepherding us to our correct destination.

Dawn eventually arrived and it was only then that one could appreciate the size of the operation. As the skies gradually lightened, the vista gradually unfolded, and it was of ships and more ships of a multitude of shapes and sizes extending to and far beyond the horizon, all tossing and rolling in a grey and far from friendly sea. By this time we were all closed up to action stations, all trying our best to put a brave face on things. It wasn't so bad for our crew as we had been in similar situations before, in the Med, but the sheer size of this operation was awe inspiring.

Just before we sailed our Skipper had called us together and had explained our part in the great design of things, which was basically, to sail to about two miles off the beach, launch our DD (Floating) tanks then hang around until the beachhead was secured then it was just a case of back to the U.K. to start the ferrying operation. All nice and simple and not involving a great deal of danger. The only proviso was that should the waves be over a certain height. It was then up to the skippers whether they launched the tanks or took them in on to the beach. The whole idea of the floating tank was to provide heavy support to the first wave of commandos and of course to have a demoralising effect on the defending troops. Can you imagine standing on say Brighton sea front early in the morning when a squadron of tanks suddenly appear out of the sea and proceed to pound the promenade to pieces? There was a quick exchange of signals in our flotilla and it was decided that it was too dangerous to launch them in such atrocious conditions and so it was a case of full speed ahead on to the beach, ditch them off and get to hell out of it as quickly as possible!

In this life there always seems to be a great difference between theory and practice and this was no different to any other. Off went the flotilla leader in cautious haste closely followed by our craft. Goodness knows how but the leader managed to avoid the many obstacles on the beach and dropped his door. We followed close behind and our bow was just passing his stern when something happened which caused his stern to slew round and our bows took a nasty knock. I must explain at this point that the ramp door was held up by two dogs, one either side, which were arms made out of at least 1″ steel plate and which slipped under a couple of pieces of steel rod which were welded to the door to form supporting pins. These dogs were released by a wheel and worm gear right forward on the bows in full view of the enemy, quite a "nice" arrangement if you hadn't to undo them and on this occasion, were released prior to going into our final run on to the beach.

By this time we were under quite a lot of fire from the defence forces who at last seemed to realise that it was our intention to invade. The order "Down Door" was given, the brakes on the door winches were released and what happened — not a ruddy thing! One of the crew nipped up top, looked at the side of the door and discovered that in the collision one of the dogs had been bent around the door and was holding it up. Things were really hotting up by this time and Jerry was starting to throw all sorts of nice things like mortars, shells and one particular heavy machine gun situated in a church tower was giving us hell. Our First Lieutenant, a Midshipman, dashed aft to get something to release the door and came back with a crow bar about 12″ long and asked for volunteers to go up on to the exposed bows to try to straighten the offending "Dog". No-one volunteered as it was immediately apparent that the only thing that would bend would be the crow bar.

A hurried consultation was held with the Officer in charge of the Canadians and it was decided that the only solution to the problem was to bring the first tank forward and to let it gradually climb up the door until its weight forced the door down. At this stage I must tell you that we had a small battery operated "comforts" radio up forward with us and amidst all this chaos the calm voice of the radio announcer said something to the effect that "We wish to announce that the second front has begun and the invasion forces are making steady

207

herman tanks coming ashore from Tank Landing Craft.

I was a Height and Range Finder in the A.T.S. and it was my job to help to plot the position of enemy aircraft in our vicinity. It was a very dangerous area, just opposite to the Portsmouth docklands. My battery was 602 Mixed Heavy Ack-Ack and we used 5.7″ anti-aircraft guns.

Enemy aircraft, especially Junkers 88's used to fly over and bomb the area. The guns used to be just behind where I was sitting and there were also "Z" batteries (small anti-aircraft type rockets). The noise used to make me believe I would go deaf! I used to pray a lot during those times. It was so dangerous. We were all sworn to secrecy. Our gunnery green faced out to the English Channel. On our right was Portsmouth harbour area. As the months crept nearer to June we all knew something big was going to take place. All the fields in the surrounding districts were filled with troops living under canvas.

It was a frightening yet exciting time, but you could not help but worry. My fiancé, Leslie, had been captured at Singapore and my brother, Maurice, was seriously wounded at El Alamein whilst fighting for the "Desert Rats", against Rommel's Afrika Corps in North Africa.

As I had not had any leave for months I was instructed to take leave during this period that included D-Day and so I was in Hugglescote, Leicestershire when "it" happened! It was still a busy area when I returned but the eye of the needle had moved on – the focal point was now Normandy. My friends said the "air had been thick with our planes" as D-Day commenced – "never seen so many!"

Shortly after D-Day I went for a walk with my friends, Lois Wedgewood from Stoke, Kathy Parker from Redcar and Rita White, also from Hugglescote. Our gunnery green was only a field away from the beach and quite often we would stroll in the sea air – with caution of course! Well, on this day we had walked from our guns, across the field and we could hear the waves lapping on to the summer sand. "Will the war be over by Christmas" chatter was going on, when to our dismay we saw the scene on the beach!

To our horror we realised the tides since D-Day had conveyed across the channel items of flotsam, some of a very personal nature.

Initially the four of us almost turned back, but as our emotions welled up inside of us, we felt we had to stay, almost out of respect, not to the items, but to the owners. Apart from a sea breeze there was no sound, but I was pleased to have the company of my friends. To my left and right lay small and larger bundles of objects. Some were still floating on the waves, whilst others appeared to roll back into the sea.

Pieces of khaki clothings and footwear left nothing to the imagination, but wallets, letters and photographs did!

The letters were dotted around the sand and although it was not possible, there was an urge to gather and return them, but the condition of them was generally poor. The photographs were curled and stained but you could make out single shots or family gatherings. We wondered if the loved ones on the photographs knew the fate of the owners.

We did not touch anything and as we departed it was as though we were leaving a memorial for the dead. We realised that these items had belonged to Fathers, Sons and Brothers of many different Nations, some of whom in recent days had probably been under canvas nearby, but now they were no longer with us.

Later that evening I sat on my bed and wrote a letter to mum and dad, explaining the heart-breaking things I had seen that day. I knew dad would understand. He had been in the Leicestershire 1/5 Battalion between 1914-19 in France.

The ending was happy. I danced outside Buckingham Palace on V.E. Day. My fiancé survived his hell on the "death railway" and we married on December 15, 1945, to have three children.

My brother survived the war and eventually became a policeman, serving at Woodhouse Eaves with his wife and daughter for many years.

I am happily married and have much to be thankful for, but every now and again my mind wanders back to the 1940's and I remember that young Private in the A.T.S. – her name – Private Betty Hatter, 210073.

Betty Kendrick, 79 Fairfield Road, Hugglescote, Coalville, Leicestershire.

I was a nurse during the Second World War at a very big hospital in Birmingham with over 1000 beds. The life was tough, with long hours and very little pay and of course during those years we dealt with air raid casualties.

However, with the invasion of Normandy we received a message from the War Office to clear certain wards and take severely wounded troops from the invasion. It was a HORRIFIC experience I shall never forget until I die. I am now 82 years old.

At that time we had no anti-biotics and all dressings had to be hand packed into drums for sterilisation – no such thing as disposables in those days! Wards had to be prepared and all lockers and beds had to be washed with disinfectant to minimise the risk of spreading infection. We worked in teams and had to be available to be on duty at any time, day or night, as the need arose.

It was a pitch black night when the first convoy arrived. Some had been flown to us in batches of 15, laying on bare metal stretchers. Others arrived by train. They had come straight from the fighting lines and some were still in their uniforms, having been evacuated after initial treatment at base hospitals. Amongst our first batch were five Polish boys who had been doing forced labour work for the Germans. They had managed to escape and get behind the Allied lines and were in a terrible condition. They were nearly starving, some badly wounded, but even so it showed on their faces that they were so glad to be out and with us in the United Kingdom.

Others were from the invasion forces – some with limbs blown off and others with burns and body wounds. Our younger doctors had been called up into the Services or sent to other hospitals, and so our hospital was left with the older medical staff. But later we were joined by French Jewish doctors who had escaped from France and had been forced to leave their families behind. They were truly wonderful.

Then suddenly there came information from the War Office that the new drug penicillin was to be released to us. It was the very first anti-biotic. It came in small ampules with each ampule containing 4 doses of 30,000 units per injection. It was then in PURE form, costing in those days £80 per ampule which was an enormous sum of money! It was so expensive that with it came explicit instructions from the War Office that it was only to be used for wounded troops. The supply was not only expensive but very limited. The effect however was miraculous. Countless lives were saved that otherwise would almost certainly have been lost. No-one had been totally certain of the outcome of its use as it was the first time it had been used, but it was so successful that one could see the results almost daily.

They were wonderful lads, and so young. And they were such good fun once they began to get better. I remember one group asking if they could take me out to a supper in the City.

"Only if you get permission from your wives!" I told them. Not only did their wives agree but they sent them money to pay for the meal! That was life in those days!

But the money wasn't needed as it turned out. When the restaurant manager saw that they were wounded soldiers and that I was a nurse he INSISTED that we have the meal "on him"! It was a wonderful evening and one I shall always remember just as I remember those young lads who came to us from the beaches of Normandy.

Miss Lillian E. Mills, 13 Greylands Park Drive, Newby, Scarborough, North Yorkshire.

When the invasion of France took place, George Formby was as anxious to follow it up as he had been in Italy following his tour of the Middle East. He sent the following telegram to General Montgomery: "Beryl and I are standing by waiting to follow you and your boys immediately the invasion starts." In the Middle East he had entertained over half-a-million troops in 91 days and travelled 24,000 miles in the process! Now they were ready to do it again.

Six ENSA concert parties, with such names as 'We're Here', 'Variety's Invaders' and 'All's Swell' were ready before the first Allied forces stormed the beaches. They were prepared to live on army rations and do their own cooking while travelling in mobile columns. It took George's party four days in a barge buffeted by rough weather, to cross the channel to Normandy. His first show, lasting two hours, was given on board a former minesweeper, H.M.S. Ambitious, for men who had not been ashore for six weeks. The men drew lots for seats in the ship's small cinema and George repeated the show for those who had been unable to get in. To get to the vessel, off the Normandy coast, he drove a 'duck' alongside. In four weeks George and Beryl gave seventy shows, some of them only a few hundred yards from enemy lines.

In dug-outs 100 yards behind the front line

George and his wife Beryl on tour in the Middle East. In one period he did 106 shows in 53 days in 15 countries and entertained over 200,000 troops. In the whole tour he entertained over 500,000 troops.

he gave six shows in three hours. George didn't demand a stage for his roadside concerts. In a forward area beyond Caen he was glad of what appeared to be a disused tank. Halfway through 'Rolling on Through France' a Canadian officer appeared and said to Beryl: "Do you mind asking George to get off my tank? I need it now to go into action."

The Rev. (now Canon) George Potts, of Birmingham, senior chaplain to the Eighth Army Corps, was assigned to conducting George and Beryl around Normandy for two weeks and he looked after them.

George wanted to get to as many troops as possible, right up in the front line. This sometimes meant his having to crawl into slit trenches just to say "Hello boys." He wasn't permitted to take his uke or sing in the slit trenches because the sound would have given away our positions to the enemy a few hundred yards away. When he crawled up, grinning, the troops would look up and say: "Good God, it's George Formby!"

The padre had no hymn books or musical accompaniment for his Sunday services at field headquarters. Hymns were sung from memory, so George asked, "Do you mind if I come along and play my uke?"

"We'd be delighted," said the padre, whose services for the first time had banjo-uke accompaniment.

"It must have sounded strange," he said. " 'Guide Me O Thou Great Redeemer' and other hymns to the strumming of a banjo-uke. I shall never forget it. I didn't know he was a Roman Catholic and he didn't mention it. George was just glad to be with the troops wherever they were and he put some rhythm into the hymns!"

He was an essentially kind, caring person.

Close to death and destruction, most people would not have given a second thought to a stray dog scratching among the ruins of a building. George saw one and could not press on without taking the terrified creature with him. Later he took it to an army cookhouse to be fed and gave it to some troops, who said they would call it George Formby! He also cared for a kitten wounded by shrapnel after rescuing it from a deserted butcher's shop in Vassy. "They're among the innocent victims of this war," he said, "and need just as much protection as humans."

227

Cpl. Walter Ray, Royal Engineers, found a bottle of rum floating in the sea. It was promptly put to use!

But among the innocent victims of Formby-propaganda was Ernest Montgomery, a 19-year-old wireless operator in the 13/18 Royal Hussars, a tank regiment – later to become chairman of the George Formby Society. He was among the first to land in Normandy and though hearing of ENSA concert parties touring the lines, never saw one of them!

"We would be told at the end of a day that if we got our equipment spick and span and everything ready for action again before nightfall, the next day we'd be able to attend a concert by George Formby or one of the other big entertainers. Then, the next morning, we'd be back in the front line. There were a lot of troops in Normandy after the invasion who never saw a show or even caught sight of an ENSA concert party. Some of the officers and NCOs would kid us along, just to get everyone ready at the double."

The first ENSA contingent, led by George, consisted of 36 artists. There was no criticism this time as there had been before of concert parties being slow off the mark. The star line-

George in his ENSA uniform packing his ukelele.

up included Flanagan and Allen, Jessie Matthews, Florence Desmond, Gertrude Lawrence, Ivor Novello and Diana Wynyard. 'Monty' was delighted to meet George and Beryl again as he had in the Middle East and entertained them as his guests. He had two dogs named 'Hitler' and 'Rommel'! Remembering that Beryl had been ill with a stomach upset in Italy, he said to her: "You don't seem too well again. Same old trouble?" And though himself a teetotaller, he gave her some brandy.

Driving through a small village after British tanks had ousted the Germans, George was stopped by an old woman who spoke a few words of English and asked him to help her dig up her herbaceous border. It was an unusual request but George wanted to be helpful and got to work with a spade. Deep down the old lady recovered bottles of champagne. She had hidden them from the Germans four years ago. George and Beryl bought six bottles, "and reet good stuff it was".

Whilst George was entertaining, Beryl was working, organising, supporting. It was all very demanding. But she also took on another job – meeting as many of the troops as she could and gathering messages that she could send to their families. The George Formby Society still has her original war-time scribble pad which is full of messages that she took from the troops to pass on to wives and sweethearts.

When reading the records of George and Beryl Formby's journeys through the hot sand of the Middle East, the heat of Italy and the dangers of Normandy, you realise what tremendous spirit and dedication they applied to their job and to keeping up the morale of the troops.

Earlier in the war there had been a dearth off "stars" to travel abroad and entertain the troops and George Formby heavily criticised these variety stars who "stayed in West End theatres instead of going to theatres of war." By 1944 all that had changed, and the Formby's willingness to go anywhere at any time was largely responsible.

If anyone wishes to receive further information about the George Formby Society, write to Stan Evans, their Editor. His own story and address appears on page 225.

mmando troops resting in a narrow lane near Caen.

targets that had been allotted to us. We put down a blanket of fire for about 20 minutes when the infantry started to land and pass through our positions. They went up the beach and into the slit trenches beyond. Fire was still coming at us and an infantryman to our front was suddenly somersaulted through the air, either through shell blast or treading on a mine. I don't know which. The beach to our immediate front was very narrow with a concrete sea wall about 4 or 5 feet high. The only way we could get off the beach was to turn right and through a hole that had been blown in the wall.

To perform this manoeuvre the tank had to reverse whilst half-turning and then complete the turn in a forward direction. We started to reverse and after a few feet came to a halt, unable to make any headway backwards or forwards. We were stuck in the sand and 4ft. of water and every minute the incoming tide made it harder to move. I told the commander I would get out and fix a towing hawser if he could call up the Troop leader to tow us out. I quickly dismounted and instantly became aware of the sounds of battle all around me! These were not audible inside the tank, what with the noise of the engine, our guns, and radio messages flashing back and forth.

My first reaction on hitting the water was to get the screen inflated again and float the tank off, but the canvas screen had been torn to ribbons. A shell had landed a few feet behind us, wrecked the screen and made a crater and we had backed straight into it! The Troop Leader's tank had now arrived and I attempted to fasten the tow rope to our front shackle but this proved impossible as it was under water and the sea kept washing me away from it. Eventually I managed to do it by telling our driver Cliff of the other tank to hold me under water by standing on me whilst I secured the tow rope as it needed two hands to fix it to the shackle. He obliged! The tow tightened as the tank pulled away, but then it became obvious that the dry sand would not support the new tank without it shedding a track. We were well and truly stuck, with the tide still rising and the Germans not being very helpful either! I unhitched the tow and the tanks moved off through the breached wall. We were now on our own. Salvaging equipment from our tank before the rising tide covered it now had to be carried out quickly. With bedding rolls, rations and sundry other items of equipment we struggled out of the tank, through the sea and through the sea wall time and again dumping our gear by the side of the gun emplacement we had recently knocked out.

My next thought was to put some dry clothing on! I had started the day dressed in my one-piece tank overalls and I had salvaged my uniform dry and intact. The hours were now passing and I knew at 3.00 p.m. our AI echelon were due to land with the first line supplies of petrol and ammunition for the squadron. I decided to make a recce along the beach to link up with any other squadron tank crews who may have come to a sticky end. I found an infantryman's discarded bicycle and rode off along the track parallel to the beach. I found three crews who had experienced similar disasters. It was now past midday and the tide had covered the tank except for the top of the turret but as the sea receded we tried to recover some of our gear but it was all ruined. Whilst doing this a photographer took a picture of the gun emplacement and I have obtained a copy because it shows two of our crew, my overalls spread on the sea wall to dry, the bicycle and our bedding rolls etc. The tank isn't visible as it was on the seaward side of the gun and hidden by it.

The two crew are the driver and the gunner (who was called Stan Moffatt) and the driver Cliff Ford. On the photo Cliff is second from the left and Stan third from the left. They are both in "tank" helmets – no brim. Stan was killed in Belgium in early September and the driver, Cliff Ford, was wounded in October. I believe he died some years ago. By mid-afternoon we saw the wheeled vehicles coming ashore and so I climbered aboard an ammo truck and we set off inland to the harbour for the night. I must say I remember feeling very vulnerable and defenceless sat on that ammunition! We stopped at a farm that night and our crew set to work to make a base for the tanks that had survived. Ammunition, petrol, rations – they were all manhandled off lorries and stacked as unobtrusively as possible around the orchard. We worked until it was too dark to see anymore and then we found a meal had been prepared – were we ready for it! It was tea and hard biscuits! When my guard duty ended I turned into my blanket under the trees in the orchard with petrol and ammunition heaped all around! One good shell amongst that lot and it would have been "bye-bye" with a vengeance! We were too tired to bother! Out of a total complement of 19 tanks the squadron lost 9 on the beach and in the fight inland on D-Day. In view of the difficulties and opposition we faced I felt that this was quite a remarkable achievement. So D-Day ended for me. We had been on the go for 22 hours in a highly charged situation and when I put my head down all thoughts left me and I lost myself in the sweet pleasure of sleep!

Wilf Taylor, formerly from Sutton Coldfield but now of
"Heatherstone," Ffostrasol, Llandysul, Dyfed, Wales.

243

s photograph is explained in Wilf Taylor's story on this page, especially the overalls drying on the wall.

Catherine with her brother Jim.

It cannot have been more than a month after my 16th birthday, that I awoke one late June morning to the sound of my mother moaning. It was more like the cry of a wounded animal as she sat rocking to and fro at the bottom of the stairs.

I heard the mattress creak in the bedroom next to mine, as my grandmother threw herself out of bed, and hurled remarkably quickly downstairs to comfort her child.

Fear had paralysed my limbs but eventually I leaned over the bannister to view the scene below.

There was my mother's silver head bent low, and gran had enveloped her in a huge bear hug. Her immense bulk filling the tiny entrance hall of our three bedroomed semi.

If mother's hair was silver, gran's was as white as driven snow, as it lay around her shoulders like some ancient matriarch.

My mother clutched in her hand the dreaded missive from the War Office. Hope had been dwindling in her heart for the last three weeks, but here it was "We regret to inform you that your husband Cpl. A. Surtees 13115148 serving with the Pioneer Corps has been killed in action." This of course had been in the Normandy landings on D-Day. I can't remember if her widow's pension papers were enclosed, but at any rate they followed shortly. The War Office didn't stand on ceremony to let you get used to the idea.

Mother and gran seemed immersed in one another, while I felt vaguely embarrassed by this unwonted display of emotion. We had never been a demonstrative family.

I went to do the only thing I could think of, boiling the kettle for a strong cup of tea. I was destined to make many more before that long summer's day was over, for the news spread like wildfire throughout the district, as bad news always does. So there were a number of callers to weep and offer words of condolence, pity for the boy of 8, my brother "A boy needs a father," but in the same breath my Father was "lucky to have Mary, such a sensible lass." It seemed I had been hearing myself called that since ever I could remember.

It always made me feel like kicking over the traces, but I just didn't know how, so I remained sensible to the end.

My poor 39 year old Father had given his life for his country, he'd gone before he'd begun to live. Mother had nothing to look back on but years of trying to make ends meet during the Hungry 30's.

Why is that day stamped so indelibly upon my memory? Firstly, it was the most dramatic thing that had ever happened in our hum-drum lives, but more importantly I had reached a turning point. I could no longer escape into that realm of childish irresponsibility, I had not wanted to grow up, not just yet awhile at any rate. But with the news of the death of my Father, I'd had adulthood thrust upon me.

Catherine and her mother.

One thing of course I do deplore,
I grew up in a cruel war.
We've cause to remember mum and me,
those D-Day landings in Normandy,
missed so much of that father mine,
he was killed aged thirty-nine.

Time enough to dry one's tears,
it's been much more than forty years,
now I have proved it is no lie,
what once has bloomed can never die.

You see I know his battle's won,
in my practical daughter and dreaming son,
returning their grandmother's selfless devotion,
proving that love is the stronger emotion.

Catherine Mary Surtees-Robinson, 37 Saffrons Court,
Compton Place Road, Eastbourne, Sussex.

June 1944 – Prime Minister Winston Churchill and General Montgomery land in Normandy.

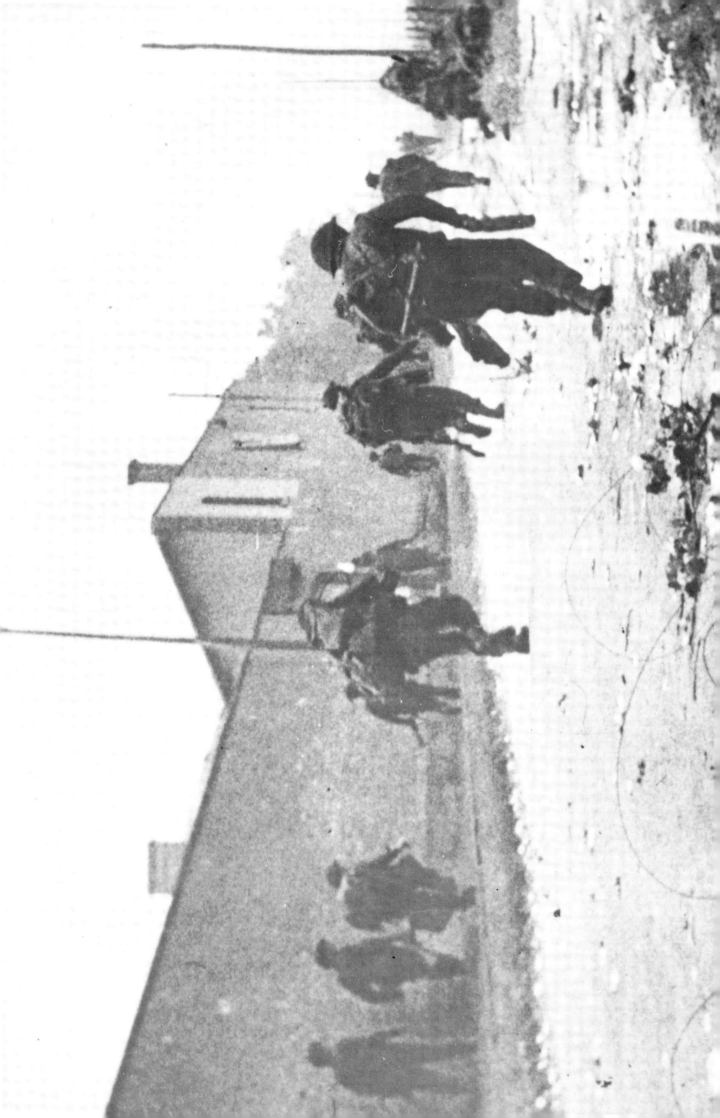

The Wartime R.A.F. was a phenomenon; it really was "A Band of Brothers" (and Sisters) and there is nothing with which to compare it except the "Pal's Battalions" of the first World War, slaughtered on the Somme in 1916, and I would not have missed a minute of my six years in the Service.

I was 18 when I joined as a wireless mechanic, lucky enough to work on Spitfires for most of my time and was sent to a Spitfire O.T.U. in 1942. "O.T.U.'s" were "Operational Training Units" to which Aircrew who had nearly finished their training were sent to gain experience on the type of Aircraft which they would fly operationally. Bomber Boys formed themselves into Crews who lived and often died together, and flew long cross-country trips, mostly by night, and carried out mock bombing raids. Fighter Boys did Formation Flying, Dog Fighting and Aerobatic exercises, went on Height Climbs to a great altitude, using Oxygen, and did some carefully supervised Low Flying. The "Low Flying" Area was always in a remote or mountainous area, so that as few people as possible would be disturbed by a Spitfire passing their bedroom windows, and any "Unauthorised" low flying was a quick passport out of the R.A.F. for the offending Pilot. The R.A.F. was very tolerant on many matters but was quite ruthless about this offence.

"Number 57 O.T.U." was at Hawarden, near Chester, although we moved a little later to Eshott in Northern Northumberland, a very beautiful part of England. I was sent to "X" Squadron, the Air Firing Flight, whose C.O. was Squadron Leader Bob Doe, one of the highest scoring Pilots of the Battle of Britain, with many victories. He was a quiet reserved man and a wonderful Air to Air shot.

Air to Air firing is an extremely difficult art and many people who flew like Angels could never hit the target at all, or allowed too much deflection and peppered the towing aircraft several hundred feet away. One of the Pupils was the famous Canadian, David "Screwball" Beurling, who was so good that he often shot the target away altogether! A Sergeant Pilot, he was very casual even by R.A.F. standards and was as likely to greet a superior Officer with "Hi Mac," rather than a salute, but when he was sent to Malta at the height of the Siege he shot down a large number of German and Italian Aircraft in a very short time, usually with a minimum expenditure of ammunition.

Most of the Pupils were from Britain or the Dominions but there were large numbers of French, Belgian, Polish and Czech Pilots as well, and many Irishmen from the officially "Neutral" Irish Free State. When the small population of Ireland is taken into account, proportionately, Ireland had more young men in the Armed Forces than any of the Nations who were actually "At War."

I knew scores of Fighter Pilots, Commissioned and Non-Commissioned. Most of them were people who conformed to the popular idea of a Fighter Boy, top tunic button undone, gaudy silk scarf, and a cap which was usually "A battered wreck, pulled on with infinite negligent rakishness." They were also gentle, kind hearted, and thoughtful people, and if these seem strange words with which to describe such doughty warriors, think of Sir Ector lamenting the dead Sir Lancelot in "Morte D'Arthur": "Ah Lancelot" he saith: "Thou wert the gentlest Knight who ever struck with sword; and thou wert the meekest man who ever sate in Hall with Ladies; and thou wert the deadliest Foe to thy sworn enemy of any Knight

who ever laid Lance in rest." "Nice types" as we used to say, and very different from the modern yuppies portrayed as Fighter Pilots in the dreadful I.T.V. Film "A Piece of Cake."

Our job as Wireless Mechanics was to look after the Radio Sets in the Spitfires, which needed little attention, as the splendid V.H.F. Radio sets had replaced the short-range and unreliable pre-war sets. Repairs were carried out in the Maintenance Wing Workshops but most of us preferred the open air life down on the Aerodrome where there was always "Bags of Activity" and advantage was taken of every moment of good weather to speed the training programme. In summer we often worked from dawn to dusk and knocked

tish infantry of 50th Division moving forward against a gun-site.

off work "Quite late at night". Everyone, W.A.A.F. and R.A.F., mucked in and helped his friends and there were no "Passengers" on "X" Squadron.

We knew that the Invasion of Europe was imminent, as in early 1944 the roads were filled with military Convoys and the sound of Aircraft filled the skies twenty four hours a day. There was a wonderful spirit everywhere, as we knew that we were a winning team about to drive the opposition off the field.

More than half of the "Foreign" Pilots were French or Belgian, although the devotion of all the "Foreign" Pilots to our Cause often exceeded our own. A Frenchman, Lieutenant Frezet, was sent to us, originally as an interpreter and Liaison Officer. He was a burly man of over thirty, bald, and looking much older, and since the average Pilot was usually under twenty, he was not considered for flying duties, although he was a Pilot of great experience. He soon showed himself to be the best Pilot on the Unit and was made an instructor. Any "Above Average" pupil who was considered to be getting a bit above himself was sent up as "Number Two" to Frezet and told "Try and stay with him." No one could.

I never hear "La Marseillaise" without thinking of Frezet. June the Sixth 1944 was a lovely day and most of our Aircraft were soon airborne on the usual exercises. We operated normally but suddenly we were elated to hear, on the Radio which every hut and Crewroom had, that the Invasion had at last begun, and listened with growing emotion, to the dry, calm

Lieutenant Frezet – Free French Air Force.

voice of Eisenhower reading his first short yet very stirring communiqué. Most people simply said, "Well, it's started, then", and went on with their work, but the whole Camp hummed with excitement, the sun shone that much brighter, and everyone smiled at his neighbour. Although there was no wild enthusiasm or show of emotion, all Europe had been waiting for this Day for four years and we knew that we stood on the threshold of great events.

Immediately after the announcement I went across to a grounded Spitfire and climbed in to the cockpit and plugged my 'Phones in (after connecting a Trolley Accumulator so that the Electrician could not accuse me of flattening the battery). We often did this when our Aircraft were airborne, to listen to the Radio chatter. Pilots were ordered to "Keep it short" but some of the repartee was worth listening to, although it sometimes made the Ops Room W.A.A.F.'s blush. I wanted to hear what was being said, as the Pilots who were flying could not have heard the momentous news, as their Radios were V.H.F. and operated on a much higher frequency than the B.B.C. and Commercial stations; much better quality of reception, too.

Frezet and most of our people were flying over the Cheviots or the Firing Range over the Farne Islands, and I heard our Ops Room Controller, Flight Lieutenant Otto Spiegelhalter, call him up, calling him by name and not using his Call Sign, which was the usual, correct, procedure. "Allo Frezet" he said in calm, unexcited tones; "Allo, Frizz, old Boy; you will be pleased to hear that the Invasion has begun. The allied armies have landed in Normandy and it is all going very well. Are you happy now, Mon vieux?"

There was a pause, and then the voice of the Frenchman came back, NOT in the measured tones we had expected. We had struck a chord we hadn't known was there, and in a voice choked with emotion we heard his reply against the background roar of the Merlin and the shriek of the wind over the cockpit hood: "Ah, merci, Spiggy; Á la Victoire! Vive La France! Enfin, 'Le jour de Gloire est arrivée,' vraiment!" He switched off hurriedly, but not before we had heard a sob, a cry which came from the depths of the soul.

That really was one of life's great moments and I felt like weeping myself. Always, on June the sixth, I think of those who that other great French Fighter Pilot Pierre Clostermann referred to as: "My dear R.A.F. friends, with your uniforms the colour of your Island mists", and remember Wordsworth's words, "Bliss it was that dawn to be alive, but to be young was very Heaven."

Alan W. Brodrick, "Sylvainne," Hall Lane, Longton, Preston, Lancashire.

h June 1944. General de Gaulle walking through the streets of Bayeaux.

It was D-Day, 1 hour and 45 minutes after 'H' hour and our L.C.T. 593 was heading towards a section of the Normandy beach not far from Ouistreham, carrying four self-propelled guns, three Sherman tanks, four half-track vehicles and eighty British soldiers of the 3rd Division. I was First Lieutenant to the C.O., Lieutenant J. F. D. E. Jones. We were in company with five other L.C.T.s.

We fired several hundred rounds from our self-propelled guns as we approached the beach and could see obstacles sticking out of the water, many of them with shells and mines attached. We managed to avoid most of them, hitting the beach at maximum speed. By this time bullets and shrapnel were flying in all directions and the noise was deafening.

After landing our men, tanks and vehicles in about two feet of water we turned the L.C.T. and we set off for home. No sooner had we set course at 'full ahead' when the mechanic appeared, reporting that we were holed in the engine room and taking water fast.

I dashed below with the mechanic and found the engine room flooding rapidly. Jagged beach obstacles had holed us in two places. The pumps were working to full capacity and we endeavoured to plug the holes with spare kit and about one hundred and forty blankets. Unfortunately, the pressure of water was too great and as it poured in one of the engines seized up. If the other did the same it would be only a matter of minutes before we sank. However, it kept going. Following instructions from the bridge we closed all water-tight doors, and I returned to the bridge. By now the stern was gradually settling lower in the water making accurate steering impossible. Return to the U.K. in this condition was out of the question. The C.O. decided to beach the craft. It was the only option, but it was the beginning of five very uncomfortable days marooned on Sword beach.

The rest of D-Day passed surprisingly quickly being occupied with securing the craft, digging a trench on the beach and finding something to eat. It took our minds off snipers in the houses along the front, firing at us whenever the opportunity arose. We had only two Oerlikon guns but we used them to good effect. During the evening we had a fright. A thick mist came rolling along the beach. Our first thoughts were that the Germans were using poison gas! We donned our gas masks and took cover, wondering what sort of gas it might be and how it would affect us. After ten minutes, taking note of the indicators on board, we were relieved to know that it was a harmless, chilling sea mist!

We did not get much sleep during the night of D-Day and as dawn broke on D+1 any rest which we did get was quickly shattered by the arrival of enemy aircraft, six Junker 88s. One was shot down by a Bofors gun on the shore road, and a member of our crew, Ordinary Seaman Townsend, hit another and set its starboard engine on fire. Later in the day men from the salvage ship 'Northland' came aboard to see if they could be of assistance. They decided to return to our stricken L.C.T. the following morning, with cement to fill the holes.

D+2 brought further troubles. We had such command of the air that enemy aircraft didn't worry us too much. It was the shelling from Le Havre which was so devastating. It came without warning, and on the beach there was nowhere to run, nowhere to hide. The shelling was intermittent and during one attack three of our crew and two salvage men were wounded. Stoker Tom Beatson died later that day from his wounds. The holes were slowly being filled with cement, the salvage men worked hard. It was a difficult job because every time the tide returned fresh cement was dislodged.

D+3 was busy. We were more or less water-tight and the 'Northland' pulled us off the beach by a length of cable almost half a mile long. The salvage vessel could not come any nearer to the shore for we were still being shelled. We watched the slack being taken out of the line. It was agonisingly slow, with shells bursting every thirty seconds in the water around us. At last the line appeared above the

...aterproofed Sherman tanks, guns and other equipment pouring ashore, followed by a "half track" vehicle.

Bomber fuselage brought back to Portsmouth from Normandy.

water and it began to take the strain. We moved slightly and a shell just missed the bows. We started to swing and another shell missed. We all expected the next one to be a direct hit but we were towed a good distance from the shore and told to drop anchor. We were now out of range of guns at Le Havre.

D+4 was a day of disappointments. It was impossible to start the engines and there was no-one who was keen to give us a tow back to the U.K. We had to spend the night at anchor.

D+5 brought the offer of a tow. We set off but towing with a long line was not successful. The thick wire hawser quickly frayed and we were worried. If it parted we would drift into minefields either side of the channel which had been swept for us as a highway to the beaches. We sent desperate signals to the towing craft, and it was decided to take us alongside. This was not an easy exercise, an L.C.T. is a cumbersome craft. We had another sleepless night, keeping close watch on the cables, renewing and repairing the protecting canvas where necessary. D+6 found us in the broad stretch of water separating the mainland from the Isle of Wight. We dropped anchor and breathed a sigh of relief. We had been lucky. Many of our friends in similar craft did not return. The obstacles on the beaches took their toll.

Our efforts were not in vain. Following a week's leave we returned to our repaired L.C.T. and made more trips to the French coast. On one occasion we brought back the fuselage of one of our planes which had been shot down. The salvaged metal was vital to the war effort.

Robert J. Pollard, 21 Saxon Close, Hythe, Kent.

I was a Regular Soldier, serving with the Hampshire Regiment and during the war I was with the 1st Battalion. After service in the Western Desert in Egypt we saw action in Sicily and Italy and if that wasn't enough we were then selected as an assault Battalion for the landings in Europe along with the other two Battalions in our Brigade, the Dorsets and the Devons. With all the replacements we had received over the years to make up for our losses I suppose we were now about two-thirds veterans and one-third "new boys" who were going to be thrown in at the deep end. There was a very heavy swell so none of us slept much that night and about 04.30 a.m. there was breakfast – for those who fancied it! A lot of us ate it even though reluctantly because we knew it could be a long time before we got another meal. For some it would really be their last.

At 05.30 a.m. we went up on to the main deck to be lowered into the flat bottomed Infantry Assault Craft, banging away on the davits. It was still fairly dark. In the Craft we sat one behind the other, in three rows, one man's chin practically resting on the pack of the man in front. We were lowered down, but as soon as we were on the water the Craft was going up and down on the swell as though we were in a demented lift. We had to try to hold position until all Craft were in formation, and before we headed for shore we were in our Craft for 1½ hours, thoroughly miserable, drenched by the spray, and feeling not a little seasick! It only needed one man to be sick and it would spread throughout the Craft. We had one! It was the only time I was ever seasick in all my years of service.

yal Marines of the 4th S.S. Brigade land at St. Aubin-sur-Mer. Bodies on the beach and 2 Landing Craft "broadside" on.

It gradually got lighter, and when we were about three miles from shore the Navy ships started their own bombardment. It took our minds off our miserable conditions and made us feel a lot happier knowing the enemy was on the end of that lot! But as we got nearer the shore the enemy added his own fire – only this time in our direction! A hell of a lot of stuff was falling around us with other Landing Craft being hit. We grounded, quite a way out because of the waves sweeping in, and the front ramp went down. The Craft never stayed grounded because one wave would sweep us in and the back surge would drag us out. Then back in again and so on, mostly at a nasty angle to the beach. A number of men were lost by Craft coming back at them whilst they were in the water,

knocking them down and going straight over them. The Officer I was close to in the Craft jumped in, was either knocked over by a wave or slipped so I followed him and gave him a hand up. Fortunately for both of us a big wave literally picked us up and carried us ashore. Our instructions were to get off the beach as quickly as possible – stop for nothing. With the flak that was coming we didn't need any second bidding! We set off at a run, not easy after being cooped up in the Assault Craft and loaded down with equipment. I remember going up the beach, between the "hedge hog" defences set in the sand, each with a mine on the seaward side. They would be covered once the tide came in. On my left as I ran was Corporal Bill Winter, already the holder of the Military Medal. He would be wounded within half-an-hour. On my right was Private Monty Bishop.

Bullets were flying everywhere but strangely with the noise of the bombardment, the wind and the sea you didn't hear them! You didn't realise anyone had been hit until you reached the sand dunes. It was only then as I looked back that I saw our men lying wounded and dead on the beach. When we reached the sand dunes we went down into a kneeling position, grateful to get our breath back. Another platoon that had just landed was trying to sort out the pill-box to our front. I noticed that Monty was leaning heavily on my right shoulder and I thought that like me he was "puffed" and pleased to have someone to lean on. But when we got orders to move forward and I got up he just fell forward on the sand. He was dead.

A bullet coming down the beach from the Sanitorium on the seafront at Le Hamel just to our right must have hit Monty as we waited. The Sanatorium, the main defence position in the area, should have been "taken out" by a low level air attack just before we landed, but because of the low cloud none of the concrete-bursting bombs found their target and the place was still bristling with guns of all types. Another thing that made our job difficult was the absence of armoured support. During "rehearsals" for the landing we had the support of "swimming tanks". These were Sherman tanks fitted with an inflated skirt which kept the tank afloat until it got to the beach where the "skirt" would be deflated and the tank revert to a conventional tracked vehicle. However, in our case the first wave of tanks launched from the Craft were immediately swamped by the heavy seas and sank. No more were launched from the Craft until Tank Landing Craft could get in and conventional tanks could get ashore.

After a great deal of hard fighting we achieved our objectives, capturing the town of Arromanches at 9.00 in the evening with an attack from the landward side. It hadn't been an easy day by any means. Our casualty list was 182 men killed and wounded out of about 550 who had set out that morning. The Commanding Officer was wounded twice in the first half-hour. When the second in Command came ashore he was killed almost immediately so the Company Commander of C Company took over Command of the Battalion. During the morning of D-Day the wind eased up, the sky cleared and by the afternoon the sun was shining. A completely different scene to when we had landed just after 7.00 a.m. that morning.

D-Day of course was just the start of some severe fighting in the Bocage of Normandy. After five weeks of almost continuous action against the best the German Army could put in the field, only myself and two other men remained of the 90 or more men of my Company who had landed that morning. The others had been killed or wounded. But before too long we were part of the chase through France and Belgium, the highlight being when we were the first infantry to liberate Brussels. A couple of days of pure heaven after what we'd been through! Why and how did I survive? I'm afraid I shall never know the answer to that!

Stanley ("Chalky") Chalk, 2 Blaxland Close, Faversham, Kent.

Bren Carrier loaded with ammunition ablaze after being hit near Touffreville.

It was all very exciting. In 1944 I was on Special Duties at Southwick House the Headquarters for planning the Second Front, or Operation Overlord as it was called. To keep our location secret we were known officially as Naval Party 1645 and all letters sent to us were sent to BFPO Reading which was miles away! The War Room, which had originally been the Library, became the meeting place for General Eisenhower, General Montgomery, Air Chief Marshal Tedder, Air Chief Marshal Leigh-Mallory, and of course Admiral Ramsay who was the Allied Naval Commander. This room is now called the Map Room and the map as it was on 6th June, 1944 still hangs on the wall. I saw it again in 1992 when attending a dinner there for the D-Day and Normandy Fellowship.

I was billeted at South Lodge next door to the village pub called The Golden Lion. My room was in the attic! Our work area was in the cellar at Southwick House where a telephone exchange had been installed together with teleprinters. The cellars were a series of whitewashed tunnels with arches leading off in different directions – one to the boiler room for central heating, then off to the left the teleprinter room, and on the right the telephone exchange. This was a very large room with a concrete floor – no windows of course as we were underground. The telephone exchange was down the centre with my table facing it. There were 14 positions for operators and the switchboard was equal in size to a civilian exchange serving a town of 45,000 people.

The most important Officers had "Clear the Line Facilities" which meant that we had authority to interrupt calls for them if the person they wanted to speak to was already

Bobby Howes receiving the British Empire Medal from King George VI.

engaged. When they called a blue lamp glowed beside their number on the board. The Exchange was manned by an equal number of Wrens and men of the Royal Corps of Signals, 21st Army Group. As the Royal Navy was the Senior Service I was in charge and I have to say that the men accepted me very well. There was a daily roster of watches and a rest room where everyone could take a rest without going off duty. The drinking of tea or smoking was strictly forbidden whilst working and certainly there was no time for conversation because the Board was constantly busy.

Before the Southwick Board became operational I had attended a Course in the use of Very High Frequency Telephones which could be used as link between the Normandy beaches and Southwick House. When this course was finished I had the job of compiling directories for the operators of the Officers of all the Armed Forces who would have a line on our Exchange. Of course this included General Montgomery and General Eisenhower!

At last the day arrived when Admiral Ramsay and his staff arrived from their London Headquarters. 21st Army Group men put up their tents in the park where they were well screened from aerial view by the trees, and General Montgomery's caravans were nearby whilst he took up residence in Broomfield House. General Eisenhower and his staff were a couple of miles away at SHAEF (Supreme Headquarters Allied Expeditionary Force) and all was ready. Then panic set in – the Naval Officers changed rooms little thinking of the chaos they were causing for us in the cellar. We didn't know where they were any longer, and so my precious directories became useless. The Army allocated a Sergeant to help me start on a new set of directories and we worked all evening to get everything updated so that by morning we were back in business. I think this was when my hair started turning grey! However, all was well and the exchange became operational without any further hold-ups. All the telephones of the Top Brass had scramblers attached, and in conducting a conversation involving secret information the caller would ask: "Can you scramble?". If the answer was yes they both switched on their scramblers and the conversation sounded like Donald Duck talking to anyone trying to listen in.

In the War Room they had a small 10 + 50 manual exchange which was manned by three Wrens I had chosen. They worked a three-watch system. I had a War Room pass, so that I could visit them if any problems arose. There was always a Royal Marine on duty at the door of the War Room to whom the pass had to be shown before entry. Wren Margaret Showell told me of one occasion when Monty went in that the Royal Marine closed the door sharpish and caught the tail of Monty's little dog in the door! But Monty just picked the dog up without a word and put him in his battledress blouse where he stayed throughout the meeting! I'll bet the Royal Marine was relieved!

In early June all personnel were called to a meeting to be told that Operation Overlord was about to begin. They were reminded of the need for strict secrecy and security and all leave was cancelled. I knew that my husband was somewhere in the area with his R.A.F. Regiment Squadron so when Monty's Equipment Sergeant, whom I knew, told me he had to go to a secret Research Station in the area I jumped at the offer to take me along. I sat in the jeep outside that Research Station praying that no-one would come along and ask what I was doing there. Thankfully all went well and we were soon on our way to Frank's Squadron H.Q. What a surprise for him when I hopped out of the jeep and said: "Hurry up if you want a trip to town Frank, we haven't got all day." He didn't wait – in seconds he was scrambling through the hedge and we headed for the nearest fish and chip shop – a real luxury evening! I never did know if the Sergeant who gave me that lift ever returned home to see his baby daughter who had been born that week as he went off to France soon after D-Day and our paths never crossed again.

I was Duty Petty Officer on the night of 5th June. It was remarkably quiet and after the previous nights cancellation because of adverse weather conditions, the operation was under way. For once the operators had time to chat amongst themselves, wondering if their boyfriends had sailed off to France and how long it would be before they met again. Would we be going to France too? Would we get any leave beforehand? Would the invasion succeed? How bad would the casualties be? All of these thoughts were bandied about, helping to pass the time – it was a very long night.

Because of the use of scramblers we could only anticipate what was happening, but a call from General Omar Bradley at about 02.00 hours gave us cause to hope that everything was going to plan. The R.A.F. had bombed the coastal batteries between Le Havre and Cherbourg and gliders had landed Airborne Divisions behind the coastline of Normandy. By the end of the Middle Watch we received news that everything was going well and at 06.30 hours the first seaborne troops were landing on the beaches. I finally went off duty at 08.00 hours, and then at about 09.30 came the BBC announcement of the landings. The Mess echoed to an almighty cheer – after all the planning the beginning of the end was in sight, our lads were in France and we had been part of it! What did I do on D-Day? I walked down the tree-lined drive to Southwick House where the red squirrels were playing, very tired but very very happy, and climbed thankfully into my bed in the attic of South Lodge.

Could I add one other note? While General Montgomery and General Eisenhower and others are well known names, the name of Admiral Sir Bertram Ramsay has rarely been brought into the limelight. He planned and was responsible for the transport across the Channel of all the invasion forces, and without his expertise and thorough work the whole operation could well have floundered. When you bear in mind his responsibility for getting the British Expeditionary Force out of Dunkirk four years earlier in 1940, I feel strongly that Britain owes a huge debt to him which has never really been recognised. I do hope you will include this little note in an attempt to remedy this omission.

Mrs. Ena ('Bobby') Howes, B.E.M. 67 Beeching Drive, Lowestoft, Suffolk.

My name was Phyllis Laura Carley then and I lived in Sidley at Bexhill-on-Sea. I was almost 13 when D-Day took place. My bedroom had a view of the sea and all my life it seemed the lightship had shone across the sea and on to my bedroom wall. Of course, in wartime we had no lights that I can recall. All we had was blackout. Anyhow on this particular night I'd heard little hoots and noises and could see flickering lights. Mum suddenly came into my bedroom and opened the window. I sat up in bed.

"What's the matter?" I said. "Something's happening," said mum. "What?" "I think it's started," she said, and I didn't UNDERSTAND! "What has?" "The Invasion." I shot out of bed. "But I thought we were all right now." Mum looked at me in frustration! "Not the

Germans – US," she said. "I think it's begun." I couldn't sleep with excitement. I think they were moving troops and equipment to Portsmouth or along the coast. At least that now explained why all those convoys of lorries had been coming down our High Street.

A few days earlier my young sister Eileen (almost 9) had nearly caused a major accident as the convoys went through. Eileen, I and my other sister Jean, (aged 11) were waiting to cross the main road. Mum was across the road going to the chemist. The noise of the tanks and lorries was earth shaking and mum didn't see or hear us. Suddenly Eileen shot across the road in front of a tank – which only missed her by slewing round sideways! The Commanding Officer was following on in his jeep and was beside himself with rage he was so furious. He stood up like a General reviewing his troops and waved his stick at us. The convoy was split in half and the soldiers were all looking out of the lorries, and my mum was so frightened and upset she was giving Eileen what for with whacks around the legs. And then I got the same when we got home and it wasn't my fault!

The day after the night of noises from boats etc. I awoke to the noise of aircraft. I will never ever forget that day. I've never seen so many planes in my life. Bombers – low. Probably Lancasters but I don't know the names of planes much. Spitfires of course but hundreds of silver shapes high in the sky. We tried to count the formations of heavy bombers flying low overhead but it was hopeless and the noise was terrific! They were still crossing overhead when we went off to school, and I can remember the children dancing and running along the streets cheering them on as they flew overhead. We yelled our heads off and waved frantically in delight. It was just so exhilarating. It seemed to go on forever and I tried to picture my dad over the other side. I prayed to God to bring him home to us.

Dad had gone over with the Inns of Court Regiment. He was in Armoured cars, one of Monty's men. He used to tell us that there was only one black beret with two badges on it and he and Monty had had a fight over it and Monty won! So that was why Monty was a General and not my dad. Do you know, we believed every word of it! After D-Day we used to look every day in the papers for the map showing how things were going because mum said that dad was the "arrowhead" of the Regiment and so we faithfully looked up each day to see where dad was. It was the arrowhead, wherever that was. We were quite confident that no German would DARE fight our dad. After all he'd nearly become a General! But we worried just the same. He was at Neimegan at the time of the Battle of Arnhem and met my cousin Kenny Oaten aged 18 only an hour before he was killed by a shell in the face. He's buried at Neimegan. When dad came back we had become a houseful of women. Poor dad! We all had to adjust but we were so glad to have him home with us again. But at least he came back. Many other poor souls didn't and I grieve for those who lost their loved ones.

With all the activity of D-Day the "in" game became wandering around looking for spy hide-outs because we were all convinced they were there – somewhere! I once led my friends into what appeared to be an empty schoolhouse and there on the wall was a map with flags on it. This was it – we'd stumbled on a spy hideout! Suddenly a deep voice asked us what we were up to. There was a U.S. Army Captain with his Sam Brown belt on. We were chucked out double quick! I now live only a few yards from that school and it STILL brings back memories of that day whenever I pass it! Another time we entered an empty house and in the fireplace someone had burned maps and things relating to France and Germany. A lot of things I remember had "Ypres" on them and I remembered had I read that name before! Of course it was from World

War I but we were only kids, the invasion of France was happening on our doorstep and we were hell bent on assisting by capturing our very own spy! We collected the "evidence" to take it to the Police Station but halfway there we realised we'd then have to own up to entering the house. So self-preservation got the better part of patriotism and we abandoned it! Anyway, we convinced ourselves, the spy was probably miles away by now seeing as he'd burned his papers! I laugh at it now but we were very serious then. That's my memory of D-Day and the effect it had on us. But the best part was that dad came home safely to us.

Mrs. Phyllis L. C. Bestley, 16 Laburnum Gardens, Pebsham, Bexhill-on-Sea, Sussex.

I was an Amphibious Vehicle Mechanic in 299 DUKW Coy,
R.A.S.C., part of the 3rd British Division. With a full
complement of DUKWs, equipment and personnel on
board L.S.T's 213 and 214, we sailed to a rendezvous in mid-
channel. At the break of dawn I decided to go up on deck
and, to my amazement, ships of every size and description
had assembled overnight in preparation for the D-Day
Invasion. The quiet was shattered by ear-splitting crashes as
salvo after salvo was fired at the coastal defences. I felt a
sense of security being part of such a massive fleet,
supported by air cover overhead. The noise was deafening
and the faces of my comrades told their own story. It was
nearing time for us to disembark. At twenty years old, it
suddenly dawned on me that I was a bit young for all this,

although I was fully trained in beach landing. I was feeling sick and, I don't mind admitting,
scared as well. As the battleships Warspite and Ramillies sailed past the L.S.T., all hell was
let loose. This was no place for a "rookie"! The coastline of Sword Beach was almost visible.

After calling us to the lower decks, the Padre conducted a short service. Afterwards, our
O.C. Major Person briefed us on the day ahead and added: "God Bless you all and may you
reach the Normandy coast safely."

We climbed aboard our DUKWs as the huge doors of the L.S.T. opened. Each DUKW
in turn moved forward slowly and went down the ramp into a very rough sea. I didn't like
the look of the sea but I tried to remain calm as we tossed around like a cork in the water.

I felt really sick and I removed my haversack and the remainder of my kit, thinking I would
eventually have to swim to survive. Visibility was deteriorating along the foreshore because of
smoke pouring from houses along the beach which were set on fire by the assault. As we
approached the last hundred yards or so, still chugging along, I could see the difficulties ahead.

The 6th Airborne Division were providing plenty of air cover – not an enemy in sight – as
they dropped thousands of troops over a wide area of the Normandy beachhead. The troops
from the initial assault, by then tired and hungry, must have thought this a Godsend.
Reinforcements were always welcome. The planes returning from the dropping zone, flying
low over the housetops, were picked off one by one by sniper fire. One plane landed along
the water's edge, another crashed into the sea on our port side, with no survivors. A few
planes crash-landed into the shallow waters and a rescue launch manned by the R.A.S.C.
was there in a flash to pick up any survivors.

After approaching the beach cautiously I could see enemy soldiers assisting the Royal
Engineers, Pioneers and the beach clearing units to tow the large metal objects, with teller
mines attached, out of the way. A flail tank was detonating as many mines as possible, so
we followed it for the remaining 30 yards before we reached sand. A temporary track was
being laid on the sand dunes directly in front of the entrance to Hermanville.

I could not believe what I saw along the dunes. The beach was littered with dead and
wounded, wrecked vehicles and many other craft which had beached. There was chaos
everywhere. This was a sight I would never forget. I can assure you that my comrades and
I were sickened and upset at seeing the loss of so many lives. On reaching the sand, I
immediately jumped out of the DUKW – why, I don't know! Dazed and shell-shocked, I
wandered round until I found the "DUKW Control Post". Many dead soldiers were laid on
a large tarpaulin; some had drowned before reaching the beach. Tank crews were lying beside

their wrecked tanks. There was worse to come as I zig-
zagged over and around the dead bodies who had perished
in front of the Hermanville strongpoint. One soldier lay
dead with his accordian by his side. Another in a crouched
position with his rifle holding him in balance, but dead.
Feeling sad and desolate I suddenly remembered the words
of Hymn 581 "The sands of time are sinking".

The complete length of Sword Beach from Ouistreham to
Lion-sur-Mer was a sitting target for occasional air attacks
and shelling. To ease the tension barrage balloons were
erected to shield us from further attacks. Large duplex drive
tanks which were causing congestion on the beach were
towed aside to make way for us. An entrance to Hermanville

was now ready to use, so cautiously we moved onto a rugged track. I remember saying: "Thank God we got off the beach." It was a real boost to all of us. A few houses by the roadside were still sheltering snipers who immediately attacked us. Fortunately, a group of commandoes appeared with bayonets at the ready and forced their way into the buildings. A few shots were fired then a yell or two. Afterwards a commando instructed us to move on to the unloading depot.

After unloading their cargo, the DUKWs returned to the beach and started to ferry the wounded to hospital ships anchored in the bay. Many vehicles were damaged by mines during the evacuation. Trees and hedgerows were almost non-existent owing to the continuous bombing and straffing during the assault. Now and again we encountered a few civilians. Many stayed in hiding to await the outcome of the day. The noise of battle was never ending as the infantry fought to consolidate the land along Perriers Ridge. The enemy were still holding on around Lion-sur-Mer.

We were now at Hermanville where we commandeered the local farmyard to set up a temporary workshop to repair and service the DUKWs as required, to keep them seaworthy. In a field nearby were about 30 dead cows but the bull was still alive. As it did not attempt to get up on its feet I assumed that it was shell shocked. Intermittent firing from the church spire accounted for the loss of many soldiers who were drawing water from a tap in the square. As a sniper could not be located it was decided, after consideration, to remove the spire by shellfire.

The first burial ground was opened in a field adjoining the workshop. A continuous convoy of lorries brought in the dead for burial. I watched the Padres removing identity discs and personal belongings which they placed in small individual containers. After the bodies were laid to rest, side by side, a service was conducted. All this was very disturbing and depressing, but made us all realise that we had survived the first ordeal. I remember saying: "Thank God for sparing me during the first day on French soil."

The farmyard buildings were made of stone and mortar. The yard contained a dwelling house, byre, implement shed and a few other barns, all in poor condition. The farm buildings survived the D-Day bombardment with little or no damage. We had a feeling that we were unwelcome probably because the farmer felt the army was responsible for the loss of his entire herd of cows. He showed no appreciation for the freedom we had brought to Normandy. It was almost dusk.

Tired and hungry, my comrades Billy and Staffy assisted me in digging a trench to secure our safety for the night. With sweat pouring from our faces we opened our emergency packs and with apples from the orchard and cider from a barrel in the farmyard shed we had an appetising meal before we decided to kip down for a well-earned rest.

At midnight a despatch delivered to O.C. Workshop informed us that the DUKW Control Post on the beach received a direct hit killing the entire H.Q. staff. This was our saddest moment of D-Day.

No wonder it was later called "The Longest Day".

Jack Patterson, Mile End, Gatehouse of Fleet, Kirkcudbrightshire, Scotland.

"Pity you couldn't have seen the garden a fortnight earlier."

*. Leach, padre to 13/18th Hussars takes a burial serrvice on 7th June 1944. The soldier died in fighting against the 21st
zer Division.*

For the most part I always felt the war had passed me by. I had the doubtful privilege of being allowed to work my time out during the war in the local mines.

At the age of eighteen perhaps I could be forgiven the feeling of indifference to what was happening around the world. Born in the Forest of Dean I had rarely been anywhere else, and I rarely allowed anything to disturb my particular kind of freedom. I traversed the Forest tracks on my way to work at Cannop Colliery, but except for occasional movement of British and American troops, the war for me was a very long way off. Of course, I followed the progress of my two elder brothers, who by the time about which I am writing were serving in Southern Italy.

My love of the "Forest of Dean" is deep and I could not conceive at that time that anything could take away my right to wander freely as I did, and continue to enjoy what was Paradise in comparison to what was happening around the world.

Often I ignored the use of transport and opted to walk the four miles to Cannop, varying my route and ignoring the more traversed tracks. I saw the change of each season, appreciating as I went each particular act of nature.

The period to which I now relate was the early spring of 1944. Everyone was anticipating that one morning we would rise to the news that a Second Front had been established across The Channel. We knew that Troops were massing at various points along the South coast, and the great presence of American troops locally was further evidence that the big day was imminent. A fairly large contingent of Americans were encamped in the "Boarts Enclosure", above Arthur and Edward colliery at Lydbrook. But for the occasional movement of transport and guards around the perimeter, we hardly knew they were there.

One evening around the middle of May I was climbing the hill on the opposite side of the valley when I experienced a strange kind of silence. The American troops had departed, leaving no trace of their ever having been there.

The thought of their obvious destination earmarked the time when I felt everything I hitherto felt about the war changed.

The eve of D-Day found me working on the nightshift, and about an hour before the shift ended next morning we received news from the surface. The radio had reported that Allied troops had landed in Normandy and were attempting to establish a bridgehead. As I walked home that beautiful spring morning I reflected on how detached from the whole mess of war I had really become. My thoughts drifted to some of the boys I had been at school with, and knew to be among those troops across the channel. I will never forget that particular morning, comparing my lot with theirs.

Gradually the news filtered through, each of those families involved awaiting that dread when the postman would call with that ominous War Office telegram. The first news I heard was of a boy of the same year in school as myself. Jack Hale wounded in action while landing in France. Another more poignant one, Donald Knight who lived near to us who I had been at school with and said farewell to on his last leave. Killed in action after landing in Normandy. The memory of those days will stay with me always. All the grief and anguish which registered on people's faces.

About a month or so later I attended my grandmother's funeral. Along with a fellow mourner I met Mr. Knight. My companion immediately shook hands with him expressing heartfelt sympathy for their sad loss. For several seconds I saw the look of terrible grief cross that gentleman's face, a face which once I knew so full of character. Then I realised the terrible cost of my particular kind of freedom. That's why I need Remembrance Day to be retained each November to remind me of the price paid to allow me to enjoy the freedom of such a wonderful area where I still feel privileged to live.

Wilfred T. Evans, 2 Kimberley Drive,
Lydney, Gloucestershire.

(Sadly we record that Wilfred Evans has died since writing this story, but his widow Joyce has agreed that we could include it, "as he was so looking forward to reading your book").

merican troops marching down an English road to embark. The soldier fourth from front is carrying a bazooka.

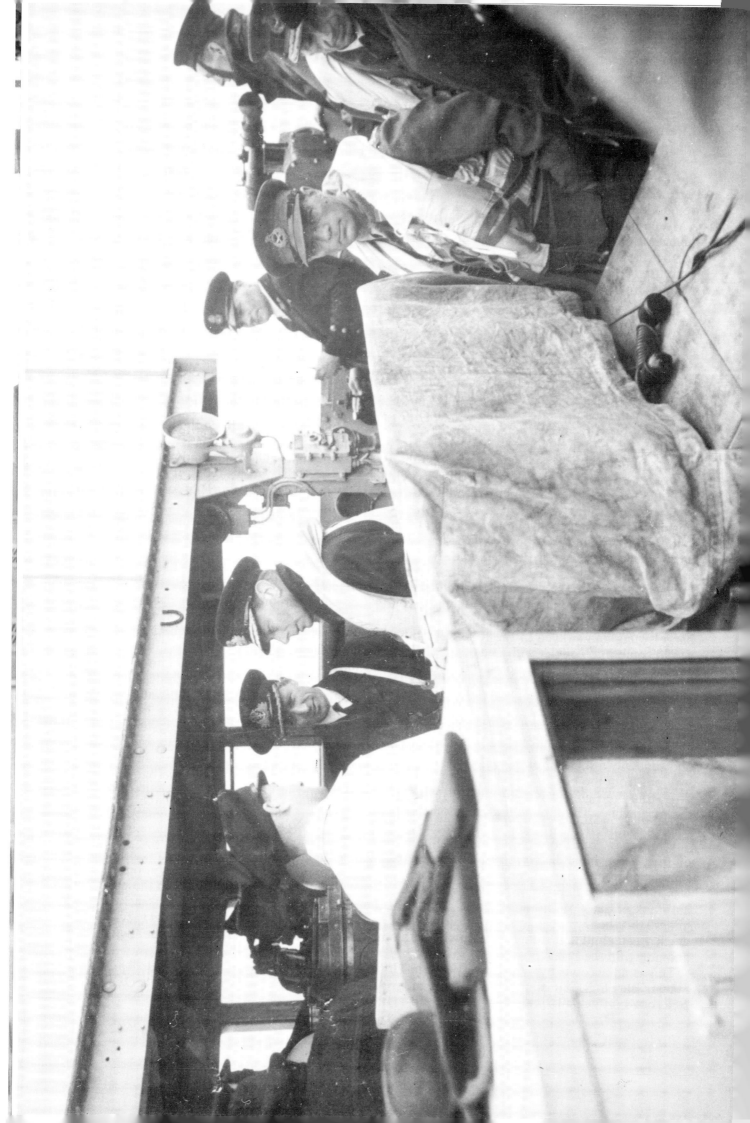

First light appears as a grey smudge. "Action Stations" is bugled. Gun crews and control parties, supply teams and damage control gangs, medical staffs and signalmen; all go swiftly to their post. Nobody talks much. Here and there a jocular "good luck" remark is passed.

Taking up our bombarding positions is no more difficult than a practice run. Our objective appears in my telescope as a replica of the photographs. The drill is perfect. Not a hitch. "Stand-by", "Shoot". My telescopic crosswires roll gently on the target. I squeeze the pistol grip, pull sharply and the ship recoils as the first salvo for the enemy roars inland. Three more salvo's rock the ship in quick succession and through the side-ports of the control tower I can see an aircraft laying a smokescreen around the battleships and cruisers. As arranged, fire is switched to a road where Panzers are expected and our guns "plaster". Landing craft move en masse towards the beaches. A few isolated enemy batteries have come to life. We close in to sniff them out. Flash! They have fired. I note their position, and put all guns on to target. The second solvo hits nicely. The battery thereafter is silent. We give it a few more nicely placed salvos for luck. Ten minutes later I have an opportunity of observing what is at once the most amazing and devastating scenes ever to be experienced. Saturation bombing. It is horrible, ghastly; nothing could possibly live under the storm of explosive rained down on that small stretch of foreshore. Deep red, ugly flashes shoot up with startling rapidity like a handful of matches thrown on to burning embers multiplied a million times.

Smoke hazes drift across the beaches. Shell splashes straddle several destroyers close inshore. We go in to give support. No flashes can be seen through the dense smoke screen. To remain without being able to return the enemy's fire will unnecessarily endanger the ship and its crew; we therefore steam out of range. With their superior manoeuvreability the destroyers remain. They weave and circle whilst maintaining continuous gunfire against the foreshore with its scattered pillboxes and landing craft traps. Meanwhile the first concentration of assault craft make for the beaches. Large craft fitted with rocket guns lay down a heavy barrage of covering fire. Few people have seen this secret weapon in action before. When fired the rockets leave behind them a short trail of red flame. A fascinating sight. Seconds later their report is heard; a short lived whoosh! like a sudden gale of wind blowing through tall trees. Every gun on the assault craft is put into action as the boats plough a white trail to the beaches.

The first line of infantry carrying boats glide ashore. Bow doors drop and a stream of Britains toughest and best trained commandos dash out to commence the invasion. What happened during the next hour is too rapid a succession of bloody events to bear clear and detailed description. The waters close inshore were whipped into spray but wave after wave of our craft surged ahead to discharge its precious load. Details of the fighting on the beaches are learned later. Splashes of information are picked up from an Officer here, a sergeant there and a corporal somewhere else.

"Warspite", "Rammillies" and "Roberts" all mounting 15" guns are having some fun with large calibre guns situated at Le Havre and on hilltops to the east of the beachhead and overlooking Ouistreham. The coastal guns can be seen flashing at intervals. The battleships are all straddled in turn. The Hun's gunnery tactics are peculiar; he does not hold a target for very long, and he ceases fire when his fall of shot appears most accurate. None of the battle wagons are hit.

Fleets of large landing craft ploughing through the main channel are now supplemented by smaller craft transporting infantry from five landing craft ships that have just arrived. The horizon is one of ships, ships and more ships. The beach is a continuous line of craft. Houses are on fire. Explosions ashore are hid in a pall of smoke covering everything behind the beaches. And to the westward is visible the smoke and flames of another landing.

From the Journal kept by George Beavis, now of 28 Highfield Road, Derby.

M. King George VI on the bridge of "Arethusa" en route to Normandy. (Kindly supplied by ex-A.B. Marcus Cross of Cupar, fe).

leading tank who immediately closed down his visor, thus making him blind to things in front! Corporal Tommy Kileen, realised what was happening and ran up the side of the road, taking two Gammon bombs from his pouches. He threw the first bomb which hit the leading tank where the turret and body meets which nearly blew the turret off. He threw the second bomb but being further away from the second tank, it fell short, landing against the tanks track which was promptly blown off. This tank now tried to escape, but only having one good track it went around in circles, so the crew baled out and tried to escape. They were shot by McGee.

Next came an attack by about a company of Panzer Grenadiers, but this was easily contained and they withdrew after losing a number of men. I was now with Sergeant Young guarding the right flank when we saw a Section of about 10 Germans break cover some 700 yards away on our western flank. We waited until they were on an open flat piece of ground, then opened fire with our rifles, which were fitted with telescopic sights. We didn't see any enemy movement on that flank for the rest of the day. It was just after this event that I saw L/Cpl. Davey laying out in an orchard, his face covered with blood and was just about to investigate when a German Panther tank appeared about 40 yards from our position, quite near to Davey. It stopped, lowered his large 88mm gun which now appeared to be pointing straight at me. I shouted a warning as I dived into a ditch, and the shell made a hole in the wall about three yards to my left but we suffered no casualties. It was later learned that Davey had realised that the Germans were all around him, so he pretended to be dead. In fact he made his way back to Pegasus Bridge as soon as it was dark and was later returned to England with his wounds. After a period in hospital, he rejoined the regiment and survived the war.

During the many attacks made by the enemy that day, (mainly by about a company strength) all were successfully dealt with at a considerable cost to the enemy, but our own casualties were now mounting. It was during one of these attacks that a German walked through the wooden door in the wall in front of us. He was just as surprised as us and immediately disappeared back through the door before we could react!

We had now been surrounded by the enemy since our arrival and so Sergeant Young and myself decided to try to get back to the canal bridge to find out the position. As we travelled along the ditch, with Sgt. Young leading, a shot rang out and he shouted that they had broken his back. I pushed him down into the ditch and fell on top of him, then examined his wound which proved to be a furrow right across his back but did not appear to have injured his spine. I gave him a Morphine injection which we all carried and dressed his wounds before returning to our position.

By 16.15 hours we had gathered 23 German prisoners and L/Cpl. Jackson volunteered to escort them down to the bridge for interrogation. He was killed by a sniper's bullet whilst returning to "A" company positions.

It was about 21.15 hours when the 2nd Battalion of the Royal Warwickshire Regiment put in an attack on Benouville in an attempt to get us out. This proved to be successful. We had been surrounded by the enemy for 17½-hours but the very gallant "A" company had held

out. We returned to the Canal Bridge, later named the "Pegasus Bridge" in honour of the men who had captured it and held it against all odds. Here we managed to get a small meal from the rations we all carried. It was whilst we were doing so that we came under sniper fire from the church tower at Le Port. Corporal Tommy Kileen asked us to give him covering fire, then picking up a P.I.A.T. (Projector Infantry Anti-Tank) gun and a case containing three bombs, he ran forward towards the church. When he was about 20 yards away he stopped and placed the butt of the P.I.A.T. on the ground, then he placed a bomb in position, and guessing the angle, he lined it up on the church tower and pressed the trigger. We watched as the bomb soared towards its target, then hit the tower quite near to the slits through which the German snipers had been firing. We ran towards the church to assist him and saw Kileen stop in the church doorway, remove his helmet and make the sign of the cross before entering! In amongst the debris of the church spire inside the church we found 12 dead German snipers. At 23.30 hours we were taken back on to our DZ (dropping zone) as reserve Company where we all dug slit trenches. I lined mine with part of a discarded parachute that I found, then climbed into the trench pulling the remainder of the parachute over me and I fell asleep about 01.00 hours, 7th June. Private McGee was awarded the Distinguished Conduct Medal, but was killed later that day. Corporal Thomas Kileen was awarded the Military Medal, and in fact survived the war. The tasks given to the 6th Airborne Division on 6th June were all successfully accomplished. The left flank of the invasion area was held secure.

I must say that we had the most wonderful support from the Royal Air Force who were masters of the skies over Normandy, and the Royal Navy who shelled everything that was asked of them. Finally, the Army personnel who fought to get ashore and advance through the enemy defences to ensure that we had the maximum support. They were all magnificent.

So ended D-Day which for myself and a million others, and it was truly a very long day!

Edgar ("Eddy") Gurney, 33 Eastern Avenue, Thorpe St. Andrew, Norwich.

"J.J.P."

Yesterday I met a man, who went in on D-Day on that Norman coast,
Who knowing of my visit, asked,
"Did they ever get them buried right?"

We couldn't stop; we left them where they fell, wrapped in grey blankets,
Some dying and some dead... rows on rows
Just where the guns had mown them down.

I often wondered how many died, who needn't, of neglect.
It doesn't bear thinking of, all that...
And the bodies floating in the sea.

Drowned long before they reached the beach, tangled in their landing gear, or
Fallen off the lifeline beyond their depth.
And every officer dead before we topped that beach.

In the end we joined the Yanks, and went into the Panzer's arms in Cambey's Wood;
Panzers three sides, our naval guns behind,
And us lot caught between the two.

If the Panzers didn't get us, our own shells did.
Whole Company gone, and Panzers too,
Boxed in that wood.

It doesn't bear thinking of, all that,
That nightmare long ago..."

"J.J.P.' is Mr. Pancott, a one-man Builder and Decorator, who one day listened to our talk of a holiday in Normandy. Then he spoke and what he said came out as blank verse. I let him go on – he was miles away, years back in the past to D-Day. I wrote it down straight away – as this is his memory. What struck me was his disbelief that all those bodies could have been buried – there were so many. He's now retired and sadly I've lost touch.

Gloria Bennett, Minster Road, Oxford.

I was in the 6th Battalion, Durham Light Infantry, and after spending six months in England on June 3rd, 1944 we were ready to embark for the invasion of the Continent. But we didn't move until the morning of the 4th. Our carriers were waterproofed for water 4ft. in depth. My mates were Ken as a gunner, and Arthur as a driver. But Ken had vanished. When we boarded the L.C.Ts. Arthur was behind me, and Ken was on another boat. He was driving a carrier full of mines, gelignite etc. Phew. I wouldn't have liked that job. We sailed the next day 5th and it was a rough sea. Quite a few chaps were sick, but I was lucky. Arriving off the coast of Normandy the next morning we

were surprised that we were not under constant air attacks. Then we nozed into the shore, Gold Beach. I took the camouflage off the carrier and warmed the engine. I was thinking, will the water be shallow enough to take the carrier, or if the water is deep will the carrier float? We knew the beach had been taken before we landed, and our job was to pass through La Riviere and push on inland. Our aircraft (Spitfires) were overhead, but one Spitfire caught the tail of another with his wing. One dropped and crashed. The other, with smoke coming from the tail, turned back across the channel.

That day we had pushed approximately twelve miles inland. We had tanks on either side of us, a bicycle Company, mixed in amongst the carriers, and 'planes above our head. Whenever we met any opposition our concentrated fire soon moved it. On the night we stopped and took up positions against counter attack.

Three carriers had to go forward, on a reccy. My Section was chosen and it was dark when we set out. We had only gone 100 yards when we came to a big gun burning in the road. Going over it I had a large piece caught in my track, and so had to stop. In the ditch near the gun was a wounded Jerry, and with him was a young Italian, about 18 years old. We tried to fix the Jerry up but we knew he was dying. The Iti worked like a slave to remove the piece of metal from round my track (voluntary) and when we went back, we left him to look after his mate. That night we withdrew, as the marching troops couldn't get up to us that night. We lagered up in a wood and I was chosen to do a stag, I did my two hours with Arthur. The next D1 morning we again started off on the column, and everything went O.K. until we reached our final objective, then as we were moving up a side road a corporal dashed up to us and said there were some Jerries coming towards the Cross Roads.

Being the leading carrier I started to go up. A motor bike dashed past with two Jerries on. A corporal stood at the cross roads, and fired his sten at them as they went past, then a truck towing an anti-tank gun came across and the corporal fired again and the truck stopped. I was only five yards away then. My crew baled out. In trying to swing the carrier round, I got stuck on the bank. It was then that our anti-tank gun hit the Jerries truck, and set it on fire. Being only five yards away from it, I baled out and lay behind my carrier. I looked round and saw everyone had fallen back, about a hundred yards. As shells etc. (from the truck) were flying quite close I decided to stop where I was! I heard another truck pull up and saw a Hun walk across the road. I wished I'd had my rifle with me. On the arrival of our tanks the Jerries surrendered. We threw a road block across the road and cut off a lot more Boche. Our carriers then carried on with my carrier leading, and we turned down the road, the same way the Jerries were going before we stopped them.

About two hundred yards down, we came to a crossroad, (Jerusalem Crossing), our final objective. Some French civilians came out and gave us some wine. Our 'planes had been flying about all the time, but one suddenly turned and faced us. Smoke came from his guns and canon and everyone dived for cover bar the French who were too horrified to move. I threw myself over the gear lever, and waited. Being the first carrier I took the brunt of the attack, and as I was lying there I suddenly felt someone sticking red hot needles in my back and side. Then I felt warm and wet,

277

I was in the 7th Armoured Division and I remember as we moved up the lane a German Staff car came down towards us! Everyone opened fire at once and it turned over and crashed. What it was doing there I'll never know. When I passed it again later in a Bren Carrier I didn't even bother to look at its occupants. There were going to be plenty more in the next few weeks that was certain.

In Villers Bocage I was sent out with four others to patrol the immediate area when suddenly I saw a tank fire from a farm yard. This was followed by a barrage from others in sheltered positions, immediately setting fire to our tank, trucks, and Bren Carriers in the narrow sunken lanes, where only minutes before our troops had been drinking tea as if on a Sunday afternoon picnic.

The scene was one of fire, smoke and continuous explosions. It was all too evident that the Germans had been waiting for us and had picked the right moment to strike which they had done with a vengeance! It was discovered later that they were Panther and Tiger tanks of a Waffen SS Heavy Tank Battalion which included a German tank "Ace" with 119 "kills" to his credit on the Russian front.

In the mayhem and confusion everyone began destroying their equipment to stop it falling into enemy hands. I began by smashing up our radios and finished by throwing my Bren gun into a pond, minus its firing pin. I then took cover under a fallen telegraph pole. I kept low enough to hide from a couple of Germans who were by now only yards from me, surveying the scene of their successful ambush from their side-car motorcycle, but still ready with their heavy machine gun.

I could have "popped-off" both of them easily, but knowing that I would almost certainly be captured if I did I decided not to do anything. There was still total confusion everywhere else – I was hidden behind my pole in an island of comparative quiet by now. But I could hear my Sergeant shouting orders and calling out, and I even saw others of my Platoon flag down a Tiger tank thinking it was one of ours arrived to help them! Shortly afterwards word had obviously got back to HQ because the area began to be bombed by British and American aircraft so I and a couple of mates who had also been hiding made a break for it and got away.

After a couple of days continuous walking we managed to get a nights kip which was a blessed relief I can tell you. The trouble was that when we woke up we found ourselves surrounded by German troops and trucks. Hundreds of troops! We had obviously been walking in the wrong direction and were now well behind the enemy lines thank you very much!

I tried to make another break for it but a German sentry, a very big chap as I remember, spotted me and fired from about 100 yards. The bullets just seemed to riddle the ground in front of me at which point I decided it might be better to stand still! I can particularly remember raising my hands and for some inexplicable reason shouting "Mum, Mum, Mum!" A maternal reflex action I suppose, just like when you were a kid and got hurt!

Before he searched me the sentry motioned with his gun in a threatening manner, and I became even more nervous than I was already! Then suddenly the penny dropped. He wanted me to discard what I had in my hand. To him I suppose it could have been a grenade, but all it was unfortunately was a pair of gloves rolled up!

Anyway my part in the fighting came to an end there and then. I was a PoW for 11 months in various Stalag and work camps in South-East Germany. I suppose it IS something to be able to say now that I fought in the Normandy invasion, but it wasn't as if I had much choice at the time! But then it was the same for everyone – the luck of the draw so to speak. You all just got on with it – no matter where or who you were!

George Benham, 62 Kelsey Avenue,
Southbourne, Nr. Emsworth, West Sussex.

…oops marching up to the front. Note Sherman tank coming round corner. The third man is carrying a map and a Thompson …b-machine gun.

I was in the American 508 Parachute Infantry Regiment and I must say here that one of my major criticisms of all our detailed briefings had to do with hedgerows. We were told that there were hedgerows but no-one explained in detail how they were to affect us. We all pictured hedgerows as dividing two fields but something that one could push through easily. This is not so. Each of the fields in this area of Normandy are not more than 50 yards square and are outlined on all four sides by hedgerows which consist of a berm of earth about three feet thick and about three feet high. From the top of this berm there are thick bushes growing to a height of six to 10 feet. In addition, each berm of earth has a drainage ditch on each side about two feet deep. What you have is thousands of little fields, each one an island unto itself. Men could be fighting and dying in one field and people could be taking a break in the next one.

Henry Le Febvre second from left, front row.

It was 02.30 on D-Day when the green light came on and I was out some 400 feet in the air above the Normandy countryside falling into that sea of tracers. Fortunately for me, I landed right in the middle of one of those 50 yard square fields. As soon as I hit the ground I heard this German, I didn't know what he was saying but I could tell by the pitch and loudness of his voice that he was really excited and that he meant business. I knew that I had to get out of my chute and away from it as soon as possible. We were loaded down with extra equipment plus having a harness that snapped around each leg at the groin and across the chest with a snap fastener. In order to minimise the opening shock these straps were very tight and under all the other equipment that we carried. Because of this and what I knew would only be a short time to get out of my chute, I used my razor-sharp knife that was attached to my jump boot to cut my way out of my harness. In my haste I also cut my way through my rifle sling. If I didn't have enough problems already, I was also confronted by a cow right next to me with a bell around its neck. It stood looking down at me moving her head and ringing the bell!

I was fortunate to be able to get out of my harness and slither about 10 yards away toward the opposite corner of the field from the Germans. Suddenly I heard the very distinct "pop" of a very pistol and I knew that in a few seconds the whole area would be flooded with the white light of a parachute flare. I got as low to the ground as possible and faced the chute. As soon as the flare came on the area was flooded with light and a hail of bullets came from the German position on the corner of the field. I saw my parachute and equipment being shot to pieces. The firing continued for the whole time the flare was lit (about 20 seconds). It seemed like an eternity to me. The only thing that saved me was the fact that I had gotten a little distance away from my chute and that my hands and face were blackened and that I was hugging the ground. When the flare went out, they didn't fire another one.

For whatever reason, they did not come into the field after me so as soon as the flare went out I started to crawl to the far corner of the field. There I ran into another pathfinder who was lost. We almost shot each other before we realised who was who! The two of us proceeded along the hedgerow into the next field when we heard the sound of German voices coming toward us. We ducked down into one of the drainage ditches along the hedgerow and waited for them to pass. Unfortunately for us they didn't pass by. Just on the other side of the hedgerow from us I heard the unmistakable sound of a machine gun being set up. The snap of the trails being extended and the sound of the bolt going back and forth as the belt was fed through. It appeared that we were in the middle of a German platoon position. We could hear

508th Command Post in Normandy.

285

them talking quite clearly just on the other side of the berm of earth. What to do?... There was no way to throw a grenade through that hedgerow. We had to whisper very quietly. I thought that we could sneak out of our position but the dry brambles and weeds would crackle loudly and we would hear "Vas is los?" and we would freeze.

I recalled from our briefing that the force landing by sea on the Normandy coast would relieve us by D-Day or D+1 so I figured that we could just stay put until the Germans were forced to move. Unfortunately for us, the sea borne invasion didn't make it to us as planned. My pathfinder friend almost got his hand stepped on by a German who was apparently going out to the platoon outpost on our side of the berm. My friends hand was on the edge of the ditch in which we were hiding and suddenly we saw these two legs go by us... Our days and nights were spent huddled together. Each move in the ditch caused a lot of noise because of the dry brambles and weeds. I was sure the

Was this the cow with the bell?

Germans would be driven out by our forces momentarily so we waited. We lived on a little water and D-Day ration chocolate bars. It was three nights before we finally heard the Germans packing up to leave.

After checking my compass for an easterly direction we started out and shortly ran into our own forces. It was a tense confrontation as everyone was jumpy. I parted company with my pathfinder friend and never saw him again. I along with many other 508ers who were scattered began rejoining the regiment with many stories of firefights, escapes, and individual exploits of courage and determination. But only five of my platoon were present for duty.

Henry Le Febvre, 618 W. Ocean Front, Balboa, California, USA.

I was with the 5th Royal Tank Regiment, 7th Armoured Division on D-Day. As we approached the coast we passed through the lines of Naval ships which were carrying out the covering bombardment. Battleships, Cruisers, Destroyers, Rocket ships sending salvoes of shells and rockets on to the land. It was at least ten times louder than our barrage that we had passed through at El Alamein!

It was impossible to hear any reply, but great splashes appeared in the water and a merchant ship near us was hit and fell behind in a pall of black smoke. As we approached the beach, our patrol vessels and aircraft dropped smoke flares to screen us as we landed, but the strong wind blew it away. All the landing craft were jockeying for a place to beach. Each Division had sent ahead beach parties to mark the landing area and also the exit from the beach. Our craft charged the beach and as the ship shuddered to a halt the large door was lowered. Our Troop leader was first, we were second. Before we started up, the instructions had been repeated. The troop leader's tank moved out, through the water and on to the special wire mesh laid out on the beach. But the driver made the error of going too near the edge of the mesh and the tank turned over on its side, and threw the left track.

After clearing up pockets of resistance that had been by-passed by the infantry of 50 Division we pushed on down the road towards St. Paul de Vernay. The road, with cornfields on each side had no hedges and as we left Trungy there was no cover for about 500 yards. Our troop was in the lead with Sergeant Cook in his Cromwell being point tank. We moved cautiously along the exposed road trying to see what was in the trees where the road disappeared in the distance. We were about half way along the road as Sergeant Cook's tank entered the trees when there was a terrific explosion. The tank literally disintegrated and the Sergeant was thrown on to the road. We moved forward and fired four a.p. shells into the area where we thought the shot had come from. Sergeant Cook staggered back down the road, and was helped behind our tank by two infantrymen but he died later.

A Company of the Essex Regiment later arrived in support. They were all spic and span and looked newly arrived from home. Not at all what we had expected. They prepared for the attack as if on the 'square'. When the arranged artillery barrage began, they began to move forward, but in open order carrying their rifles at the port position. We could hardly believe what we were seeing.

286

In just a few minutes the line was massacred. The ones that were left fell back. They formed up again as an Officer came running up shouting: "Send them in on their bellies." This time they made use of the waist high corn, as the enemy flame throwers moved forward. It took the remainder of the day and most of the night to clear the woods as the enemy counter attacked time and again. Enemy tanks came up in support, and enemy infantry were attempting to attach grenades to the side of the tanks. Two enemy tanks were put out of action by the infantry with their Piat Guns. In the darkness, one enemy tank Commander passed through our lines and destroyed two of our reserve tanks before he was disposed of.

We left the Infantry to carry out the final clearing up, when we were due for replenishment. Forming up on the road where we had previously lost Sergeant Cook and his crew, we made our way to the rendezvous. As we turned into the area where the replenishment lorries were gathered, a sniper shot Sergeant Major Knight as he stood in the turret of his tank.

Without rest, but with a little breakfast, we moved off leaving the Essex Regiment to clear the area and the nearby village of Ellon. We had been ordered to try to expand the bridgehead by moving down some secondary roads which would lead us to our objective which was Villers Bocage.

With the element of surprise we passed through several small villages overcoming the opposition, despite the noise made by the tanks as they approached. We had travelled 12 miles before we encountered serious opposition. As we entered the village of Livry, an anti tank gun opened fire from the side of the square.

We were carrying some infantry with us. It was necessary to dismount them and mount an organised attack on the village and we attacked from all sides. The anti-tank gun was knocked out and several enemy taken prisoner. We stayed in the village for the night, awaiting replenishment, and infantry patrols made contact with the American Army on our right.

The lead was now to be taken over by the 4th City of London Yeomanry, one of the other two tank regiments in our Brigade. As we moved along towards the main road to Villers Bocage, 4th C.L.Y. passed by us and we then followed them. We were now moving out of the enclosed bocage country, and as the 4th C.L.Y. entered Briquessard, we moved off across the open fields to be on their left flank as they attacked Amaye-sur-Seulles.

We took up positions along the top of the hill, and around midday received a message that the 4th C.L.Y. had reached their objective and had entered Villers Bocage. But around 14.00 hours firing was heard and the air became full of messages! The enemy, who had been constantly delayed by our air attacks, had at last arrived and were endeavouring to make Villers Bocage their headquarters!

Our leading column, who had earlier reported that they were in charge of the town, had found that the enemy tanks had allowed them to pass, and when all the tanks were in the town, had fired on the infantry half-track following behind, completely blocking the road. The last message received from the 4th C.L.Y. Squadron Commander was that his Squadron was completely surrounded by enemy tanks and infantry, and that he would have to surrender.

Despite fierce fighting we were in fact finally able to relieve the 4th C.L.Y. who came forward to help with supporting fire, and the Germans finally decided to call it a day. But it was touch and go.

It was to be 30th June before we were pulled out of this front line for the first time since we had arrived over three weeks earlier!

S. Storer, 85 Hereford Close,
Barwell, Leicestershire.

I was a sergeant in A Troop, 322 Battery, 103 Regiment of the Royal Artillery. We landed on Sword Beach at 07.45 am and as our Rhino transport dropped the ramp I suddenly found the water coming up round my legs! By the time I was off the ramp it was up to my waist and I remember the chap with me was standing on the seat with his head out through the trap shouting "Keep her going sarge or we'll all bloody well drown."

We followed the space between the white tapes that amazingly were already in place showing where it was clear of mines, and made it quickly to the road that ran parallel to the beach where we had to wait whilst the Sussex Yeomanry got into action with some German tanks on the high ground behind Hermanville. I must say they soon sorted them out, but it was terrible to see a tank catch fire. You still have feelings whether it's the enemy or not.

Other vehicles of our Troop were arriving but we couldn't take up our proper position as it was still in enemy hands; so we didn't hang about but put the gun legs down where we were, ready for action just in case. It was just as well we did because we'd only just finished when the Bombardier shouted "Enemy aircraft!" and we were attacked. We had to engage them through open sights but we hit a JU88 which blew up and crashed on the beach. Shells were also falling around us by this time from the German guns inland. We couldn't respond to that because we had no information of where to fire so we ran for cover.

Two of us ran for a trench left by the Germans and I remember seeing the chap with me run into it and then get straight out! When I looked to see why I found it was full of German troops who had been occupying it – all dead. No wonder he got out so quick!

So we sheltered behind a high wall where we saw the Royal Marine Commandos carrying their dead and wounded out of the firing. I heard a Sergeant say "We don't want that one, he's a bloody German" and they just left the body – that's what war does to you. They'd all been caught by mortar fire which was still striking the wall.

Later we got back to our vehicle and gun and it was then that we saw the first German prisoners-of-war coming in. There were a lot and they seemed to be mostly young boys and old men, but perhaps they weren't old. Perhaps they'd just been through an awful hammering that made them look it. I know what we went through was bad enough but I certainly wouldn't have wanted to be on the end of what they'd had!

About mid-day we moved on to Colleville where we suffered from snipers which in many ways was the worst of the lot. But then a plane came over and bombed us and without thinking I dived for cover under my lorry. Fortunately the bombs missed and no-one was injured but the covers on the vehicles were torn to ribbons. It was only then I remembered that my lorry was half-loaded with petrol so if we had been hit there wouldn't have been much of me left!

Insofar as the landing itself is concerned we had no end of trouble. Regimental records show that A Troop was divebombed on our LST and the lift was jammed causing delay in unloading. The Regiment landed as and when it could and not always according to the timetable arrangements! In some cases the guns had unloaded and landed before the recce parties had arrived! The records show that at the time when 16 guns should have been ashore there was only 1 Gun and 1 Radar – such were the opposition and problems. But we persevered – and we made it!

W. A. "Bill" Rogers,
8 Norman Taylor House,
Hope Road, Deal, Kent.

This must surely be a unique photograph of THE two outstanding men of D-Day. Taken at Pegasus Bridge it shows Major John Howard DSO on the left and Sgt. Major Stan Hollis, the only V.C. of D-Day, on the right.

The legendary exploits of Major Howard are already well documented and we record them in our tribute to Den Brotheridge on page xiii. Major Howard of the "Ox. and Bucks" was in Command of that first group of gliders to land at 00.16 on D-Day to seize and hold the bridge over the Caen Canal. Within minutes both the Caen Canal and the nearby Orne River bridges had been taken with only nominal losses and were successfully held until the Allied Forces could move up from the beaches.

Sergeant-Major Hollis was in the Green Howards and landed at Gold Beach near La Riviere. Before 09.30, under continuous fire, he had charged a hidden pillbox which was about to ambush the three leading platoons of Green Howards. He thrust his Sten gun inside the slit opening, swinging it horizontally to cover the interior, and followed that with a hand grenade. Ten German troops surrendered to him – the rest were dead.

He then saw that pillbox had a trench leading to another pillbox 30 yards away where 18 more German troops surrendered, and as the trench was narrow they did so by filing past him! In minutes he had neutralised over 30 enemy troops and saved at least three platoons of Green Howards, and probably the rest of his Company, being mown down.

Just over two hours later at Crepon, he led two Bren gunners on an attack on a field-gun holding up the advance. They had to crawl through a field of ripe rhubarb at full height! However they were spotted and fired on at point blank range, but the guns were not sufficiently depressed and the shells shot over them. They had to retreat, but when Stan got back he saw the other two were still pinned down and now in imminent danger.

There wasn't time to crawl back, so he snatched up a Bren gun and charged, firing from the hip. His sudden action earned its own reward, distracting the German guns to allow his colleagues to escape. Then weaving, dodging, tripping and stumbling through the rhubarb he also got back, followed all the way by machine gun fire.

He was hit on six different occasions during the war but survived, despite having a metal plate inserted in his head, and later went to sea with the Canadian Merchant Navy. After that he took a pub at North Ormesby near Middlesbrough – inevitably called "The Green Howard"! He died in the early 1970's – the only V.C. of D-Day.

Casualties – 6th June to 31st August, 1944

	Killed	Wounded	Missing	Total
Allied Army.........................	36,976	153,475	19,221	209,672

Allied Air Force ....Killed or Missing: 16,714. Aircraft Lost: 4,101

German Forces ....Estimated at 200,000 Killed or Missing

---

A TRUE STORY – Security was so tight that absolutely nothing was allowed to interfere with convoys heading for the docks. Somehow a laundry van accidentally got into a convoy at Maidenhead, and couldn't get out for 60 miles until they reached Southampton! Wonder what his customers thought?

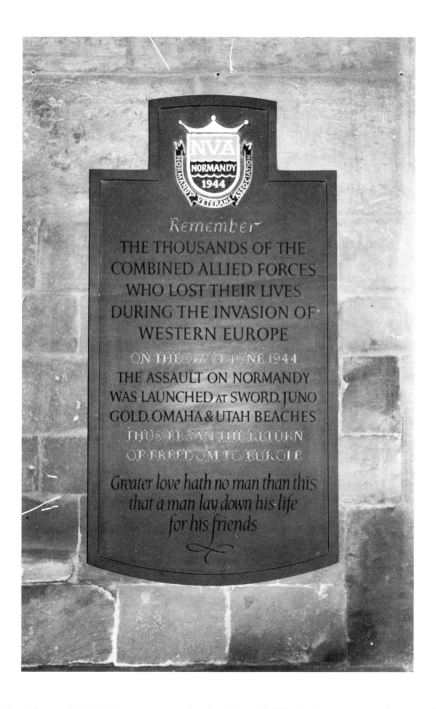

This Memorial Tablet was made by David Kindesley, a professional stonemason, and was presented to Canterbury Cathedral in 1989 by Branch No. 33 (East Kent Branch) of the Normandy Veteran's Association, to mark the 45th anniversary of D-Day. It is made of Normandy green slate and was unveiled by Her Majesty Queen Elizabeth the Queen Mother. The wording was composed by Mr. Arthur T. Palmer, Chairman of the Branch, and will always remain as part of the Cathedral to keep alive, by the many pilgrims and tourists who visit the Mother Church of England, the memory of the sacrifices of 6th June, 1944.

Daily

No. 15,006   ONE PENNY   FOR KI

BEACHHEAD V

Savage Fighting in Caen Str
100 Miles Across and Troop

THE first historic day of Europe's liberation has gone completely in favour of the Allies. Our troops and tanks are firmly ashore at many points along 100 miles of the Normandy coast from Cherbourg to Le Havre. They are 10 miles inland at Caen, five miles inland at the base of the Cherbourg Peninsu One report also puts Lisieux, 15 m from the coast south of Le Havre, British hands. German coastal batter have been silenced by 10,000 tons bombs and the shells of 600 warsh Casualties among both airborne a

'WEST WALL' IS BREAC
IN FIRST HOURS

TWENTY-FOUR hours have sufficed to smash the first fortifications of Hitler's vaunted West Wall. The Allied navies and air forces, operating in unheard-of strength, have put the first wave of General Montgomery's armies safely ashore on the magnificent beaches of Normandy, according to plan.

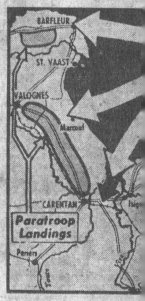

MAP shows the layout of operations, the beac already established, and the paratroops landed. definite news has emerged

MIDNIGHT COMMUNIQUE
Vian of the Cossack in Command

AN Allied communiqué issued at midnight said reports of operations so far show that our forces succeeded in their initial landings.

Here is the text of it:—

Before midnight on 5th June, 1944, Allied night bombers opened the assault. Their attacks were in very great strength and continued until dawn.

Between 6.30 and 7.30 a.m. two naval task forces, commanded by Rear-Admiral Sir Philip Vian, K.B.E., D.S.O., flying his flag in H.M.S. Scylla (Captain T. M. Brownrigg, C.B.E., R.N.), and Rear-Admiral Alan Goodrich Kirk, U.S.N., in U.S.S. Augusta (Captain

"Impregnable" strongpoints, built up over three years by the famous Todt organisation, crumbled in a few hours under the rain of bombs and shells.

Minesweepers have swept away the mines. Engineers have cleared the underwater "fences," "pyramids," and "hedgehogs." Troops and guns and tanks are flowing on to the shore of France.

German opposition will stiffen now and on succeeding days, but the first crucial phase has been carried through by the matchless skill of our sailors, soldiers, and airmen.

It is too early yet for the design of the invasion to take shape, but obvious objectives are the great ports of Cherbourg and Le Havre, which in peace handled Transatlantic traffic.

Roughly halfway between them General Montgomery has struck for the town of Caen, ten miles inland, which dominates roads and railways radiating all over Northern Normandy. Our troops are officially reported to be fighting in its streets.

Pilots returning late last night said our troops were moving inland. There was no longer any opposition on the beaches. "We saw our tanks

ENGL